Rescued by Grace

CALLED TO SERVE IN INDIA

PAULINE ROBINS

Ark House Press
arkhousepress.com

Cataloguing in Publication Data:
Title: Rescued By Grace
ISBN: 978-1-7637394-4-4 (pbk)
Subjects: REL012040 RELIGION / Christian Living / Inspirational; REL012170 RELIGION / Christian Living / Personal Memoirs; REL045000 RELIGION / Christian Ministry / Missions;

Design by initiateagency.com

"The God who made the world and everything in it is the Lord of heaven and earth and does not live in temples built by human hands. And he is not served by human hands, as if he needed anything. Rather, he himself gives everyone life and breath and everything else. From one man he made all the nations, that they should inhabit the whole earth; and he marked out their appointed times in history and the boundaries of their lands. God did this so that they would seek him and perhaps reach out for him and find him, though he is not far from any one of us." Acts 17:24-27

Table of Contents

Acknowledgements

I have kept journals for many years. I am using them to write this brief account of my story. I trust that what I have written is an accurate summary of what truly happened. Much of it explains my journey with God and the lessons He has taught me. I humbly pray that you will be encouraged when you read how God's grace is sufficient for all our needs.

I acknowledge the help of editors Pamela Harvey, PhD, and Neil Hockey, PhD, who journeyed with me and offered comments and improvements. I am grateful to George Abou-Sleiman (BA), whose critiques encouraged greater emotional expression while retaining the authenticity of my voice. I thank proofreaders Robyn Heazlewood and Denise Miller for correcting my first draft and helping me avoid recurring mistakes.

My sister Janice was the first to recognise my love for storytelling. In 1986 she gifted me a writing course which I regrettably did not pursue. However, the encouragement of others has reignited my passion for writing. I share my stories with the hope that they will evoke laughter and tears but, most importantly, inspire awe at the extraordinary grace of our God who accomplishes His purposes through ordinary people like you and me.

Foreword

It is a pleasure for me to write this foreword for Mrs Pauline Robins for her new book "Rescued by Grace" giving an account of the Lord's calling to missionary service in India and beyond.

Pauline has an amazing story to tell as she obeys the call of God upon her life, experiencing the matchless grace of God throughout her journey of faith and trust in her Saviour.

When Pauline eventually retired from active missionary service, she joined the Queensland Missionary Advisory Council (QMAC), of which I was a member. This Council very much appreciated the task that Pauline took to write a monthly newsletter to send to all the Queensland AMT missionaries serving overseas, giving them the local news to keep them up to date with what was happening back in Australia. Every Christmas, the missionaries also received a New Year calendar. At that time, we recognised the specific gifting that Pauline had in storytelling and communicating through writing.

Pauline truly had a heart to faithfully serve the Lord in cross-cultural ministry and sacrificially committed her life to this task. This new book will be an inspiration to all who read this testimony to the wonderful grace of God.

In her closing thoughts Pauline says, "I have written this book to reflect on my life's journey. I am astonished at how God has dealt with me through

His abundant grace." I'm sure we can all agree with this reflection in our own life's journey. Samuel Rutherford says it so well in one of his hymns: - "With mercy and with judgment my web of time He wove."

I have enjoyed reading Pauline's previous book on the wonderful heritage of the Peninsula Palms Retirement Village (PPRV) Anthology at Rothwell since its inception in the early 1990s. I highly recommend her new publication, "Rescued by Grace".

Roland Heazlewood
Mueller Community Church
Rothwell. Queensland.

Family Connections

William Hodgkinson (1829-1890) was born in Lancashire, England, and arrived in Australia in October 1863. He married and had a son, Albert Edward Hodgkinson (1876-1937). A.E. Hodgkinson married Florence Edith Smith (1885-1964). Her father was William John Smith, who married Anna Margaretha Dorothea Hinz, born in Germany. A.E. Hodgkinson and Florence Edith's first child was Albert William Hodgkinson, Pauline's father.

Albert William Hodgkinson married Amy Helena Fleetwood in 1925.
They had five children who lived

Margaret = Eric Flint: **Gary**

Laurel = Maxie Trathen: Guy 1975 = Amanda: Lily

: Sam

Brendan 1979

Zoe 1980

Janice = D. Graham Pearce: **Vicki** = Malcolm: Dean 1997

Adam 2000

Aimee 2001

Lindsay – Marion

Julie = Nabil: Naomi 1994
Rayana 1996
Elina 1998
George 2000

Pauline = Frederick J. Robins = 1995
His children: Mark 1957 = Helen: Melissa & Scott
Jennifer 1962 = Neville: Gareth, Tamara, Joshua & Benjamin
Leonie 1964 = Vladik: Melanie & Lachlan and Denzil (twins)

Gweneth = Russell Todd: **Jeffrey** 1964 = Merryl: Caleb 1995 – Amy: Grace 2021
Robyn 1981 = Michael: Hugo 2005 Henry 2007
Robyn – Mark

Raymond = Janice Lemon: **Ian** 1973 = Kylie: Nathan, Joshua & Zak
Leslie 1975

Map of India

300 km
200 mi
© d-maps.com
Jammu and Kashmir
Himachal Pradesh
Chandigarh
Punjab
Uttarakhand
Haryana
Delhi
Arunachal Pradesh
Sikkim
Uttar Pradesh
Rajasthan
Assam
Nagaland
Bihar
Meghalaya
Manipur
Jharkhand
Tripura
Gujarat
Madhya Pradesh
West Bengal
Mizoram
Daman and Diu
Chhattisgarh
Orissa
Dadra and Nagar Haveli
Maharashtra
Telangana
Goa
Andhra Pradesh
Karnataka
Pondicherry
Tamil Nadu
Andaman and Nicobar Islands
Kerala
Lakshadweep

Prelude

The storm broke overhead, sending lightning across the landscape and shivers down my spine. I was a scared six-year-old, but I was on a rescue mission despite my fears. There were orphan ducklings alone in the dark as we had enjoyed roast duck for Christmas. I crept across the wooden floor of the back veranda to where the old dog was tethered to the inside railing. He was whining in protest. I patted him as I passed, grabbed my dad's old sack coat, and stepped out into the fury of the tropical storm.

Rain was pounding down on the tin roof of the hastily erected pen. Leaning inside the structure I grabbed a handful of drenched ducklings. Returning to the kitchen at the back of the house, I lay them down in front of the wooden stove. Warmth still radiated from the burning coal. There were more ducklings to rescue.

I ventured into the rain once more to get them. This time the remaining ducklings had become stiff with cold. A light appeared in the kitchen. Someone was up and had lit the kerosene lamp. It was my mum looking ghostly in a long white homemade nightgown. 'I was about to do the same thing,' she whispered.

Relieved and happy, I watched her quickly open the oven door to become a tray, spread an old towel, and carefully put the stiff ducklings in the warmth of the dying wood fire. The gentle light fell on my mum's face, revealing her tired expression and concern for those near-frozen ducklings.

This was my mum, and my heart squeezed with love for her. The action of rescuing the ducklings seemed to set in motion a pattern for my life. I was on a mission to rescue those threatened and in need.

Chapter 1

A Country Kid's Wonderland

To the praise of the glory of His grace
which He freely bestowed...
Ephesians 1:6

My early childhood in Rockhampton was mainly happy and carefree. The bush was our backyard. My four siblings and I were skinny, energetic children with freckles and straight brown hair. We possessed a sense of being loved and a passion for the bush.

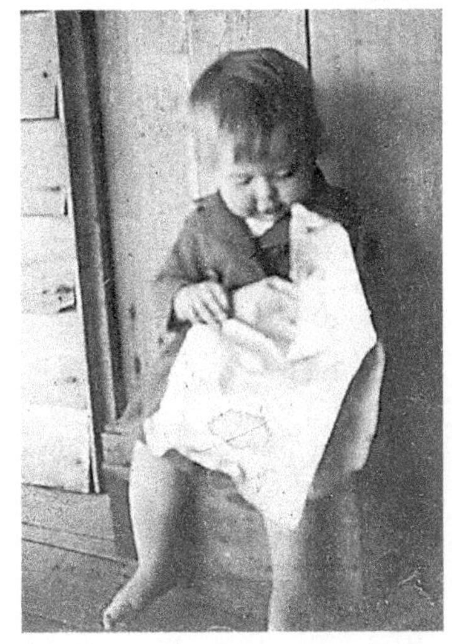

Pauline - the fascination begins

In Pink Lily and the early days in Koongal, a suburb of Rockhampton, we spent hours walking around the bush. When Mum saw us heading off, she would call out, 'Make sure you are home before dark.' How dramatically different our lives spent in childhood were to those of this twenty-first generation; there seemed to be no such thing as 'Stranger Danger' and no sense of being bored.

Not having many toys, no computers or TV, we played outside, making cubby houses or finding adventure in the bush. We roamed around freely.

Sometimes we gathered wild passion fruit or jujubes from the trees growing wild, carefully avoiding the thorny branches. The jujube fruit is smaller than a plum and has been used medicinally for thousands of years. Although we could eat the fruit fresh, we liked them boiled up in a tin can on our campfire; incredibly delicious were the "snotty gobbles" – the overripe, slimy ones!

We played traditional children's games like jacks using five knuckle-bones, marbles, hopscotch, and skipping. As we walked along the long dusty road to and from school, a favourite game to play was 'follow the leader.' One child would be chosen as leader and the others had to do what the leader did, whether skipping, hopping, clapping one's hands, and so on. It certainly made the walk home more enjoyable.

I am glad I was privileged to experience the bush without its harshness. Having the bush as our playground and enjoying its creatures has impregnated my thoughts with images still alive today. Later I wrote poetry to capture some of the magic I often felt. I am sure that my siblings shared the same feelings.

During World War II, my dad worked at the Rockhampton Aerodrome at night as the airport was being substantially upgraded. We were living at Pink Lily, a rural area near Rockhampton. Our house was on the lagoon banks on which pink lilies floated. A large US Military camp was spread across the Rockhampton region. As a youngster, I sometimes went with old Jo Mumford in the horse and dray to collect scraps for our pigs from the nearby US camp.

My two sisters Margaret, Janice, and I attended the Pink Lily School, a one-teacher school with about thirty pupils. It opened on September 9, 1872, and closed on April 30 1971. I attended school when I was five and was the only one in my class. I think I got into trouble the first day for talking because I remember being banished to the shelter shed and feeling very sorry for myself. Having a trench drill every week made us acutely aware of the war raging in the Pacific.

During these War years, Mum and Dad worked hard to make a living. We owned two cows and Dad used to hire a horse and plough. Initially, Dad grew vegetables, which he sold door to door and further afield. When there were too many vegetables, he bought pigs to eat the leftovers!

This was how Helena Stud Piggery in Pink Lily began. Dad raised pigs for breeding purposes, mainly Berkshire and Tamworth, although he also had Large Whites. His Berkshire boar with the grand name of Helena Trump, *Cap* for short, was awarded the Grand Champion pig at the Royal Exhibition in Brisbane and champion at country shows on more than one occasion. *Cap* was so tame that he would oblige the people at the Royal Show by grunting into the microphone and following Dad around the ring in the grand parade. Newspaper cuttings have captured these moments for us to enjoy. One caption reads, "The only pig ever to appear in a Grand Parade." Almost as good as *Babe*!

Dad was a successful farmer and toured outback Country Shows judging pigs. A newspaper wrote about the Stud, *"Helena Stud Piggery has had outstanding success. It has gone a long way in a scant five years. Few studs have begun so modestly, and few have won success in so short a period as the Helena Stud Piggery, the property of A. W. Hodgkinson of Pink Lily, Rockhampton. The stud was started in November 1932 with a Berkshire boar, Gatton Royal, bred by the Gatton College, and a Berkshire sow, Roselock Damsel, bred by Messrs Porter and Sons of Wandal. There are now 150 pigs at Helena Stud, including some very high-class Tamworth studs....*" The date for this excerpt is not known.

When Mum and I went back to look at the Pink Lily house in 1990, the giant tamarind tree was still standing in the corner of the paddock. It was up this tree, at the age of six that I nimbly climbed when chased by an angry bull that I had been teasing. In 1990 we saw that the old house had been raised on high blocks. A couple of ancient structures still straddled the fence, which Dad used as a run platform to load pigs into a truck.

When the war ended, I was eight years old. By this time we had moved to Dunbar Street, Koongal, at the foot of the Berserker Range. My four-year-old baby sister Gweneth was unhappy with moving into a strange house and cried, "I wanna go home." In December 1946 excitement punctured the air when my brother Raymond was born after four girls. My aunties were delighted and shouted, 'It's a boy.'

Dad had secured employment at the Lakes Creek Meat Works, making sausages and other small goods. However, it was not long before Dad erected the sign *Helena Stud* near our driveway on Dunbar Street. Besides working at the Meatworks, Dad again started a successful business with Mum. The house was on about two acres of flat land. At first Dad put in crops, which he entered in the Rockhampton Agricultural Show. He won in the garden exhibit one year when he copied the back of a two-shilling piece. Instead of a kangaroo and an emu he had a cured pig and stuffed turkey. On the shield he glued various grains that he had grown. I was very proud of his achievement.

The two cows often escaped and wandered off up onto the low hills of the Berserker Range. My job was usually to find them and bring them home for milking. This was a job I liked except on cold mornings when the frost was crisp on the grass, and the spider webs were wet and clingy with crystal dewdrops. They fed on carrot weed and other bushes that tainted the milk when the cows got loose. We screwed up our noses as children do, at the taste. We had a couple of pigs and Dad was given wild pigs to fatten up for a friend for Christmas.

As children, we feasted on fresh produce from the gardens and enjoyed digging up peanuts when they were ready to eat. Creamy milk and eggs, along with roast chicken, were readily available. Mum and Dad rarely disciplined us by spanking. If we were caught fighting, we were sent to weed the gardens. We became friends again in a very short time, with Dad becoming enemy number one because we hated weeding. Another time I was sent to the bathroom, and Mum closed the door. I must have been furious for I emptied a talcum tin of power all over the bathroom floor. Mum took off her slipper and gave me a whack on the bottom. Another time I connected all the float watering systems in the fowl runs, creating a fantastic waterway scheme. Dad was so mad. He took off his belt, but this hampered him as he chased me, and I was able to escape.

Christmas was an exciting time. On Christmas Eve, after putting an empty pillowcase at the end of our beds Mum went to the pictures (movies) with Dad. When they returned home, they filled our pillowcases. The presents did not cost much, but we enjoyed simple things like a game of snakes and ladders and a Christmas stocking with lollies. One time Janice's present was a rag doll with yellow wool for hair. We rarely received this kind of gift. I so wanted that doll for myself. I took it and climbed up one of the pine trees, and I wouldn't come down.

After seeing the film "Lassie Come Home", my eldest sister Margaret acquired three Scotch Collie pedigree dogs. Lassie, Laddie, and Queeny had pups, which were sold off. The dogs were sometimes entered into the Show. If the bitches had too many puppies to feed, we would top up their feeds with diluted cow's milk. When bottle-feeding them I would hold them up by the scruff of the neck to see the size of their tummies. If rounded and fat, I would say, 'You've had enough.'

When we moved from the bush school in Pink Lily to the much bigger school at Lakes Creek, we were struck down by childhood diseases, one after another. Mum did all the nursing and doctoring. The Lakes Creek State School was opened in 1895 on its current site. We finished our schooling there. I liked school, especially starting a new exercise book. There was something magical about all the blank pages waiting to be filled in. History was my favourite subject. The pie man came to the school gate every day and the government provided milk for all the school children. Janice and I later attended Kerr's Commercial College to prepare for office work.

Dad worked long hours at two jobs at the Meat Works and on the poultry farm. We children had jobs of cleaning out pens, throwing grain to the free-range fowls, or collecting eggs to put in the incubator. Gradually Dad built up his successful business, hatching up to one thousand-day-old chickens a week and rearing pullets to sell off as laying pullets. We kept mainly Rhode Island Reds, White Leghorns, Black Australorps, and Australorps-Leghorn crosses. Later, Dad built an abattoir to dress and sell dressed poultry.

Often I was on a rescue mission. One night I was woken by a cat's cry from the kitchen downstairs. I crept down the back stairs and was so angry when I saw a big carpet snake swallowing one of our little kittens. The cries were coming from its mother. I rushed upstairs and shook Dad awake, and he killed it. Even though I performed major surgery on the snake, the kitten was dead, understandably!

We had homing pigeons which were let out once a day. When hawks gathered around, my antennas went to alert mode. With great agility a hawk would drive the pigeons down and down until they flew into a high fence, and then the hawk would pounce. A dingo came down out of the hills and went on a killing spree until Dad soon stopped that. Kookaburras came after the chickens, so Dad used his shotgun. Dad had a system of running warm water under pens in one shed during winter. He had to dismantle the system as rats were chewing off the chickens' legs when they poked through the wire flooring.

Dad's other pride was his prized roosters and drakes. This pride was affirmed and validated when one of his Muscovy drakes was awarded the grand championship. One day the agonising squawk of a frog reached my ears. A drake had a large green tree frog in its bill. Soon, with Shang eye in hand, I was ready to attack. Out flew the stone and wham, I hit the target for once. Imagine my dismay when I examined the unconscious drake only to find it was Dad's champion. With trepidation I waited for Dad to come home from work. Would he punish me? I didn't think he would feel sympathy for the frog. This was his prize Muscovy drake. I didn't pray for God to rescue me, for I didn't know how. A little later, to my astonishment, I saw the drake walking around. Relief flooded my senses. I thought, 'Mum's the word'. It was a close call. So, the frog lived to croak again, the drake lived to win again, and I continued to miss – again!

There is much about suffering that I find difficult to accept, for example, what went on in the incubator shed. The thousands of day-old chicks hatched in a large incubator. Dad gave them only two extra days of grace to hatch. Some eggs, with a chicken's beak protruding, were thrown down a deep dry well in the orchard. Dad killed the crippled ones. One day, while looking for something to do, I heard a chicken chirping in a tin of discarded eggs. A little chicken dad had wounded but failed to kill was chirping pitifully. I rescued it and looked after it until I could release it.

One day Dad entered the kitchen and said, 'I don't know what is wrong with Pauline's pet. It keeps turning summersaults.' I knew what was wrong. The poor thing was brain-damaged.

During the long hours in the incubator shed sorting and testing the fertility of the incubator eggs, Dad listened to the ABC radio, acquiring knowledge about many subjects. He was a jack-of-all-trades, a successful breeder and farmer, a builder, a plumber, and an electrician, and he mended our shoes. He made candy for our school fetes and could make a batch of delicious scones. When I was studying physics in 1970 in preparation for further study at the College of Nursing in Melbourne, he amazed me by answering my questions on hydraulics and other related subjects. He was respected in the community. However, his success was made possible because Mum handled the business side, keeping accounts, answering letters, and acquiring customers in outback towns.

Despite their busyness, Dad and Mum kept their sense of humour and took time to go to the movies even though Dad probably snored, and Mum felt compelled to dig him in the ribs occasionally. At least it was 'time out' for two busy people.

Our dad had black, slightly curly hair and slanting blue eyes. I think he could be described as a 'colourful character'. He told a good yarn and would stand with his hands tucked into the back of his trousers as he had a 'chin wag.' Around the farm he whistled heartily. He sometimes screeched like a cockatoo on the open road in his T-model Ford instead of using a horn! However, he could not stand 'tomfoolery' and would kick the empty feed tins around if frustrated. Dad would lean over and twist our ear lobes if we kids misbehaved at the table. That worked wonders! For a lark he would heat his teaspoon in his cup of tea and then put it on our leg under the table. Many customers fell foul to Dad's trick of shaking hands while he caught hold of the electric fence wire that kept the pigs in the orchard. Dad did not touch alcohol or smoke. All jokes aside, Dad lived for his 'Better Half,' meaning Mum and his kids. Mum called him 'Albert', Dad's family called him 'Bert', and his friends called him 'Jerry'.

In contrast our mother, Amy, seemed prim and proper to us. She always dressed nicely and she loved her jewellery. Her great sense of humour saved her. We loved her laughter when we told funny stories. We would turn one of Shakespeare's dramas into a comedy and act it out in the kitchen. Mum would be in stitches. Her thick brown, slightly curly hair offset her dancing hazel eyes.

Mum loved beautiful things, and she taught us the value of looking after what we had, making things last, and being considerate of others. Mum was a keen gardener, so her garden was often a colourful display of annuals such as delphiniums, dahlias, flocks, stocks, lilies, and roses. During dry spells, hotels sometimes asked her to supply flowers. Gardening required a great effort on Mum's part because of Rockhampton's harsh climate, but she had chicken manure which was an excellent fertiliser. Two peacocks strutted around the garden and were later joined by a pet curlew.

Parents sometimes brought their children to the farm to see the farm animals, especially the large variety of birds, including parrots, pigeons, quails, turkeys, ducks, and my brother Raymond's pet crow. The proud peacock would fan its tail to show off its beautiful feathers. The peacocks roosted in the pine trees at night and made a terrible noise if startled.

Dad retired from the Lakes Creek Meatworks and retired as a farmer a few years later. Countless ribbons and prizes bear testimony to Dad's success. While other breeders kept their best stock in special cages all year, Dad's entries were taken from the fowl runs the day before being judged. He selected those in prime condition by running his expert eye over the birds and fowls. Then he quickly gave them a shampoo, rubbed oil onto their legs and combs, plucked out stray feathers, and cleaned their toenails. Such was his judgement and expertise that he often won major prizes. Even in the Meatworks as a small-goods man, Dad won an Australia-wide competition for a sausage he entered and received the award of three hundred pounds! It must have proved a good recipe with commercial value. This would have been in about 1950. With this money, Dad built a large kitchen underneath our high-block house.

By 1971 the farm in Dunbar Street was surrounded by houses as Dad had already sold off some of the land and it was time to move on. Dad pulled down the sheds and fences and sold the house and land. They received enough money to buy a snug house at 16 Face Street, Park Avenue, and a new blue Marina car.

Growing up in such a family where respect and love were shown to each member was a blessing. Although we were not church-going, we firmly understood right from wrong. When I stole a sixpence as a nine-year-old, I felt very guilty. It happened like this. The houses, when built, were not sparrow-proof. Sparrows built their nests under the roofing, and lice would crawl down the walls. Neighbours asked me to climb up into the ceiling and rid the place of the nests. One neighbour, the Collins family, asked for my help. I went up the manhole and quickly found the nest. No one was in the bedroom, so I took a sixpence from a purse lying on the bed. No one saw me. But God did. And this holy God hates sin. It is an antithesis of His very nature. This God grieves because sin has marred his beautiful world and set man in rebellion against God.

GOD'S RESCUE PLAN

This amazing God would reveal himself to me as the God who forgives sin and puts a rescue plan in motion. He sent his Son to save guilty humanity. This God loved me as I moved around in my childhood world. He knew me even when I was being formed in that secret place.

I didn't know that this God created the world I enjoyed. He made the trees to climb, the moon to watch rising over the mountain, and the blossoms pregnant with a perfume that wafted on the breezes that fan us on a hot day. This God would put his hand on my family, and amid our trials, he would bless us. Such was his amazing grace so freely bestowed.

Chapter 2

In the Shadows of Innocence

In him (Jesus), we have redemption through his blood, the forgiveness of sins, in accordance with the riches of God's grace. Eph 1:7.

As we step out of the last chapter of what seemed an idyllic early childhood, I am struggling with this next chapter in my life; it is not easy to share something that touches one deeply. I was now an eleven-year-old child in 1948 with the same sense of adventure and zest for life. But this time, I was meeting human predators out to destroy the innocence of children. Instead of being the rescuer, I needed to be rescued.

In the 1940s-50s, my family operated as a typical, busy family. Sex was never discussed. So, the emotions I felt at the abuse could not be brought out in words, nor could the powerlessness that accompanied it. It was a betrayal of trust. My older sister felt the ramifications of these evil acts by the perpetrator more destructively. This abuse occurred when the two of us went on holiday on two or three occasions to the same place.

I was unaware that the initial grooming event could make me vulnerable and submissive to future abuse. When it happened again at fifteen on my first job working in a Photo Studio in East Street, I was filled with self-disgust, but underneath that was sickening anger, shame, and a stifled cry for justice. Professionals tell us that trauma victims often blame themselves.

Consequently, wounds were well hidden, deep in my inner being, underneath my energetic lifestyle. I was unaware of the prevalence and impact of child sexual abuse. It was a surprise that such a thing could happen. Mercifully, later in my journey as a believer, God showed me that the past is not set in cement; we can go back and forgive those who have sinned against us. The decision to forgive others is crucial to our mental health. It may not happen for some years, but it needs to happen. God's grace is enough for us to forgive others. Forgiving is the pathway to healing and victory.

Forgive one another, just as God forgave you
because of what Christ has done. Eph 4:32

The Australian culture in the 1940s-50s minimised and denied that such a criminal act occurred. It wasn't until the 1970s that child abuse emerged as a significant social and political issue in Australia.

Years later I shared it with my parents, and I wish I had not done so. I caused them unnecessary distress. The perpetrator was dead, so what good could come from them knowing?

Furthermore, during those years I was unaware that there was a God who saw everything, heard everything, and knew everything. A God who knew me even though I did not know Him. Though we were sent infrequently to the Anglican Church Sunday School, I did not hear a clear message of the grace and mercy of a loving God. I did not know Him personally. One day, when I told my Mum that I wanted to be religious, she sent my two older sisters and me along to be confirmed – to confirm the promises made at our baptism. The only problem was we had never been christened or baptised!

I was indignant when I discovered this and complained, 'Mum, you have brought us up like a bunch of heathens.' In response to this, Mum sent Margaret, Janice, and me to be baptised, attend confirmation classes, and, on Sundays, take Holy Communion. Gweneth and Raymond were also baptised. However, the following Easter brought the same question: 'Why did Jesus need to die?' 'Is it true that the real me lives on after death?' I still did not understand the difference between being religious and having a personal relationship with God. God put such a longing in my heart to know Him. I longed to experience God's love and forgiveness.

Thankfully, God was quietly working to bring me into a place of blessing. In 1952 after my first failed attempt at a job, I found one I enjoyed. It wasn't typing and shorthand for which I had been trained at Kerr's Commercial College, but a job working with numbers. When I began employment in the large office of the Lakes Creek Meatworks, I was offered a position on the comptometers. The Meatworks sold consignments of beef overseas, and the clerks in the shipping department needed their accounts checked. These accounts were in foreign currencies, and the four comptometer operators ensured that the charges and conversion rates were correct. We also checked the clerks' payments of the hundreds of salaries paid out by the main office.

This is where I met Jo White, the boss's secretary. Jo attended a Christian Brethren church meeting in the ALP Hall in Park Avenue. Today, many of these brethren churches go under the name 'Christian Community Churches of Australia'. They form a network of Open Brethren churches or 'assemblies' in Australia. They do not form a denomination in the organisational sense but rather a network of like-minded autonomous local churches.

Jo invited me one night to hear Mr Roger Griffith from Brisbane, who was doing a series of bible teaching. I reluctantly arranged to go to the meeting. Mr Griffith was a retired schoolteacher. He used a visual aid, a large chart showing God's great plan of salvation stretching across the centuries. He explained that God desired to RESCUE those who cried out to him.

Initially I felt awkward and out of place, but my heart was soon captured by the words from a verse in the Gospel of John: *Behold, the lamb of God who takes away the sin of the world.* (John 1:29). I thought, is that why Jesus died – to take away my sin?

Roger Griffith went on to explain why God sent his Son, Jesus. Jesus was the Rescuer. Through his sacrifice of dying on the cross, he bore the punishment for our sins. If we confess our sins and need, God will forgive us. This all flowed out of God's love and grace for us, the people he created perfect but who had gone astray.

> *For it is by grace, you have been saved, through faith –*
> *and this not of yourselves, it is a gift of God....* Eph 2:8

Roger Griffith graciously pleaded for us to respond to this great love. He quoted another verse that shook me to the very core! This verse was from the last book of the Bible, describing what takes place at the time of the great judgment. *Anyone whose name was not found written in the book of life was thrown into the lake of fire.* Rev 15:20

I didn't know much about the Bible, but I had heard of the lake of fire! My father used to warn us, 'If you kids keep playing up, Old Nick will come and take you to the lake of fire.' Dad's theology was not crash hot, but those words were enough to quieten us down. I could have walked away from that meeting thinking, 'hogwash'. But no. I had met the God who sees me, loves me, will forgive me, and make me clean.

Jesus came to rescue me. God was offering me salvation, a gift I didn't deserve, but because of His amazing grace I could experience this unconditional act of His kindness and mercy.

It seemed all too good to be true. This was a gift! There was no way I could earn it. So, in 1953 I asked Jesus to come into my heart and life, to cleanse me from all sin, and to give me the gift of eternal life in heaven.

'God, thank you for forgiving me.'

I was so excited. This was what and whom I was searching for. I told my sisters, Janice and Gweneth, and asked them to come to the Sunday service. They too accepted the Lord Jesus as their personal Saviour.

And so my two sisters, Janice and Gweneth, and I began our journey of faith in a personal God and our Saviour, Jesus. I eagerly read the Bible and found the answers to many of my questions. Each morning we read God's Word and prayed for our family. We used the devotional 'Streams in the Desert' by Mrs Charles Cowman. We were ignorant of the enormity of the steps just taken, but God kept us in his care until we understood what being a Christian meant. Janice, Gweneth, and I were baptised in the Fitzroy River on a cold July morning. This time our baptism was a declaration of our desire to live a life of obedience to the Lord Jesus.

A whole new world opened to us. We became enthusiastically involved in church activities like Sunday School, Boys and Girls Rallies, and Children's camps. My sister Janice would zip around in the little van, picking up children. We visited the neighbourhood houses and gathered a group of youngsters with whom we spent time. We took them to activities where they could hear the gospel. We did fun things together, like climbing the Berserker Range and having billy tea in the shade of gum trees.

Mum and Dad didn't object to our new way of life, but they might have been puzzled by the degree of our commitment. It took them a few years to understand and enter into the assurance of salvation in Christ.

God's grace rescued me and instead of tears, I had an inward joy because I knew God loved me. I wanted others to experience the joy of sins forgiven and have a personal relationship with God.

Chapter 3

Bridging Worlds – Embracing the Call

He has saved us and called us to a holy life
– not because of anything we have done but
because of his own purpose and grace.
2 Timothy 1:9

After working in the large office at Lakes Creek for three years, I left to go and work in Sydney when I was nineteen, leaving home in Easter 1957. On my second day there I secured a fantastic job working on the comptometers for Qantas Airlines. I was among the employees who moved into the new Qantas building on Hunter Street. Looking back, the reasons for going to Sydney seem insignificant. Perhaps it was the urge to spread my wings or God directing my path.

While attending a church in Burwood, I went to a youth camp where I saw the film "*Brands from the Burning.*" The film hinted at the terrible Hindu practice of sati – the burning of the widow with the body of her dead husband on the funeral pyre, which is now illegal in India. Equally important, the film gave a graphic picture of rejecting the truth of the Creator God and turning to idols made by man. I was moved to tears.

Like Nehemiah, who was distressed on hearing of the plight of the Jews, I was distressed on hearing the plight of the women in India, hopelessly trapped in a caste system. They did not know that the Creator God loved them. They did not realise that they were of value – that Jesus had given his life to bring them back to God. They were dying without hearing the good news of the gospel. The hymn sung was:

Rescue the perishing, care for the dying,
Snatch them in pity from sin and the grave;
Weep o'er the erring one, lift up the fallen,
Jesus is merciful. Jesus will save.
Down in the human heart, crushed by the tempter,
Feelings lie buried that grace can restore;
Touched by a loving heart, wakened by kindness,
Cords that were broken will vibrate once more.

I desired to tell these women of the liberating truth of the gospel. I felt a call upon my life to serve the Lord in this vast land of India. I spoke with the Burwood Church elders and made my desire known. This is the reason I decided to do my nursing training. I needed a pathway into the lives of these women. I knew my mother would be apprehensive about all this, so I gently tried to break it. At first, she was upset, but given time for reflection, she quietly accepted my decision. I left Sydney in 1958 to be nearer home and started nursing training at the Tannachy Private Hospital in Rockhampton. However, after eight months I realised this training was not what I needed for India. I applied to a recommended Sydney hospital but, on arrival in Sydney was surprised I was not accepted in their next intake. I had three months to fill in before starting training. I thought, 'Now what?'

LUTANDA CHILDREN'S HOME

Keith Young of Wattle Park Chapel in Melbourne, whose mother was working at the Lutanda Children's Home in Pennant Hills, Sydney, knew of me and told me of their dire need for staff at Lutanda. The Lord seemed to have arranged this, so I met with the staff, offered my help, and cared for a dormitory of little boys and girls at the other end of the building. They certainly kept me on my toes. I remember helping to make about fifty school lunches each morning and washing dozens of school socks.

The weeks I spent as a houseparent to these children drew from me unique relationships with some of them. I remember one family: a girl of about eleven with a younger brother. My heart went out to them on visiting days, for no one came to see them. Their father was in prison. I kept in touch with Caroline, the young girl, for many years. She eventually married.

ST GEORGE HOSPITAL, KOGARAH, SYDNEY

At last, the day came to start my four-year training at the St George Hospital in Kogarah. It proved to be an excellent training school. Many nursing students came in from the country towns and a few were Christians. Before long I ran a weekly Bible study and sought to build up attendance at the Nurses Christian Movement meeting held once a month in the Nurses' Quarters. NCM had become a national organisation in 1928 and was well-accepted in hospitals. Soon we had fifty to sixty nurses coming regularly to

Pauline as student nurse

the NCM meetings. I roomed with Sue Hampson to acquire a larger bedroom for nurses to gather for the weekly Bible Studies.

Still a rescuer at heart, I helped a nurse who accidentally locked herself out of her bedroom, and this wasn't the first time. I knew the matron kept keys in a tall flowerpot outside her bedroom. Quickly running up the back stairs, I grabbed the planter, rushed down a flight of stairs, scooped up the keys, opened the nurse's door, and rushed back to replace the keys and planter. Another time, I sat in the nurses' mess with a meal that looked remarkably like vomit. It was disgusting. I told the staff, 'I am not going to eat this. I am asking Matron Harper to come to show her what you are giving nurses to eat.' The kitchen staff took more care with our meals after that.

When my sister Gweneth came to St George to begin as a student nurse, she trained a Verse-Speaking Choir to perform in our outreach programs. Though Gweneth, Janice, and I had learned the Art of Speech for several years, Gweneth was the gifted one at recitation. We also formed a singing choir, and Matron Harper permitted us to wear our uniforms when we were invited to perform at Youth Meetings in Churches. We did look very smart, wearing red capes and black stockings.

A representative from a TV Show asked us to perform on TV. However, I declined as I was unsure of Matron Harper's response. We went to nearby Nursing Homes to perform. In 1962 I arranged a big event to which the Doctors, Matron Harper, and the Tutor Sisters, Sister McGuire and Sister Cush, were invited. A Christian Eye Specialist gave an inspirational message on the wonder of sight, the eye's structure, and the value of spiritual sight. One of our Christian nurses, Rosemary Snodgrass, became the Hospital's Director of Nursing from 1984 to 91.

These proved to be satisfying years of ministry and training, learning to face my human frailties and experiencing God's grace. On Sundays I attended the Bexley Gospel Hall during a day off. Dr Victor Wilson and his wife Daphne often asked me home for a hot dinner. I don't think I stopped talking at the dinner table! My mind was always alert and I was naturally enthusiastic – full of stories. Later, when I was working in the hospital in Ambajipeta, Dr Wilson sent me parcels of new surgical gloves and little gadgets put to good use. I felt blessed when food parcels, sometimes from my parents and sometimes from praying friends, arrived after months in the post.

After completing four years of general training in Sydney and a year of midwifery training at the Brisbane Women's Hospital, God led me to relieve Sister Isa Black for several months at the Doomadgee Mission near Burketown — a series of events pointed in this direction.

DOOMADGEE MISSION

Doomadgee Community lies in the far northwest corner of Queensland, one hundred and forty miles from the Northern Territory. The mission commenced in 1933 by the Akehurst family with the support of the Christian Brethren Churches.

In 1964 the living and working conditions in the hospital were still very basic. The hospital's walls were corrugated iron, and the floor was concrete. There was a kitchen with a wood stove and a sink. In the centre of the building was a ward with six beds. Adjacent to this was my room with a bed and kerosene refrigerator. Another smaller room led off from mine and into the labour ward. I shared the bathroom with the patients and the outhouse out the back.

By day the flies landed in their hundreds as soon as anyone stood still. By night the mosquitoes buzzed noisily, trying to get at me through the net. I often swallowed a fly! I revelled professionally and spiritually with each challenge during those long, hot months. I was on my own – treating and delivering babies, suturing wounds, extracting teeth, diagnosing, and being on call 24/7. The Flying Doctor, based in Cloncurry, came when I called him on the two-way radio.

The Aboriginal mothers in the camp were strongly encouraged to bring their babies to the hospital every morning and late afternoon because if they did, they would receive porridge and custard topped with puree apricots. Bottles of milk feed for the day were poured into sparkling clean tomato sauce bottles. In addition to this, they received freshly squeezed orange juice. The babies looked very healthy and bonny.

One night a mother brought her feverish baby to the hospital. I held up the lantern but could not see the baby clearly as the glass was dirty. When dawn broke, I became aware that the baby was very ill. Suddenly the little fellow had a seizure indicative of meningitis. I tried to contact the Flying Doctor but was unsuccessful. However, a cattle property owner picked up my signal. I relayed to him that I had a "case of meningitis" and for him to contact the Flying Doctor. Another mother came rushing in within the hour with her toddler, also convulsing. The Flying Doctor's plane landed an hour later, and both babies were airlifted to the Mt Isa Hospital. Sadly, the little boy with meningitis died. The second little toddler had eaten some poisonous plant and thankfully recovered.

I had to diligently monitor those with raised temperatures for the next few weeks. This was complicated by the fact that an influenza epidemic hit Doomadgee. The Flying Doctor came down hard and said we had to hospitalise anyone with an elevated temperature. I had to accommodate more than thirty patients in the jailhouse, girls' dormitory, and even the labour ward to monitor them for signs of meningitis. If a child was brought at night with a high fever and showing signs of cerebral irritation, I put the child in a cardboard carton in my bed with me under the net. I followed the instructions given by the Flying Doctor, giving the antibiotics and sponging the baby between naps. At first light I contacted the Flying Doctor. We had three more cases of meningitis and thankfully saved the babies. We made the ABC News!

I was supported during such times by a missionary nurse, Isabel Strahan. Rob and Isabel were serving at Doomadgee and Isabel was able to help occasionally. I rescued old blind Maggie from the camp one day and gave her a much-needed bath. As I poured the warm, soapy water over her, she sang in her tribal language, punctuated with, "Thank you, Jesus. Thank you, Jesus." Maggie sent me a little live crocodile as a thank-you gift. What was I to do with a crocodile? I named him Bo-Bo and kept him in the bath. Feeding him proved a problem. His teeth were very sharp. I needed to finely chop the meat and ease it between his teeth.

After a few weeks of feeding Bo-Bo and putting him into a bucket whenever someone needed a bath, I sent him home to my parents! I put him into a container with wet rags and wrote on the outside of the tin, 'My name is Bo-Bo. I like fingers.' When it arrived in Rockhampton, a dumbfounded TAA officer asked my dad to come and collect it – post-haste. My dad kept Bo-Bo for a while but then had Bo-Bo mummified and placed on the wall at the entrance to our home.

One night when it was pitch black, I heard shuffling on the veranda. It was uncommon to have folk around at night, although sometimes crocodile shooters ended up on our roads. I found a man and woman holding on to a poor soul, a young mother who had developed post-natal depression. During that day, she tried to harm her baby. They explained the situation and then melted away into the darkness. The hospital door did not lock. No matter how often I tucked her in bed, she would climb out again. I was desperately tired, so I climbed into bed with her under the net. I tied our ankles together and then tried to get some sleep. As soon as it was dawn, I called the Flying Doctor. I didn't hear how she recovered from her post-natal depression.

Aboriginal folk go walkabout. They walk off abruptly into the bush. This is due to the spiritual ties indigenous people have with their land. Going walkabout is not a good idea when taking daily insulin injections. I had one such fellow and, on his return, he gave me a curlew to sweeten me up. However, this curlew had a broken leg as his dog had mauled it. I carefully splinted the leg, and the curlew soon became a pet. I named him Jacky.

I taught Jacky to dance, a fatal error of judgment as he would put out his wings and waltz down the veranda, making a loud noise as he went.

On the way to school, children would call him to follow them to morning prayers. After a few noisy sessions, Mr Hockey said, "You must do something about that curlew." So, I did. I sent Jacky home to my parents! My parents had him as a pet for many years. He followed my mum as she gardened, alert to catch an insect. But Jacky should have been called Jaqueline as he laid an egg.

The Doomadgee Mission was a working cattle property and I sometimes watched as they broke in wild horses. Massive dust storms were not unusual. Everything in the hospital would be covered with thick dust as there was no way to keep it out. There are two seasons in the far north – the Wet and the Dry. With the first downpour of monsoonal rain, I found the hospital tank was full of holes. My white uniform soon took on a pale cream colour from the river water.

On Sunday afternoon I took my turn to be 'on duty', minding the teenage girls from the dormitory as they swam in the river. The sound of their laughter filled the air. At night the sky was brilliantly lit with a myriad of stars. During the summer days the temperature soared into the hundreds. A mid-day rest was impossible because of the flies, as they were always looking for a place to land.

When I was at Doomadgee, no alcohol was allowed on the property, which was a relief. Drinking alcohol can lead to domestic violence. Although often exhausted, I just went quietly about my work, accepting the situation. My recollections of my experiences are positive ones, except for the exhaustion. Some of the fatigue came from caring for a long-staying patient on bed rest because of a damaged heart. Most nights I needed to get up at least three times to meet her needs.

The Aboriginal women were shy, but they would listen when I sat on a wooden box under a shady tree and talked informally about Jesus. I was grateful to Gwen, a lovely Christian Aboriginal girl who helped me in the hospital.

During those months I proved the Lord faithful financially and in many difficult situations. Being dependent on Him when I needed a level of skill for which I had not received training stood me in good stead for what lay ahead of me in India.

As a thank-you gift, the school children, under the guidance of the principal Lionel Fawssett, gave me a large book of their exceptional artwork. Along with this were sewing samples and a pocket of letters neatly written by the children. I did not expect such a show of appreciation. I treasure that book and still look at it occasionally.

AT THE CROSSROADS

When I came to a crossroad, the Lord often took me to the same text in the Bible – the gospel of John, chapter 21, verses 15-17. This describes the encounter between Jesus and Peter after Christ's resurrection and after Peter had denied being a follower of Jesus three times. The Lord Jesus asked Peter three times, "*Do you love Me more than these?*" The fishermen among the disciples had returned to their former trade of catching fish. But this was not Jesus' intention for them. He had called them to '*follow Me, and I will make you fishers of men*'. (Matt 4:19).

This same question challenged my heart. I could give a resounding 'Yes' to *'Do you love Me?'*, but the challenge for me was in the *'more than these*?' To love Him more than anyone else or anything? Was I prepared to let God direct my life? Was I willing to commit myself to a ministry of pastoral care and encouragement by teaching God's Word to bring hope? A life of compassion for those who needed it? Moreover, God had gifted me with the ability to teach and a passion for communicating the life-giving words of Jesus. So many opportunities had opened up for me to do this, not only among the nursing students but also as I travelled extensively throughout eastern Australia, telling of my call to serve God in India.

In 1965 I was at a crossroad where my loves competed with each other. I knew one love needed to go. I had continued in a friendship with a Christian man even though I knew there was no future in it. I had not been brave or honest enough to end it. I had tried explaining my reasons but failed to be adamant about my commitment to overseas service in India. Consequently, when it came to crunch time, the friendship ended in hurt feelings on both sides.

I dearly love my family. How could I bear to leave my parents and siblings? Yet my love for the Lord Jesus had to be supreme, more sacrificial. The Lord tested me on this commitment more than once in future years, just as he tested Abraham's faith. Abraham did not fail, whereas at this crossroad in 1965, I had to come to the place where I needed God's transforming power to love people as God loves. God's love doesn't fail to seek the best for the recipient. The early church used the word 'agape' to describe this kind of sacrificial loving.

From the day of my conversion, I have loved God's Word. I studied with the Emmaus Correspondence School and attended many conferences.

It was a joy to learn verses and speak at women's gatherings. I knew we needed God's Word written on our hearts to prepare us for the enemy's attack and the trials of life. It is the Sword of the Spirit that we use in spiritual warfare. Beyond that, the Word of God tells us how to live wisely as we seek to honour Christ selflessly.

How I needed God's grace and promises in the years ahead. Indeed, I was ever mindful that I was bringing into situations the trappings of my old life: old patterns of thinking, reacting and behaving. I often felt I was falling far from what people thought of me. I felt like a failure until I recognised the danger of putting labels on myself. A label would only lock me into a place that wouldn't allow change. Instead, I say, 'I have failed,' and ask God to help me correct my wrong attitudes and actions.

Years later, when reading Marjory Foyle's book '*Honourably Wounded*,' I better understood the stresses I encountered on the mission field and what is necessary to come to terms with them. Amy Carmichael wrote:

Give me a love that leads the way,
The faith that nothing can dismay,
The hope that no disappointment tires,
The passion that will burn like fire,
Let me not sink to be a clod,
Make me thy fuel, Flame of God.

From my child-like need to want to be good, the Lord brought me into a place of dependence on his grace. God's grace, this unmerited favour of God, is to be the framework through which my entire life must be lived. I experience God's grace when enabled to forgive others and his forgiveness when I sin against Him.

I read once that God's grace does not just call us to salvation but also servanthood. His grace distributes our talents and spiritual gifts so that we can serve others. Everyone has this calling in their lives.

Each of you should use whatever gift you have
received to serve others, as faithful stewards
of God's grace in its various forms.
1 Peter 4:10

Chapter 4

India – At Last

And the God of all grace, who called you to his eternal glory in Christ, after you have suffered a little while, will himself restore you and make you strong, firm and steadfast.
I Peter 5:10

By mid-1965 I was ready to obey God's call to serve Him in India. I had been writing to two hospitals in India. One was in Kerala State and the other was up the eastern coast in the Godavari Delta in Andhra Pradesh State. Both had a School of Nursing that taught in English. I was prompted to go to Kerala when I heard that Mary Bardsley, a missionary nursing sister at the Thiruvalla Medical Mission hospital in Kerala, had fractured her leg in England and could not return to Kerala until she was well enough. Two other missionary nurses were working in the TMM hospital. Muriel Pitts was the Nursing Superintendent and Mary Miller was the senior Nurse Educator.

My home assembly in North Rockhampton, where I was nurtured during the first three years after my conversion, had suffered a church split in 1964. It meant that I needed commendation from another church for missionary service. A church commends a missionary candidate deemed suitable both practically and spiritually to fulfil the role chosen by the candidate. The commending church gives reasons for this — for example, details of the candidate's previous involvement in ministry. A commissioning service may follow this commendation. The sending church's declaration commends other churches to pray and support the candidate as the Lord directs. Annerley Assembly, now Village Avenue Community Church, which I attended while doing midwifery training at the Royal Brisbane Women's Hospital in Brisbane, commended me with an endorsement by the Bexley Assembly in Sydney.

I sailed for India in August 1965 on the P&O ocean liner, the *"Arcadia"*, leaving on a bitter winter's day. Snow had fallen on the Blue Mountains and outer suburbs of Sydney. Mum and Dad looked so miserable standing on the pier waving goodbye. Mum was ill with an influenza virus and had travelled down from Rockhampton. I still feel an ache in my heart as I relive that scene. I was leaving home and would not be coming back for five years. This was a significant emotional loss, for I loved my family dearly.

I travelled with Don and Mavis Adams and their four children. Don and Mavis were returning to Kerala after their furlough. Don acquired good berths on A deck. When I decided to try to eat lunch in the dining room for the first time, a giant wave hit the ship, and crockery smashed everywhere. I quickly retreated. We disembarked in Bombay after eighteen days on the high seas. I was so glad to be off that rolling ship as I felt seasick most of the time.

At the Bombay railway station, I sensed the first assault of India upon my soul. The platforms were crowded; beggars were pleading for help; a cacophony of noise filled the air, and the sights and smells assailed my senses.

I felt overwhelmed as I sat minding all the luggage while Don and Mavis sorted out our ongoing travel. God opened my eyes, and I saw them, the women of India. A mother was hurrying along with a child straddled on her hip. A little girl dressed in rags sat begging. Another girl was sleeping on a bench. The rich wore colourful saris, but their needs were the same. They needed Jesus. They needed to know God's love. My heart cried out, "O Lord Jesus, Good Shepherd, you look compassionately at these lost ones. Help me never to lose compassion. Enable me always to see them with your eyes. I see humanity broken and in need. Your healing power can restore us to what You intended us to be. Give me pathways into lives to bring your healing power. I pray in Jesus' Name."

KERALA STATE – 1965-1970

We caught a train from Bombay to Vellore Medical College, where Mavis's sister and her husband, Dr Frank Garlick, worked. Then we travelled down to Kerala State by train. My eyes feasted on the sea of green – large paddy fields edged by coconut trees. Kerala receives prolific heavy rain in June, hence all the greenery. There is so much beauty to enchant any nature lover. Kerala is often referred to as 'God's own Country'.

I saw a baby elephant being washed in a stream and excited schoolchildren strolling home from school. Houses were painted in pastel colours or whitewashed. I noticed that the houses had pitched roofs covered by tiles. Heavy traffic choked the roads while drivers swerved and beeped their horns. I enjoyed all I saw through the train window.

The plan was for me to study the Malayalam (മലയാളം) language while staying with Don and Mavis in the Boys' Home in Irinjalakuda. Then I would move to Thrissur to stay with Edith Wallace and Phyllis Treasure in the Rehoboth Girls' Orphanage. This time I engaged an experienced Hindu language teacher for the next six months. I soon acquired a taste for the curries of India and felt blessed to be in a safe environment as I adjusted to the Indian culture. Stripped of things familiar, every day dawned with a new awakening. Soon came the realisation that the missionaries encountered many heartaches as they sought to meet the overwhelming needs so nakedly evident around them.

I worked on the language eight hours a day. Often I was in tears, but I persevered. I had a lazy tongue, so it was difficult for me to roll an 'r' and make other strange combinations of sounds. There were three 'r' sounds in the Malayalam language! It was a great day when I rolled my first 'r'. It happened like this. I felt frustrated with my Hindu language teacher, who made me learn grammar words in the Malayalam language. After the lesson as I sounded forth as I sometimes do, I stopped and shouted, "Wow, did you hear that? I just rolled the 'r'."

I loved my time at the Rehoboth Orphanage in Thrissur, interacting with the girls. The word Rehoboth was a name given to a well Isaac built. In Genesis 26:22, Isaac said, 'The Lord has made room for us…' which happened at the Orphanage. Needy children came and found a home. Many brought up in Rehoboth Orphanage can testify to this home's influence. Phyllis Treasure and others accepted all who came and were able to make a difference for over a thousand individuals and their families. Many came to faith in Christ, and some became wives of Indian evangelists and pastors. Phyllis, born in 1934 in New Zealand and trained as a Home Science teacher, is still at Rehoboth and mummy to many who love her dearly.

While studying Malayalam, I attended evening prayers in the Shala (Sanskrit for *abode*), a large hall where the children met to sing songs by heart. They were bright, energetic children who quickly crept into my heart. They called me Pauly Aunty. Phyllis arranged suitable marriages for her girls. Some returned to Rehoboth during pregnancy with their first child and stayed for three months following delivery, as is the Indian custom. This ensures that the mother receives the rest and care she needs.

I have visited Rehoboth a few times since my language study in 1965-66, and I am amazed at how much Malayalam I can still remember. In 2006 while there, I taught English at the Rehoboth Theological Institute. I used grammatical markers from the Book of Romans, thus showing the young men how to put a sermon together. Another time, I was asked to speak at a Kerala Conference for Women, where about five hundred Christians had gathered for fellowship.

VISIT TO TAMIL NADU

While at Rehoboth in 1966, I heard about a Welsh missionary doctor working in an isolated area in Tamil Nadu State. As I needed a break from language study, I wrote to express my interest, and we decided on a meeting point. What an adventure it proved to be. A hair-raising bus ride up a mountain range and down the other side brought me to the designated village where I was to meet the missionary. The people around me were speaking Tamil, a classical language of India. It is also Sri Lanka's official language.

With relief and feeling rather travel-worn, I saw a white woman and greeted her. Without too much fuss, she pointed to a bicycle. Oh no, I hadn't ridden one for years. I bravely mounted the very old-looking contraption. A young boy followed with my baggage. The way to her hospital was on a narrow, rutted path between paddy fields. All seemed to be going well until my sandal strap snapped, my foot slipped, and I lost control. I had to decide between a paddy field with water or the other side. I chose the other side – a wrong choice. I ended up in a briar patch. For days I was picking out prickles.

We arrived at rather primitive-looking buildings, and immediately, the doctor (I cannot remember her name) was called to a case of a man with a massive abscess on his neck. She asked me to hold the kidney dish. Before this, I felt anything but well, and the smell of E. Coli pus pouring out was too much. She said, 'You have turned green.' I nodded and made my escape.

The next humiliating experience was when we went swimming in a big well, with steps down on the inside wall to the water. I'm not fond of heights, but I persuaded myself I could do this. When I jumped in, dozens of frogs jumped out and sat on the bricks, blinking at me. I have a phobia of frogs. I cannot stand them getting hurt, but I cannot stand them. An earnest prayer ascended to heaven! I smiled bravely and stayed put, hoping the frogs would do the same. When I did exit up the narrow steps, I did so safely without any green encounters.

I began to realise that this Welsh Doctor was unique as were her treatments. I laughed at her antics as she walked around the ward waving a Lippes Loop used in contraception. Someone said her first case in a village was delivering a buffalo's calf.

The Welsh missionary doctor wanted me to see more of Tamil Nadu State. Phyllis Treasure was to meet us at a given point on our journey south. We were going to Amy Carmichael Orphanage – the safe home called Dohnavur Fellowship that Amy had opened to rescue girls from being trafficked in Hindu temples. These desperate rescues started one day when a little seven-year-old girl called Preena jumped onto Amy's lap, clung to her neck and cried, "Please help me! Please don't send me back." The little girl had escaped from the Hindu temple in the middle of the night.

Amy served in India for fifty-five years without a furlough and died in 1951. She spent the last twenty years of her life bedridden, during which time she wrote several books and poems. Her dedication has inspired others to serve on the mission fields. Other missionaries at Dohnavur were carrying on with this ministry. The compound and buildings were beautifully kept, and the girls must have felt safe in such an enclosure. It was all very impressive.

We travelled to Cape Comorin, sometimes called 'Land's End'. Both Marco Polo and Ptolemy have mentioned this area in their accounts. My Welsh doctor friend intended to swim, and I didn't give it much thought and went in after her in my clothes while Phyllis sensibly sat on the sand.

Oh no, there were rip currents, and I went with them as the waves ran back into the sea. Knowing I was in trouble, I struck out for the shore, swallowing seawater, but energised by adrenalin and another more divine source, I made it to shore. God must have assigned a special angel to look after me on this trip.

The subsequent humiliation was when we climbed up a nearby tower to see the view. When I came out of the manhole onto the flat roof, I found no railing. Unable to stand up because of my acrophobia, I called out, 'I can see everything from here. What a beautiful sight'! I was glad when this adventure was finally over.

CHRISTIANITY IN INDIA

The major religion of India is Hinduism, followed by Islam, then by Christianity. A census in 2011 documented that there were twenty-seven million Christians in India, a total population of 1.3 billion. Although the origins of Christianity in India remain unclear, there is a general scholarly consensus that Christianity was rooted in India by the 6th century AD, including some communities that used Syriac liturgically. Many articles by scholars have explained the origins of Christianity in India and the reasons for Syriac Liturgy. It makes fascinating reading. It is possible that Christianity existed as far back as the 1st century.

Some historians claim that St Thomas, one of Jesus' disciples, came to India and was martyred there. When I was in India in 2005, I visited where Thomas first ministered in Kerala and saw the impressive structure built by the Mar Thoma Syrian Church to honour him. Being in Kodungallur on the Malabar coast in the Thrissur district of Kerala, I had the joy of preaching in the shadow of this wealth of history.

Catholics account for sixty per cent of all Christians in Kerala. The Kerala brethren church movement officially started in 1898 amidst persecution. Many of the first members of the brethren church came out of the Jacobite church and were primarily descendants of the early Syrian Christians. Early on there was a zeal for mission work. However, after a generation many lower-caste brethren who were added to the church joined other Christian movements. However, today there are about six hundred brethren churches in Kerala and Malayalee missionaries from Kerala serve the Lord in northern India.

There are astonishing and vast differences between living as a Christian and living as a Hindu in India. These stark contrasts are highlighted when we read stories of early missionaries to India like Amy Carmichael and Mother Teresa or Mary Reed, a missionary to lepers.

Mother Teresa's work and dedication can be summed up by the following excerpt from her Nobel Peace Prize acceptance speech: 'I choose the poverty of our poor people. But I am grateful to receive (the Nobel) in the name of the hungry, the naked, the homeless, the crippled, the blind, the lepers, of all people who feel unwanted, unloved, and uncared-for throughout society, people that have become a burden to society.'

A young missionary martyred by Auca Indians in South America wrote, 'He is no fool who gives what he cannot keep to gain what he cannot lose.' What is ours to keep? Our houses? – they may burn down; our health? – disease may cripple us; our families? – they may desert us; our ministry? – it may be terminated. However, if we reject God, we lose our own souls. But we cannot lose our salvation when truly born again; we cannot lose God's love or forgiveness. Instead, we gain so much when we wholly follow Jesus. We walk with purpose in every step. We gain the fellowship of Christ's company; we drink deep of the well of forgiveness; we live overshadowed by God's grace; we gain the satisfaction of helping others and living healthy lives.

In 1966, having completed the period set aside for language study, I travelled down to the Hospital in Thiruvalla.

Chapter 5

My Bittersweet Journey

And God is able to make all grace abound to you so that having all sufficiency in all things at all times, you may abound in every good work. 2 Cor: 9:8

THIRUVALLA MEDICAL MISSION (1966-1970)

Thiruvalla Medical Mission (TMM) Hospital began as a dream in the heart of Dewan Bahadur Dr V. Varghese, the Chief Physician of the King of Travancore. When Dr Varghese retired from his royal position, he began to give shape to this vision. By 1935 he had established a hospital built on a woody hillock near the Thiruvalla Railway Station. As an ardent Christian, he read and studied the works of early missionaries closely. The life that most impressed him was that of George Mueller, a prayer warrior and a leader of the orphanage movement in England. Inspired by George Mueller's faith, Dr Varghese prayed earnestly for someone to take on the responsibility of the hospital. In 1940, Dr and Mrs A.S. Churchward, Brethren missionaries from New Zealand, arrived and took on the service as a divine commission. In those days hospitals were few and far between. A nurses' training course was established in 1943 to fulfil patient care needs.

From that dream many years ago, TMM offers medical and other services in almost every branch of human health requirements.

I started working in the Thiruvalla (Malayalam = തിരുവല്ല) Medical Mission Hospital in 1966 as the Midwifery Nurse Educator. I was in charge of the midwifery wards, which had fifty beds. Each year I trained sixteen students in English.

Muriel Pitts was then the Director of Nursing and Mary Miller oversaw the School of Nursing. After they retired to England, Mary Bardsley was in charge. I found that I loved teaching and midwifery.

About eight hundred applications came in for the sixteen seats offered for midwifery training. We chose about fifty candidates from these applications, whom we saw personally and put them through an intensive interview involving seven tests.

The Kerala government had strict rules that we had to follow. One candidate had to be of the Islamic faith, ten from the outcast community, and the rest were accepted on merit. Many Christians in India come from outcast communities, so I chose Christians to fulfil this category. This meant that I could offer opportunities for training among our orphan girls.

A government representative visited the hospital to review the potential candidates chosen. I developed the midwifery curriculum and enjoyed seeing these nurses grow professionally and in their Christian faith. During the week we conducted Bible Studies in the Nurses' Home, and I taught Sunday School in Malayalam. To start with, I had to learn the Bible story by heart! Then I would tell the story using visual aids.

I revelled in the professional challenges and learned many lessons that humbled me. One case in particular comes to mind. I was conducting a problematic labour case and didn't notice that the student assisting me was the gentle Muslim nurse who sometimes fainted at the sight of blood. There was plenty of blood, and I needed her to keep swabbing so that I could see where to suture. Looking up in exasperation, I saw who was assisting me and thought, 'Oh no, not you again.' Later, when I relived the scene, I repented. The Lord has never said to me, 'Oh no, not you again.' Instead, the Lord encourages me and urges me to keep trying. He never gives up on me, and he never will.

TMM - My midwifery student

Snakebite is prevalent in Kerala, and about fifty-eight thousand victims die every year. Russell vipers live in grassy areas, and their venom breaks down the clotting mechanism of human blood. A pregnant woman, out gathering grass for her buffalo at dusk, was bitten by a Russell viper and was transported to our hospital. Victims soon go into kidney failure. Her pregnancy complicated this. We delivered a dead full-term baby and saved her during the initial bleed. However, she later went into kidney failure, and we could not save her.

Dr Brian Smith, a godly Australian obstetrician and gynaecologist, was interested in treating snakebite victims. Brian gave large doses of anti-serum and had success in many cases. Dr Gilmore Davis primarily attended general surgery. Both missionary Doctors' children were sent away to the Nilgiris Hills to the mission school in Ootacamund. This was especially traumatic when the child in question was only five years old. Hebron International School in Ooty still functions as a Christian ministry.

I remember another obstetrical case because it was so unusual. I called Dr Brian Smith to do a forceps delivery on a pregnant woman who came after outside interference. When I touched her arm, I felt a strange sensation under her skin: air in the subcutaneous tissue. Immediately I realised that we probably had a case of Gas Gangrene for I had heard others talk about this condition. Dr Smith ordered the room to be thoroughly cleansed, and we waited for the pathology test results. Clostridium perfringens bacteria was detected, so the prognosis was not good. The young mother and her baby died.

An incident occurred when agitated citizens in the Kerala communist party surrounded our hospital. They would not let patients or staff in or out. At times we felt that our lives were being threatened. It was stressful when slogans and lies were shouted over the loudspeakers, causing unrest. The matter was finally resolved when a certain person was reinstated.

Part of the requirements for our midwives in training was working for 2-3 months in Public Health Centres. This meant that we needed to visit them to ensure they were safe. Two nurses were stationed in each centre. Mary Bardsley had just taken delivery of a green Volkswagen shipped from England. As we travelled, the narrow roads wound in and out of villages and paddy fields. Suddenly, Mary accidentally hit an older woman carrying a huge clay pot. The old lady fell over, and I got out to see if she was okay.

People oozed from huts, and I noticed red communist flags flying from coconut trees. The villagers became angry and Mary took fright and drove off in her new car, leaving me to face the crowd. I offered money for the clay pot, worth about three rupees. The older woman was okay. No matter how much I offered, the crowd's anger did not die down.

I said to the Lord, 'Lord, I need a miracle. I need rescuing.' And a miracle arrived! What happened was too unusual to be anything but a miracle. A big lorry rolled up, and a rather large man climbed out and came to my rescue. I explained what had happened. He quietly told me, 'Give one hundred rupees, then come immediately and climb into my lorry.' I quickly obeyed. He took me to where Mary had parked some distance away. Other missionaries had similar experiences on the roads, and one couple had been involved in a court case for years.

The years spent in Kerala were rewarding in one way but stressful in another. A distressing problem reared its ugly head, and I didn't know how to deal with it. I eventually proved that I was incapable of handling it. Even though I had made it known, no further discussion occurred to bring relief. Because it involved others, I can't elaborate on the nature of the problem. These were the days when most missionaries had little member care and few pastoral visits from the commending church or mission body.

An adequate support system is essential before going to the field. My letters about the ministry were published in the Mission's magazine, and fellow believers interested in mission enterprise sent enough financial assistance to meet my needs. Living in India proved to be much cheaper than living in Australia. None of this support was promised beforehand. Back then, those working under the umbrella of Australian Missionary Tidings stepped out in faith, wholly relying on the Lord.

With time the stressful problem reared seemingly inescapably on my horizon. I felt very fragmented. To whom could I go? The limbic system of my brain, especially the amygdala, was taking over. That is not good because it can lie to us. I felt trapped within the situation and could not see a way out. Looking back on that testing time, I marvelled at how the Lord graciously made a way to a far more adventurous opportunity.

At the time God in his mercy again reminded me that there was One who is a God who sees everything, hears everything and knows everything. What amazing grace and mercy I have found in my loving God. I belong in God's family and he is my Heavenly Father. Why did he not save me from my difficulties? Why does he allow bad things to happen to his children? King David asked these kinds of questions when he was downcast and desperate. That is why his psalms are so encouraging to us. He would weave his way through his emotions and often finish with a song of praise.

I could write a whole chapter on what I have discovered. Time and time again, I have been moved to rest in the truth that God is in control. No one should go to the mission field without believing God is sovereign. We are so vulnerable to attack by our enemy out to frustrate God's good intentions. We must believe that nothing can touch us unless the Lord permits it. God is not the author of evil but He does use, direct, limit, and prevent evil. He is the One who can bring good out of the tragedies of life.

The prophet Malachi assures us that God's children are His treasured possessions. As the Potter, God carefully moulds the clay. He knows how long to keep us on the wheel and how much we can take. He has in mind the end product, a vessel shaped to honour his Name. And during that shaping, the Lord continues to work out his purposes and rescue us by his grace.

Chapter 6

Grace Given to Press On

Yet the Lord longs to be gracious to you; therefore, he will rise up to show you compassion. For the Lord is a God of justice. Blessed are all those who wait for him!
Isaiah 30:18

I press on toward the goal to win the prize for which God has called me heavenward in Christ Jesus. This verse from Philippians chapter three, verse fourteen, has inspired me for many years. Trials in life can stifle our joy and steal our desire to follow the Lord Jesus wholeheartedly. The Lord challenged me to trust him and press on toward the goal he had called me. I left Thiruvalla in December 1969 for furlough. I was issued a one-year visa and a No Objection to Return (NOTR), a necessary document allowing a missionary to return.

I arrived at the Rockhampton airport, where Mum and Dad were waiting for me. It was so good to see them again and hug them. Mum was surprised to see that I wasn't brown or shrivelled up! I laughed when she mentioned this a few days later. As we drove home, I blurted out, 'Where are all the people?' Ours was the only car on the road!

I had six short weeks with my parents in Rockhampton because I wanted to further my nursing career. During these six weeks Mr Royce Sadler, a lecturer at Rockhampton University, gave me a crash course in physics and chemistry, which I had not covered at college. Because I loved teaching, I intended to become a qualified educator, and I needed to have a grounding in these two subjects. I was sad that I only had a short time with my parents before leaving for Melbourne in February 1970. I was so thankful that I was admitted to study for a diploma in Nurse Education. I did not have the money to cover the expense but the amount I needed arrived in the post. I had not let my need be known. I held the cheque and thanked God for his Father's care. How amazing is our God? I took this as God's stamp of approval.

COLLEGE OF NURSING AUSTRALIA, MELBOURNE

I studied Physiology, Midwifery, Educational Psychology, Microbiology, Public Health, Teaching Practice, and Training School Administration at a university level. This then proved to be a very intensive one-year course. Often, I had little sleep because of the amount of study necessary. The Lord helped me and I gained credits while a few students failed. Failing an exam is not always the student's fault. This could have happened because too much material was introduced in a one-year course, or the level of expertise was unrealistic.

I was sorely tested in the two-week study break in September, granted before the final five exams. June and Kevin McKay ran a children's camp at Yarra Junction, and the study leader suddenly dropped out. I am not sure how they heard about me. I received a plea to help. After a struggle, I said

I would take the studies. Not having time to prepare, I used the Jungle Doctor stories and stories about India. I was able to draw the animals to illustrate. We even had an Indian meal sitting on the floor and eating with our fingers!

While at the College my accommodation in Melbourne was with another student in the home of a Messianic Jew returning to Europe on a preaching tour. His secretary was in the house with me and Angie, another college student. During this time I had contact with Jewish folk who came for our fellowship morning teas. I came to love the Jewish people, little realising that my future ministry would be with our esteemed doctor, Dr Irene Leeser. Her father was Jewish and a doctor. Dr Irene Leeser started the medical work in Ambajipeta in 1967.

I needed an extension on my one-year visa and thankfully, the Indian Consul granted me six months. This enabled me to visit the churches supporting the work in India and spend time resting and being with family. To tell about my work in India I travelled extensively, even as far as Tasmania and Atherton in north Queensland. On this trip north I joined my sister Gweneth and brother-in-law Russell Todd, missionaries serving in PNG.

The thought of leaving my parents again weighed heavily on me. They needed the care of a Rockhampton evangelical church. After praying about this need, I took them with my brother Raymond to the High Street Baptist Church. Later, my brother met his future wife at the Lakes Creek Baptist Church, and I attended their marriage in May 1971.

The Lord encouraged me in my commitment to press on, and my praying partners supported me. I was ready to return to India by June 1971, but it wasn't to Kerala. Mr David Burt, a Tasmanian missionary working in the Godavari Delta, Andhra Pradesh State, let it be known that there was a real need at the Women's Hospital in Ambajipeta as the medical work was mushrooming. Letters of encouragement and welcome set me on a new path. Looking back, I can see how the Lord prepared me for this next step of faith.

RESILIENCE IN MOTION

I booked my flight to India. On my arrival, I planned to travel to the Nilgiris Hills to Oatacamund in Tamil Nadu State to meet with Dr Leeser and Sylvia Wright from the Ambajipeta Hospital in the Godavari Delta. I had yet to meet them before this. I was to travel with them by car to visit the hospital work at Sankeshwar, Karnataka State, where Edna Ramage worked, then straight across India to the East Godavari District in Andhra Pradesh State. This memorable trip included places to eat and a bed for the night. One night we had one large bed to share, and I kept Rene (Dr Leeser) and Sylvia awake, for I was sure bed bugs were biting me.

One hotel we ate in was a shack with pigs roaming outside. It was a busy 'hotel' which was a good indication that the food was good. The young boys serving the customers used the curtain that divided our cubicle from the rest to wipe their hands on their way past! The food was hot and tasty and we scored no after-effects.

When we finally arrived in East Godavari, I feasted my eyes on the vast green paddy fields edged by coconut trees. To this day the area has rich soil and a plentiful water supply which supports five million people in small villages. It was similar to Kerala, which also has paddy fields. Ambajipeta's population is about thirty thousand, but it overflows into nearby villages.

On arrival in Ambajipeta we were greeted by many who were thankful that Dr Leeser and Sylvia were back in their area. Driving through the hospital gates, the driver stopped before a gracious two-story bungalow, and my heart warmed to all I saw.

This bungalow was built by Mr Brown, a missionary to the Godavari in 1900, and it became my home for many years. On the second story there were two large bedrooms with bathrooms for Rene (Dr Leeser) and I. Sylvia had a bedroom and bathroom on the ground floor. The rooms on the ground floor and verandas were pathed with huge grey slate stones, which would have been transported from areas far away. Ambajipeta is on an island without stones and with water that is only about thirty metres underground.

Mr Brown's safari hat was still hung on the hat rack, and a rod for the punkah (a fan system operated by a punkah wallah sitting outside the room) was still stretched across the dining room ceiling. It was like stepping back fifty years in time. I was excited, felt blessed and at home.

Thirteen-year-old Ratnam served our meals which Joseph cooked in an outside kitchen. The stove was made out of mud and cow dung. There was so much to learn, but I was excited about this new adventure and thankful to God for this open door of service. God had been so gracious to me, leading me to fulfil his purpose, as it says in Ephesians 2:10.

For we are God's workmanship, created in
Christ Jesus to do good works, which God
prepared in advance for us to do.

Chapter 7

God's Gracious Care

For we know that in all things God works for the good of those who love him, who have been called according to his purpose. Romans 8:28

AMBAJIPETA WOMEN'S HOSPITAL (1971-1986)

Trusting in God's providential care gives confidence and comfort. Our Almighty and loving God's absolute control gives comfort because He is a good and gracious God. He works to bring good out of all things for those who love him. Lovers of God are in his care and can, therefore, face the future confidently knowing that things are not happening merely by chance. God is present and active in our lives to fulfil his purposes.

All this is for your benefit, so that the grace that is reaching more and more people may cause thanksgiving to overflow to the glory of God. 2 Cor 4:15

In July 1971 I was ready to serve among the Telugu-speaking people of Andhra Pradesh State. This makes me wonder; perhaps I should have gone to the Godavari District in the first place. Changing states meant starting again – learning a second language with an entirely different script. However, on reflection, if I had joined the School of Nursing in 1965 in Narsapur, West Godavari, I don't think I would have become involved in the medical work in Ambajipeta, East Godavari, which didn't commence until 1967. I loved teaching and training nurses, and the School of Nursing in Narsapur would have attracted me significantly.

Ambajipeta is a village in the East Godavari District in the fertile Godavari Delta, with a man-made canal system. The source of this system is the great Godavari River. The whole area is beautifully green with vast rice fields, coconut trees, bananas, sugar cane and other crops. My soul absorbed all the beauty. The mouth of the Godavari River opens into the Bay of Bengal in the east. I have crossed over this wide river in a long skinny canoe in the company of a fat buffalo that protested all the way. All I could think about was, 'The water looks too dirty to swim in.'

Protestant missionaries arrived in the Godavari District as early as 1800. Anthony Norris Groves (1795 – 1853) has been described as the 'father of faith missions.' He was one of the earlier missionaries who worked in the Godavari District. As a missionary, he aimed to help indigenous converts form their churches without dependence on foreign training, authorisation or finance.

His ideas eventually found wide acceptance in evangelical circles. In 1900 another missionary, Mr Brown, had a stately bungalow built on the five-acre compound in Ambajipeta and another smaller building of two rooms with a wide veranda where a small medical clinic was conducted. When this small building was pulled down, we built the present Children's Ward. Gifts from Australia funded this two-storey building.

In 1967 Dr Irene Leeser, who was working at the Narsapur Hospital in West Godavari, felt God's unmistakable call to 'cross over the river.' This was a call to start a hospital on the east side of the river. This she did and discovered Mr Brown's large, abandoned bungalow in the village of Ambajipeta. This proved to be an ideal place to start a medical work. It was on a busy bus route. Sylvia Wright, a trained nurse from New Zealand who had worked in the Narsapur hospital and other ministries, joined Dr Leeser in 1969, and of course, I joined them in 1971.

Mrs Afra Cooper, an elder missionary, was initially with Dr Leeser until Sylvia arrived. A Hindu man named Appa Rao was employed to attend to the carpentry jobs needed. The bungalow needed repairs, and the bats needed to be chased out! Appa Rao, who once made idols, became a Christian and later an elder in the Ambajipeta church. He faithfully oversaw all the building projects as the hospital expanded.

Dr Irene Leeser's father, Dr Otto Leeser, was Jewish and had been working as a doctor in Frankfurt, Germany. His wife was German, the daughter of the Ambassador to Turkey and Iran. He understood Hitler's evil intentions and wisely took his family to England. Dr Irene Leeser has a brother, a Quaker. The Quaker social workers helped Jewish people escape from Nazi Europe.

Dr Leeser qualified in post-graduate obstetrics and gynaecology in Edinburgh. Due to her quiet manner and medical skills, many patients sometimes travelled vast distances to be treated in our hospital in Ambajipeta. Her goal was to treat the women who came with real needs and to see churches established in the many villages throughout East Godavari. Before she retired in 1997, she witnessed this happening. Dr Irene Leeser MBE was born in 1926 and was transported to Glory in 2017.

Sylvia Wright was from a loving Christian New Zealand family of five girls. She was competent, spoke Telugu fluently and was a great colleague to work with, as she had a lively sense of humour and boundless energy. During those thirty years of service, Sylvia gave the kind of support Dr Leeser needed, seeing most patients who attended the Outpatient clinics and assisting in the village and church ministries.

In 1971 as medical work mushroomed, Dr Leeser (Rene) and Sylvia saw my coming as an answer to prayer. Rene and Sylvia were carrying a heavy workload. Consequently, I determined to learn the Telugu language and sit for the language exam in six months instead of one year. With the Lord's help, I was able to do this.

Telugu has a phonetic writing system with 56 basic letters and over 400 combinations of letters. Unlike Malayalam, Telugu verbs must agree with the subjects regarding gender, person, and number. I am so grateful that I was thoroughly taught English grammar at school.

I continued with my language teacher for another year while working full-time in the wards. My goal was to learn about twenty new words a day, and I could only do this with the help of a tape recorder. My language teacher was a Hindu man who recorded new words for me to practise. Occasionally I squatted in the smoky kitchens as the relatives of patients cooked curries and practised my Telugu. When correcting my lessons, my Hindu teacher learned much about the Creator-God and Saviour. Yet, sadly, I don't think this changed his thinking about the Biblical concept of God and salvation in any way. I was called to his house when he was dying and felt so sad when standing at his bedside. Later, I heard that the Narsapur Hindu language teacher was baptised as a believer. He had taught several missionaries, and God wonderfully opened his heart to believe in Jesus.

I did not sit for any more exams and sometimes felt frustrated when unable to express the Bible knowledge stored in my brain. Sylvia had sat for two exams and had more language skills than I had. Rene was very quiet and left most of the speaking engagements to Sylvia.

Even before we had the help of Indian Doctors, Rene and Sylvia saw more than five hundred outpatients a day. After an exhausting day in outpatients, Rene went to the operating theatre to attend the listed surgery. I supervised the labour wards and in-patient section, which was challenging, especially in preventing cross-infection. Few patients knew the germ theory that microorganisms, known as pathogens, lead to contagious diseases.

As more patients came and more buildings were erected, the hospital complex ended up with two hundred beds, three theatres, a paediatric ward and a postoperative ward. The large Outpatient section housed a large waiting hall, medical storeroom, laboratory, and consulting rooms.

I learnt so much during those happy and productive years. Dr Leeser trusted me to handle uncomplicated forceps deliveries and other more complicated procedures.

I first reported these cases to her. Some cases required a Vacuum Extraction when childbirth lasted too long and were not progressing near the second stage. My being able to help in this way meant that Rene could continue seeing the outpatients who had paid more to see her.

Sylvia Wright Dr Leeser Pauline

Sylvia saw the bulk of the outpatients but sent those who needed surgery or a more precise diagnosis to Rene. Sylvia and I gave the anaesthetics in emergency cases. Before any procedure, we would pray for God's help.

This is our confidence in approaching God;
if we ask anything according to his
will, he hears us. 1 John 5:14

It soon became evident that most registered Nurse-Midwives had received very little training. Prevention of cross-infection was high on the list, and I attacked this by giving classes. They were amazed and hopefully convinced, when I introduced them to the minuscule world seen through a microscope. Many were not taught the signs of foetal distress during labour. After designing and printing labour charts, I supervised the nurses in keeping accurate records. By nature, the female staff were respectful and willing to learn. I loved spending time with them in their kitchen while they cooked their curries. They would give me a plate and let me sample some of their cooking. It was my joy to encourage them to serve the Lord Jesus.

Sylvia and I were on call at night when Dr Leeser needed to operate. We were on duty six days a week from 7 a.m. to 7 p.m. After our evening meal at 7 p.m., we returned to the wards to check with the night staff and attend to any problems. We were a good team as we had varied gifts and could complement each other. Sundays, we spent differently.

I am very thankful for the wonderful colleagues the Lord gave me and their encouragement. They rarely clipped my wings when I drew up plans for new buildings or suggested a more efficient way of handling some administration problem. However, I wondered what they thought about the Baby Show I organised. About five hundred mothers brought their beautiful babies along. It was a howling success! The goal was to promote the Baby Clinic, which was started in the Outpatient Department. Nurses wearing four different coloured ribbons divided the babies into four age groups, with the mother wearing the appropriate colour. The judge was from another village, and the baby who won was so bonnie. I think the Amalapuram Lion's Club members gave every baby a gift.

Sylvia felt uneasy about pulling teeth without anaesthetic, but one of her helpers, whose tooth was aching badly, said, 'Why do you worry so much about it, Amma? When you pull the tooth out, it's as if you pull out the pain.' Sylvia had so much energy. She was responsible for visiting the two clinics weekly in Chakalipalem and Nedunuru. Sometimes, at Chakalipalem, so many people came that she often finished by candlelight. I never heard Sylvia complain about such things. On hot, humid days, the only dry part of her uniform was the hem section.

On Sylvia's return one day from Chakalipalem Clinic, she arrived with a little 4 lb newborn. A young, unwed girl came to the clinic because of abdominal pain and delivered a baby under a nearby bush! She then ran off. Meanwhile, back at the hospital, a Christian woman had her third stillbirth in our labour ward, and I wanted so much to comfort her. The stigma of infertility and childlessness is a burden too heavy to bear. I thanked God when Sylvia handed me the little abandoned baby. I knew God had compassionately answered prayer. I met the woman's grieving husband standing outside the ward. I said, 'Look what I have. Do you think your wife would want her?' He looked surprised and said, 'Yes'. The young woman and the baby bonded beautifully. Now, as a mother, she could breastfeed God's love gift to her. At such times, God reveals his heart.

The LORD is gracious and compassionate,
slow to anger and rich in love.
Psalm 145:8

We enjoyed going out to the villages on Sundays. To reach one isolated area, we waded through shallow water and walked through tobacco fields to a dusty little village where many eager women were waiting for us. Sometimes, gurgling babies are thrust into our arms to be named. This is a joyous ceremony when giving a child a name, and it is incredible how one's mind goes blank trying to think of a suitable name. On one occasion I gave a rather grumpy-looking boy the name 'king of joy' and to a girl, 'daughter of peace' even though her eyes were brimming with mischief. Rene was often caught out. The same name would pop into her head. There must be many men named Prakasha Rao living in the Godavari!

The East Godavari Delta area is a fertile, beautiful area with hundreds of little villages and five million people. Children ooze out of the village huts and houses and greet us as we walk in from where we park the car. Most are from poor families, but everyone is smiling and happy to see us. The girls with brightly coloured flowers caught in their plaited jet-black hair greet us shyly while the boys energetically path the way through closely packed huts and gardens.

Some huts seem to balance precariously on the edge of rice paddy fields. Coconut palms provide some shade from the hot sun. Telugu children are beautiful. They appear gentle and care for their younger siblings, often straddling a younger child on their hip. As I looked at these children, the words of Jesus came to mind, *'Let the little children come to Me.'*

THE LITTLE BOY WITH THE RED BOW TIE

I like telling stories; this one about the little boy with the red bow tie is one of my favourites. In our hospital nursery we had one child, like all others, precious to God. In some twisted way, this child was left in our care. The child's mother was admitted in an advanced stage of tuberculosis and soon came into labour. She had an elderly mother as her near relative to cook for her. They were cared for on an open veranda because the patient was highly infectious. Clothed in old saris with little money, they sat dazed by their surroundings.

I drew near to this sick young woman as I knew she was dying. While she was breathing with difficulty trying to hold onto life, I gently talked about Jesus and how he loved her. She had little strength left and died soon after delivering a baby boy.

Once the elderly woman knew her daughter had died, she fled and left us with the body and the baby. We buried the mother behind the hospital on the canal bank and put the baby in our nursery. We called him Johnny. Johnny was a beautiful child. However, he did not thrive. This could have been due to 'multi-handling' as different staff members handled him on their shifts. A baby doesn't thrive when this happens. I tied up an old sheet like a hammock, and Johnny's incessant crying would cease for a while when tucked inside. What he needed most was a loving mother.

It was a happy day when a Pentecostal pastor shyly approached me with his equally shy wife and asked about Johnny. They had a house but no children. After I asked a few pointed questions, I took them to see Johnny, and it was love at first sight. Kamala agreed to stay in the hospital with Johnny to be instructed on feeding him with buffalo milk and caring for him. He also needed his vaccination of B.C.G. for tuberculosis and OPV for Polio.

Every year approximately one and a half million children die in India from diseases preventable through vaccination. These vaccinations are free of cost in Government hospitals and Primary Health Centres nationwide.

The joy on Kamala's face on the day of discharge was achingly beautiful. Imagine my delight when the Pastor brought Johnny to see me on his first birthday. He was sporting a little red bow tie as Kamala had dressed him so lovingly. He put his hands together when his dad said 'Salaam', the greeting used by Christians and Muslims in our area. When he came on his second birthday again wearing a red bow tie, he greeted me and said a little Bible verse. His father brought him back several times, and each time, Johnny said a Bible verse and had on a red bow tie. I wonder if Johnny is a pastor today, searching out children and telling them that Jesus loves them.

Rene, Sylvia, and I visited most of the more than fifty Sunday Schools our hospital's staff or associates ran. Our Sunday visits also encouraged the teachers, and we gave out prizes at their annual celebrations.

Some of the children memorised chapters of the Bible. The first prize among the girls and boys was a Telugu Bible. They received material to make a shirt or a skirt if they already had one. Every child received a gift. We bought hundreds of metres of good quality brightly coloured material, which Sylvia cut into pieces of different sizes. Some children received beanies or woollen vests sent out by ministry partners. These folk were mainly older Christian women who knitted outfits for premature babies and young children. We do have a cool, damp season around Nov-Jan.

I loved listening to children telling a Bible story with an Indian flavour. One young boy's idea of the prodigal son's wicked, wasteful behaviour was, 'He lived having a Gold Spot (fizzy orange drink) every day. Not working but sitting under a whirling fan.' That, to him, was decadence!

Many children capture one's heart. Poor children aged six or seven work in sidewalk huts serving coffee and tea or selling pitiful wares. Tragically a few children are purposely maimed to become beggars. The more favoured children are dressed neatly, crowded onto rickshaws, and transported to school. As more than half of the population in India lives in villages, education in these rural areas is essential to growing the economy. In many homes children must pursue a good education. It is one way to lift families out of poverty. Many Indian children are multilingual. Brought up in a highly competitive environment, many achieve academic brilliance.

Our Lord God loves children, yet millions die because of poverty or neglect. Mothers die in childbirth. God wants the world to know that he is a God who cares. He is a good God who hears human cries. He sees us in our need. Remember the story in Genesis chapter twenty-one of Hagar's son Ishmael in the desert scene when he was dying of thirst? Hagar put her young son under a bush and sobbed, "I cannot watch him die." God heard. God also heard the young boy crying and opened their eyes to see a well of thirst-quenching water. When I think about this for a moment, I marvel at such a God in tune with all that is happening in his world. God is the God who hears – "Yishmael". Before this, In Genesis 16:13, Hagar fled when Sarah acted harshly towards her servant Hagar. The Angel of the Lord appeared to Hagar. This may seem strange as Hagar was not an Israelite. It shows that God values the marginalised and oppressed. Hagar acknowledged God as El Roi, the "God who sees".

This compassionate God welcomes millions of little children into heaven. They drink from the river of the water of life flowing from the throne of God and the Lamb (Jesus). In that future time, as recorded in the book of Revelation, we read that there will be no more evil, tears, or pain. The Lord Jesus will reign supreme.

HAVE GUN. WILL TRAVEL

The following account may surprise you. When I first considered what I should do to equip myself for mission work in India, I looked at some practical steps I needed to take. Do I need to learn to ride a horse? Shoot a gun? Walk over a narrow bridge? What would it be like living in an Indian village and learning a language?

I had an enthusiastic English Grammar teacher in Grades 6 and 7. I remember Mr Cunningham well because he sometimes spat when he shouted! I also learned screeds of poetry and prose when attending Elocution lessons with Mrs Pugh from age ten to fifteen. All this helped learning a language. I have always been quick and sometimes impulsive and excitable, and my speech could not keep up with the thoughts flying through my mind. Mrs Pugh wrote in my report, “You are just saying words. Think of the meaning.” Later in India, I learned hand and head movements from the locals, which assisted me in communicating more effectively. And a few of my dramatics thrown into the mix helped immensely!

Now, back to the preparations I undertook. When I went to Rockhampton for a month’s leave during my nursing training, my brother hired a horse for me to learn how to ride. Ha! Ha! I enthusiastically saddled this horse and set out down Dunbar Street with interested neighbours watching the goings-on. I felt like a real cowgirl until the horse put down its head to munch on grass, and I sailed gracefully over its head and landed flat on my face.

The wily mare had resisted as I tightened the girth, and the saddle was, therefore, not secure. In other words, he was a girthy horse. I magnanimously forgave the creature and set off for the bush, running along Tozet’s Creek. I think this horse had it in for me. I had forgiven him, but he still harboured a vengeful spirit. He took off, trying to wipe me off under low-hanging tree branches. Finally, we ended up in long elephant grass, running along the creek’s bank. I think he knew about the wasp nest. I was starting to feel more confident when wham, angry wasps flew out and bit me on my face in several places. I now know what it feels like to be ‘moon-faced’. I decided that day that I did not need to learn to ride a horse!

I’d rather not tell you how I walked over narrow bridges in India. It is embarrassing to admit that I suffer from acrophobia – I am scared of heights. My Indian friends must have secretly laughed at my antics. Sylvia helped me on several occasions when I closed my eyes, and she led me across. I was much more successful with handling a gun. My young brother Raymond had a rifle and my father had a shotgun. Raymond taught me the basics, and I could shoot reasonably well. I happily put a tick to that on my list.

You may well ask why a missionary would need a gun. Did you know that about twenty-five thousand Indians die every year from bites from rabid dogs and, less infrequently, rabid monkeys? Rabies is a fatal viral infection that targets the brain and nervous system. The public health system would need to vaccinate every dog to eradicate rabies, an impossible task. In India thousands of stray dogs roam the streets. Because Hindus firmly believe that animals possess souls and humans are in different states of physical and spiritual evolution, killing any animal, whether a rat, snake, or dog, is a sin. Yet what do you do when a stray dog wanders into the hospital compound showing signs of rabies? At first the hospital carpenters would beat them to death, which was a cruel way to solve the problem. Consequently, I asked one of the medical sales clerks to buy me a rifle in Bombay.

Before owning a gun, I had a close encounter, but not with a flying object. Instead, it was a rabid dog, and nobody was around to help me. The dog was not suffering from the furious type of rabies but the paralytic kind. He looked sick, and infected saliva was dripping from his relaxed jaws. I lassoed it with rope, then thought this was not good enough – a chain around the neck would be better. Taking a plank from the carpenter's shed, I lay it across his head and held it down with my foot as I slipped the chain around the dog's neck. I tied the rope to the end of the chain, dragged the dog along, and threw him into a large pit at the back of the compound. The men could deal with the dog later. But in doing this, my arm with a small scratch was smeared with the dog's saliva.

Dr Leeser ordered the vaccine from the Pasteur Institute of India in Coonoor. I underwent the painful procedure of having the daily dose of five ccs of vaccine injected into my rectus abdominis (Abdominal muscles) for ten days. I needed that gun. To further protect ourselves, I also vaccinated our two pet dogs.

The first chance to use the gun proved to be a real adventure. The dreaded words rabid dog (Picci kukka పిచ్చి కుక్క) reached me, and I ran to the bungalow for the gun. By this time the dog was in a crowded ward. Everyone was up on the beds. This included patients, relatives, children, and me jumping from bed to bed. The beds were close together as this was a sought-after ward near the Labour Wards. In vain I tried to get a clear shot. God heard my prayer, for the dog took off down to the back of the compound, where I could do the deadly deed. Not without compassion, I may add.

Another time the staff called me to chase off some monkeys, which were causing havoc on the tiled rooves and pulling flowers off the coconut trees. These monkeys had hitched a ride on lorries coming from West Godavari. Before this, we were free of monkeys on our island on the east side of the Godavari River. This troop of monkeys was an easy target as they had big red bottoms – a couple of near-misses – and they soon took off. Monkeys are sacred animals to the Hindus, so I aimed only to frighten them.

The next cry for help came from Joyce Harding, a missionary in charge of a Girls' Home in West Godavari. A troop of monkeys had moved in and frightened the girls, making it almost impossible for them to spread out washing on the flat rooves of buildings or get water from taps. I sent back a message, 'Have Gun. Will travel.'

I set out on the three-hour bus trip with my gun slung over my shoulder. I received some confused looks on the bus. After being warmly welcomed by Joyce Harding and her laughing girls, I was shown to a bedroom. The plan was to stage my attack at dawn. It took three dawn raids to convince the monkeys to move on. I don't know what happened to that gun when I left India.

OPPORTUNITIES GALORE

Not long after I arrived in Ambajipeta, a Sunday School Rally was held under the enthusiastic guidance of Mrs Mary Short, wife of Dr Short of the Bethesda Leprosy Hospital in Narsapur. It soon became apparent that this would be a memorable weekend with three hundred children drawn from Sunday schools throughout the Godavari Delta. The children were keen to win a prize for saying a memory verse or telling a Bible story. Twenty Sunday school teachers participated in the workshop. They were taught methods of teaching, especially the use of visual aids.

Concerned elders of the brethren churches in the Godavari Delta also met to discuss the problems occurring in some fellowships. Pastors were being tempted to accept foreign money to join other missions.

I was asked to help in a students' camp in Narsapur, West Godavari, about a three-hour drive from Ambajipeta. We were comfortably accommodated in tents in a beautiful spot by the sea. After Bible studies under the trees, we spent an hour in the ocean. Most of the girls had never been swimming before, so my job was to keep them safe. We wore old clothes instead of swimming costumes. A message arrived saying to stay put as no buses were running due to a curfew in Narsapur. We rose at 4 am on Monday morning and started the long trek back to Narsapur in the moonlight. The men brought the tents back on bullock carts.

In the early 1970s as there were no doctors to relieve Dr Leeser, we closed the hospital for the hot month of June to go to the Nilgiris Hills for a break. By then, Rene (Dr Leeser) and Sylvia were exhausted after seeing six hundred patients in Out-Patients five days a week. Closing our hospital meant discharging patients or sending them on to other hospitals. The staff all took their holiday during this time. Somewhat refreshed, we returned, and the hospital soon filled up again until we were trying to find a space for another patient. The hospital staff also returned happier, more rested, with a new zeal to serve the Lord. We had the difficult task of turning away jobless folk asking for employment as nurses, ayahs, cleaners or office workers. Many were hungry, but we didn't have a place for them.

Our time on the Nilgiris Hills in the Montauban Missionary Home in Ootacamund was as if we lived in the 1880s. The missionaries gathered in the lounge room in the evenings. A wood fire warmed the cold mountain air. We all dressed for dinner in our best clothes, which often smelled of mothballs as they were kept in trunks in the Home until the next holiday. A bell would sound, and a butler would announce that dinner was being served. In the dining room, our meal was served by men in fancy butler-like gear. It was all very English and formal, and I found watching all the interactions fascinating.

During the first week of our stay on the Hills, we were sick until our bodies adjusted to the cold mountain air and rich food. Once recovered we enjoyed chocolate from Ooty's famous chocolate shop and a masala dosa at the Curry House, which was my favourite. Masala dosa is a crisp and aromatic crepe stuffed with spiced potato. Just writing about it makes my mouth water. Tourists flock to Ootacamund, Ooty, for it is a beautiful hill station.

Mark and Alex Ronalds and their family still serve the Lord at the Hebron School in Ootacamund. What a unique experience their children will have. Ootacamund is a beautiful part of India. The lush green tea plantations, vast meadows, towering mountains, and sparking waterfalls make it a must-see destination. Hebron is an international, Christian, Co-educational Residential School. It was founded in 1899 to serve Christian workers in Southeast Asia.

We certainly needed that summer break. Some weeks in the hospital were hectic. One Sunday we could not visit the village churches because of problem cases. We performed four Caesarean Sections, three forceps deliveries, and several normal deliveries. We were so thankful for the prayers of those on the home front; we needed strength and wisdom.

From time to time, we admitted children suffering from tetanus and were thankful when the preventative vaccine was available, for not many survived. In December 1973 we started giving tetanus toxoid injections to antenatal patients because so many pregnant women deliver in their homes, attended by unskilled and often ignorant village women. These tetanus injections protected both the mother and newborn. We performed tubal ligations as a form of Family Planning as the Government encourage parents to have no more than three children. The government paid for both delivery and surgery if the women consented to undergo tubal ligation.

Since 1975, Indian doctors have been employed at the hospital. These doctors learned many new skills from Dr Leeser. Regrettably, once the lady doctors had gained specific skills, they left to set up their own practices, and Dr Leeser would then have to train others.

At least now, we could leave the hospital in the hands of the Indian Doctors while we had our one-month refreshing break in the Nilgiri Hills. The city of Ootacamund is 7,400 feet above sea level. The Nilgiri Hills were originally the home of the Toda people, a small pastoral tribal community said to be guardians of the Nilgiris. India has the largest number of tribal groups compared to other countries. Every tribe is different and has its own culture and secret customs. I was fascinated with the Toda tribe. They believe the first Toda woman was created from the rib of the first Toda man. Sound familiar? They wear clothes beautifully embroidered and live in a small hamlet in an oval-shaped hut with a pent-shaped roof and one small sliding door. There are about one hundred million tribal Indigenous people in India.

We had a tribal woman come to our Ambajipeta hospital and deliver a big baby boy with a harelip and cleft palate. She wouldn't take an upstairs bed as it was too far from the ground! Though we showed her how to feed her baby during her stay, she returned with a malnourished infant several weeks later. She couldn't keep him. I knew of a Christian couple, landowners, who desperately wanted a boy. When they came, I showed them the little boy, and they said, 'Yes, Amma'. The new mother stayed until she felt confident in feeding the little fellow. I advised them to take him to Kakinada to have his harelip and cleft palate repaired. They regularly returned to the Baby Clinic. Village folk believe the moon's eclipse causes a harelip and cleft palate. When we did have an eclipse, I found the antenatal patients sleeping under their beds! And only to strengthen this belief, amazingly, we did have such a baby born that same day with a harelip.

My brother Raymond sent a portable generator, which was a great help in supplying light to the operating theatres when they were without power. It stood outside the main theatre door and was readily available. In April 1976 we rejoiced in the gift of money to buy a large generator and build a shed to house it. The generous gift came from the Melbourne Deepdene Assembly, which I attended while at the College of Nursing in 1970. Power cuts happened without warning, even in the middle of surgery. It was not uncommon at night to finish off an operation by torchlight. Intubating an infant is a challenging procedure. Doing it under torchlight is even more difficult.

Some of the babies delivered were quite premature. We did not have any special equipment to nurse them. We tried our best to keep them warm with the knitted outfits sent from our home countries and using hot water bottles, but often we failed to keep them alive. I mourned every little one lost. Aware of this, Dr Leeser comforted me by saying, 'They are now with Jesus, safe from the corruption in this world.'

One day I walked into the nursery to find a man, possibly a grandfather, sitting cross-legged with a pot on top of a tiny primus stove. In the pot, honey and his gold ring were being heated. His idea was to put this mixture of honey and gold off the ring into his grandchild's mouth to give the child a good character. I could tell he was a high-caste man and that I needed to show respect for this ceremony, but there were oxygen cylinders close by! I asked him to continue away from the oxygen cylinders. He understood and moved to a safer distance.

In the 1970s preeclampsia was a real problem, with some patients going into the next stage of eclamptic fits. Many had not received antenatal supervision. Despite handling complicated cases and having no blood bank, many patients were saved and went home well. We would have about three maternal deaths yearly, mostly from haemorrhages following other complications. If we needed blood for the transfusion, we would send one of the relatives with two test tubes of the patient's blood to Amalapuram, several kilometres away. The blood was tested and cross-matched in their laboratory. The relative would return by bicycle with the bottle of blood packed in ice and sawdust. We had a case of a Christian woman with a retained dead foetus, and her blood was not clotting. If this was due to afibrinogenemia, we were in trouble. We gave blood transfusions. I am sure God answered our prayers, for she lived.

In third-world countries we see so much suffering. Being a rescuer at heart, I grieved when we couldn't save a patient. There is a mystery in all suffering, and it is hard to come to terms with it. As a Christian I understand that suffering can result from humans exercising their free will. Though God created the world good and man and woman good, suffering entered this beautiful world through man's disobedience. Consequently, suffering has become a part of our human fabric of existence.

Suffering is not good in itself. However, good can come out of the experience of suffering. In his book *The Problem of Pain,* C.S. Lewis has a quote: "I suggest to you that it is because God loves us that he gives us the gift of suffering. Pain is God's megaphone to rouse a deaf world. You see, we are like blocks of stone out of which the Sculptor carves the forms of men. The blows of his chisel, which hurt us so much, are what might us perfect." Some Christians become too discouraged and disillusioned and give up on walking with God altogether.

As a child I collected caterpillars from oleander bushes. I kept them in a wired cage and fed them leaves, which they ate voraciously. Their next stage fascinated me. A caterpillar would weave itself into a cocoon or chrysalis which hung seemingly in limbo on the underside of a leaf. Then one day when the time was right, it would split open the cocoon and a vision of exquisite fragility would emerge. For a few moments it would hang, letting its wings fall limply. I would watch in wonder as this new creation became a beautiful butterfly with painted wings that would enjoy the ecstasy of flight when released.

Thinking back on this, I now see it as a metaphor for life. The cocoon is like the trials of life when one feels isolated while going through the dark passage of pain. However, for the butterfly, the cocoon is not only a prison but a place of transformation. Is the cocoon of suffering not only a place of pain but a creative place where you are changing into a more authentic human being, humbled, alive, and freer?

I saw some remarkable obstetrical cases. One was an abdominal pregnancy where the foetus grew inside the abdomen instead of the uterus. The placenta had attached itself to organs, including the bowel. It was a miracle of God's grace that this patient lived. A group of godly women prayed on such occasions outside the theatre. When I was conducting a low forceps delivery on what seemed to be a very large baby, I heard a crack. It was a mercy that the pubic bone separated, for the baby was huge. We called him Goliath!

Another day, a labouring woman arrived in a bullock cart with twin babies kicking around in the straw and the placenta still inside. The staff and I pulled her onto a trolley and soon had an IV infusion running as she was haemorrhaging. On closer inspection I found a case of uterine prolapse. The swollen cervix was sitting outside, covered with straw! Without scrubbing I put on sterile gloves and picked off the straw. I changed my gloves to replace what had slipped out. Holding it inside with a gloved hand, I placed the other hand on the abdomen as I waited for contractions from the Syntocinon IV infusion before manually removing the placenta. The nurses put up a blood substitute. We gave an antibiotic, a tetanus shot, and cortisone. During the whole procedure, I felt the Lord enabling me. Mother and babies made a good recovery.

Another time a high-caste Brahmin woman arrived in strong labour. I tried to take an obstetrical history. I found out later that this was her seventeenth pregnancy. I sent a message to Dr Leeser saying we urgently needed her. While preparing the woman for a caesarean section, I felt the uterus tear when my hand was on her abdomen. Though we rushed her to the theatre, the mother died as did her baby. In the 1970s patients often arrived after being handled by simple village women, and we were left to try to save lives or conduct complex cases.

Every patient heard the Good News of Salvation while with us. However, many may have added Jesus to the list of their many gods. Before going home, they would give a small fruit gift, pay their bill, and then return to their village. The patients who returned to the hospital often understood the message and came to faith in Christ Jesus. We got to know some Hindu and Muslim patients so well that some asked us to visit their village.

Chapter 8

Without Vision, the People Perish

For the Son of Man came to seek and to save the lost.
By grace are you saved through faith…
Luke 19:10; Eph 2:8-9

DR LEESER'S VISION

What motivates missionaries to serve on mission fields? God gives them a vision of people perishing because they have not trusted in our Creator God's way of salvation. God's Word teaches that everyone receives salvation the same way: through believing in Jesus, God's Son as Saviour and Lord. We cannot earn God's acceptance. This is Good News for the many worldwide who strive by bowing to false gods and those caught in the web of false beliefs.

God gave Dr Leeser a vision to establish churches of Christ-followers throughout the East Godavari District. On Sundays we visited the village churches after morning hospital rounds and attended to any patients experiencing difficulties. On our return we fasted and prayed until it was time to retire.

Our Christian hospital staff commenced Sunday schools in many villages and from this ministry, churches were established. Christian hospital male staff acted as pastors in these village churches on the weekends. On Monday nights we showed the Jungle Doctor film strips in surrounding villages. About six hundred or more Hindu folk would gather to listen to the simple message. As the Lord blessed these methods, more than thirty churches were established in East Godavari. God blessed the work, and Dr Leeser saw her vision realised.

Dr Leeser, through an energetic pastor, started a ministry among the Koya tribal folk dwelling in the hill area many kilometres from our hospital. The Koya folk are farmers by occupation, but most of their food supplies are from the forests. They make bamboo furniture including mats for fencing, dustpans, and baskets. Koya folk kept their livestock inside as tigers and bears roamed the forest region.

They had little access to medical care. The pastor travelled for about three hours on three buses to reach this isolated hill region. He could only enter with Government permission as tribal communities are under the Government's protection. He visited each household and wrote down the names and symptoms of those needing treatment. He returned the list to Dr Leeser, who dispensed the necessary tablets. It worked as a remote-controlled clinic! Most folks needed treatment for anaemia, vitamin deficiency, worm infestation, infertility or other women's problems. Infertility would be treated with homoeopathic tablets along with vitamins and iron tablets. The pastor was able to help meet their needs and pray with those who wanted prayer.

Dr Leeser's father was skilful in using homoeopathic medicine and had written a comprehensive book in German about its uses. Rene (Dr Leeser) used homoeopathic treatment successfully for many skin diseases and infertility. We routinely popped the small round sugar pills containing arnica into a baby's mouth following a traumatic delivery, and they loved the sugar flavour. When I returned later on mission trips in 2005-6, I noticed that the Indian doctors were following Rene's use of homoeopathic medicine for infertility.

Lyn and Pauline

Through meeting the needs of the Koya community and sharing the Good News of God's love expressed through Jesus, many came to faith in Him.

On my last visit to India in 2007, I wanted to see this area again and meet with those who had become Christians.

Lyn Harrison and I were taken to the little building erected for worship and were greeted by a group of smiling believers. Previously, in 1986 I was privileged to lead the Koya women down into the water to be baptised by the pastor.

During the 1970s – 80s the gospel was faithfully preached. Though not directly involved in most evangelistic outreaches, we three missionaries worked as a team with the many active staff members and pastors. Krupadanam, a hospital clerk, had seen blessing and encouraged the believers in Konkapilli village. Both he and his sister are musical. John Victor, responsible for looking after the hospital's medical stores, goes to a delightful spot called Mummidivaram. A temple is nearby and the Hindu festivals provide an excellent opportunity to distribute tracts and gospels. Paul, who works in the maintenance department, helps John Victor. We were able to encourage and pray for pastors and, on occasion, give them money to reach their goals. As with us, we knew that the Lord would use these men as long as they faithfully walked with the Lord.

When we visited the churches, Dr Leeser gave out homespun saris to the widows in the congregations. Four evangelists came to preach in the Out-Patients building during clinics. Their messages were broadcast into the wards. The Godavari district was also blessed by evangelical messages over the radio network.

Though often exhausted, we had the joy of knowing that the love of God was changing people's lives. We would not have been able to meet our commitments if we didn't have the support of our Indian friends. Three widow Christian women looked after our personal needs. Kamala and Naomi lived in little huts on the edge of a road and came each day to see to our needs. Marthamma lived on the hospital compound and was the mother of a family working there. Coming to our big, airy bungalow to care for our needs was a blessing to them. The wages we gave were the only money they received. They did not receive a government aged pension.

A dhobi washed and ironed our uniforms. Joseph, our cook, was an elder in the Ambajipeta church. He was an excellent Bible teacher. The stove was made of mud and cow manure, and the kitchen outside was separate from the bungalow. Young Ratnam, our table boy, served us and washed the dishes. We lived eating basic curry and rice for our midday meal and more of a Western meal at night. When food parcels from our home countries arrived after months in the post, we picked out the weevils and enjoyed the rest.

We had a small rice paddy field, and patients sometimes gave us gifts like bananas, delicious mangoes or a chicken. One day, Joseph cooked the rooster we had been given, and when Rene cut into it, out fell a bullet! It was the rooster I had shot and wounded because he was causing havoc in our rice field.

A COFFIN UNDER HER BED

Let me share this story. Jesus' friend Lazarus was sick. His sisters sent a message to Jesus, *'Lord, the one you love is sick.'* Wouldn't you rush to be with them if you received such a message? I know I would. Jesus didn't. He wanted to reveal himself as the source of true life. He had a higher purpose, so he delayed two days. His friend Lazarus died, and Jesus wept at his tomb. Imagining the scene described in the Gospel of John chapter eleven shows how much Jesus cares. One of the reasons for the delay was that God intended his Son, Jesus, to be glorified by raising Lazarus from the dead. When Jesus stood before the tomb, he called out, *"Lazarus, come out!"* and the dead man came out! Jesus proclaimed, "*I am the resurrection and the life. He who believes in me will live, even though he dies.*"

This resurrection is so different from the Hindu belief in reincarnation. Jesus' followers will be resurrected when Christ returns the second time, as He promised. We will have a transformed body that is perfect in every way. The Hindu believes he goes through an endless cycle of rebirth into a new form of existence as a human, animal, or even a plant. This may take hundreds of rebirths. Karma (good luck or bad luck) means that the sum of a person's actions in this and previous states of existence decides their fate in future existences.

Christians believe that when they die, they immediately enter life in Heaven. Our bodies have incredible value because God created us wonderfully and skilfully in his image. Like God, humans have intelligence – a mind to think, reason, and plan – and the capacity to love and communicate in languages. Jesus not only died to redeem our souls but also our bodies.

Imagine you are an elderly outcaste widow, and you are sitting on a mat underneath a tree drinking in this message of salvation that Jesus came to give. You hear of the crucifixion and resurrection of the Lord Jesus. You hear that God loves you when nobody else even cares. Wouldn't you be drawn to Jesus? Wouldn't you want to forsake your man-made gods and follow Him? Such an Indian woman did follow when God opened her heart to believe. To ensure that she would be buried as a Christian and not burnt as a Hindu, she asked Sylvia to bring a coffin to put under her bed, ready for when she died. The hospital carpenters made the coffin and secured it on top of the Ambassador, the hospital car, and Sylvia delivered it safely to the rejoicing new believer.

I have seen so much death. I have had to bow before its power. Babies, though so much wanted, died. I mourned their death until Dr Leeser said, 'They have gone to be with Jesus. They will not be trapped in a system of unbelief.' The Bible teaches that the last enemy to be destroyed is death. Until then, death will stalk our streets. Children and the elderly will die, but death has already been defeated for the followers of Jesus and little children. Death is now but a gateway to everlasting life for all who love Jesus. But for those who are strangers to Him, only judgment awaits.

Before the national immunisation programmes in India started in 1985, we admitted cases of tetanus. Children came spasming with tetanus until exhaustion claimed them. I had a separate room built for such infectious cases. We called it the Shanti Guthi – the Room of Peace. One such case with tetanus was the young son of our waterman. We could not save him. He had fallen off his bike and hurt his leg. Without washing the wound, coffee powder had been rubbed in to stop the bleeding, trapping the road dirt inside and the pathogen.

Sometimes, mothers would bring their babies too late. They first visited the temple priest and came to us as a last resort. We would say that our medicine wouldn't work unless we cut off the charms tied on by the Hindu priests. If the child died, the wailing was terrible to hear. When calm was finally restored, we called a rickshaw to take the mother home, as her husband would be working in the fields. We gently covered the baby to hide that the baby was dead. If the rickshaw wallah had known, he might have refused to take her or charged an exorbitant fare. Death would contaminate his rickshaw, and it must be ritualistically cleansed.

Dr Victor Wilson of Bexley Assembly in Sydney sent me unused medical equipment discarded in Australia because the sterile pack had been opened. Still, it was invaluable to us in India. I often tried to find a vein to connect intravenous fluid to babies with diarrhoea and vomiting. Dr Victor sent butterfly needles, which are ideal for securing intravenous fluid lines. Dr Leeser didn't like suturing children, so I was pleased to receive micro-surgical needles with the thread already attached. Using this type of needle for suturing meant less scarring. Little plastic clamps arrived and replaced our heavy stainless-steel clamps to clip catheters. Disposable Australian gloves were used many times because of the excellent quality of the rubber. There are so many practical ways that sending churches can meet the needs of their missionaries. I have been blessed to have friends who met our needs.

As I look back on the years I spent in Ambajipeta, I remember the frustrations I faced every day as I sought to keep the hospital surroundings clean and tidy and the standard of nursing care comparable to the expectations of the relatives of patients. Every patient had a relative staying with her to cook her meals in the individual kitchens we provided. This was necessary to maintain caste integrity. Brahmins, the priestly caste, boast of eating purely vegetarian food. Others from the outcaste community eat mutton (goat), fish and chicken if they can afford it.

The wards were often crowded. Sometimes there were three to five people to each bed – the patient, her baby and her youngest child, the relative and maybe her youngest child and grandma who couldn't be left at home. I remember one time when two grandmas wanted to stay. I said, 'Okay, sleep under the bed, but don't let your feet poke out!'

At night the relatives spread mats on the floor to sleep. If no outside locked-up kitchens were available, some relatives tried to keep the wood under the bed to prevent it from being stolen. This was not acceptable. The cleaning woman could not satisfactorily mop the floor, and scorpions sometimes crawled out of the wood. The beds were also close together. As the hospital stay was often of short duration, staff became tired of repeating the same instructions.

The way relatives hung out their washing caused me another headache. They would drape it over whatever they thought was a good spot. Then, how they washed dirty baby rag nappies at the clean well made my blood boil. Sometimes, the babies had diarrhoea. The toilets made me despair, but I won't describe those.

The constant clash in defeating the pathogens and my role in winning this battle created tension in me. The image of me as a supervisor who was always on the warpath did not go well with the idea of a compassionate missionary, loving people. This caused me concern and I often felt I was falling short. Someone once said, 'To be disappointed in oneself is to have trusted oneself.' I had to roll the burden onto my Saviour, who knew I desired to represent Him faithfully and give the best patient care possible. We rarely had an empty bed. Indeed this was a testimony to patient satisfaction.

Blessed with good Biblical teachings in the past, we kept coming to our divine counsellor when we arose every morning at 5 a.m. to be strengthened for a new day. I loved my nursing experience and was rewarded when a patient responded to my smile, or I saw the fear leave her eyes. The distressed woman felt safe. A rumour went around the villages, 'God is in that place.' Infertile women were getting pregnant, mothers went home with live babies, and people listened to the preaching over loudspeakers three times a day. Four evangelists, Prasad, Paul, Solomon, and Satyanundum, travelled miles on their bicycles to preach in the Out-Patients building.

Every day seemed to bring challenges demanding godly wisdom and sustaining grace. The Lord blessed me during my time in Sydney at the Capernwray Conferences when Major Ian Thomas opened my mind to the need to live out the life of Christ within. One of his statements was profound. 'My goal is to make the invisible Christ visible.' At a similar conference, I received another glimpse of how a Christian should be. The Canadian guest speaker was Mr Gayle Erwin, author of the book *The Jesus Style*, which was translated into thirty-five languages. Every missionary candidate needs to read his book. Several of us at this conference gathered around the dinner table, airing our theological knowledge. Gayle Erwin walked in. What did Gayle do? He picked up a broom and swept the floor! We read the gospels and see many situations when Jesus served humbly, even washing his disciples' feet.

When the two hundred beds were occupied, the hospital was a busy place to supervise. The cleaners were women who came from the outcaste community. I felt sorry for them having to deal with filth every day. I started a weekly meeting and encouraged them to learn Scripture verses. A godly Christian ayah, Vidyavathi, helped me. The women were illiterate but they tried so hard. I gave out pieces of scented soap and talcum powder as rewards.

Sylvia remembers a story about me, which she tells with great delight. She was in the Out-Patient building and heard me 'blowing my top' at the back of the children's ward. It was in the early days when we had children hospitalised with paralysis from polio. Now, with vaccination, this disease is mainly controlled. A granny had dug a hole and filled it with water and cow dung. She put her five-year-old grandson in it with a stick across for him to hold onto. He was to move his legs around in the slosh. I told the grandma what I felt about this kind of therapy in no uncertain terms. Trying to calm me down, the old granny said, 'It's all right, Amma. I am going to clean him up afterwards!'

I needed to supervise the twenty-five nurse-midwives and the thirty ayahs. Most were professing Christians. These ayahs were village girls whom we trained on the job to assist the nurses. I cried over some of the things I discovered, like the morning when I counted the number of injections a nurse had given and the number of needles she used. She had used the same needle on more than one patient. We didn't have disposable equipment. This nurse was one of my senior nurses. That day, I lost it. I went to the bungalow to recover and pray. As I returned to the wards, the nurse met me in tears and asked my forgiveness. I was in tears, asking her for forgiveness for my show of temper. We hugged, and that was it.

Another time I decided to check on their taking of blood pressure as I doubted some of the readings. They were getting diastolic readings without using a stethoscope. I also discovered they were trying to count a foetal heartbeat using the Telugu numerals, which are much longer than English numerals. So, this required me to teach them how to count a fast foetal heart using English numerals.

It became known how good our nurses were after being with us. When they applied for a position of responsibility in city hospitals, they were snatched up. Occasionally I trained staff sent to me from outside centres. This was all in the Telugu language and stretched me considerably. I used chalk drawings to illustrate more complex concepts like surface tension, the kinds of blood cells and the importance of haemoglobin. Some subjects proved too challenging to teach. I repeated English terms until they understood. Some of my drawings, like the foetus playing skipping with the umbilical cord, produced a laugh. I always found them most eager to learn. The nurses gave Public Health and Infant Care teaching using visual aids to groups of patients and relatives.

The nurses were good at preaching the gospel. We placed mats on the ground under the mango tree or in the wards and invited the women to sit for a while. The staff used colourful flashcards of Bible stories that Sylvia's sister, Winsome, had sent from Japan. Hindu festivals, Christmas and Easter, provided the background to explain the way of salvation offered by Jesus. Hindus believe they must go through hundreds of lives (re-births) before reaching salvation (deliverance). How simple yet profound is the way back to the Creator God, as the Bible explains it.

A few nurses invited us to their villages to meet new believers. On one mission trip in 2006, when visiting a village church, I found about one hundred women sitting on mats, all new believers, but they had no Bibles. Obtaining one hundred Telugu Bibles through the Bible Society was not difficult. Just imagine the joy when they receive such a gift. About seventy per cent of women and girls are literate in the Delta area. If older Bible teachers in a church gathering could not read, the younger ones read the verses for them. Indeed, God's Word is active and life-giving.

It was best to leave the gospel preaching to the Telugu Christians. We mainly took the nurses' and doctors' Bible studies. However, we did tell Bible stories at the Sunday School celebrations. Sylvia was asked to speak at women's conferences. Just occasionally I was called upon suddenly. Once I was asked to advise the married couple at a nurse's wedding. I can laugh about it now, but, at the time, I was shaking like a leaf and very dependent on the Lord. The couple nodded wisely, so perhaps they understood something of what I said. At least the Bible verses would have challenged them.

My two colleagues and I did have some good laughs together. Sylvia was in a village and was shown to a hastily erected bathing area. When she was bathing, a little boy peeped in and shouted, 'She is white all over.'

Then there were the toilets we sat on. Showing great care when we visited their village, they would erect a temporary shelter. One time, I nearly died laughing. An oversized throne-like chair with a hole poked in it sat over a hole in the ground. Then there was the time when I signalled to the women that I needed the toilet, and one conducted me outside to what they had prepared. The woven leaf structure stood grandly under a coconut tree. However, in their enthusiasm, they had laced up the four sides. There was no way in!

Sunday Communion was another, sometimes challenging experience. I don't want to sound irreverent, but the 'bread' occasionally offered for Communion was sometimes tricky to deal with. On one occasion, the 'bread' was harder than a dog biscuit. I had this piece in my mouth with my cheeks poking out either side, and it wouldn't melt. I hid under my sari until I successfully dealt with it. But how sweet was the fellowship of those village believers? They went without to provide a delicious curry and rice meal for us.

Nothing fazed these village folk. When we were sitting on mats between rows of houses in one worship service, a bullock cart came along, and we moved to let it pass. The bullock did its jobbies on the way through. The women quickly scooped it up, put it safely by, washed their hands, and we continued the service. Dung is valuable. It is mixed with straw for fuel or blended with mud to smear on the walls or floors of houses.

Sylvia could almost tell a different joke every day. Rene was so quiet in comparison, yet she had a quaint sense of humour. She loved Winnie the Pooh and sometimes, after a tough day, we read Pooh Bear at the evening dinner table. Our God gave his created humans a sense of humour. Laughter releases feel-good brain chemicals, so-called endorphins that make one feel good. Emotional tears release stress hormones. We are indeed fearfully and wonderfully made.

We tried to follow a routine in the hospital and manage our responsibilities. After our evening meal we checked with the night staff and dealt with any complicated cases. At 9:30 pm, Rene, Sylvia, and I had Bible reading and prayer time together, then went to bed, hoping we would not be called during the night. Breakfast was served at 6 am. Following breakfast, we walked to the hospital across the garden. We visited every inpatient with Rene as she ordered the necessary treatment. Then we went to staff prayers in the Outpatient Building at 7.30 am.

About two hundred patients would be waiting to be seen by this time. At 8 a.m. Rene and Sylvia commenced seeing outpatients. I returned to the wards to supervise nursing care, examine all new admissions and examine all patients in the Labour Ward. We had a coffee break at about 10 am and a meal break at 12.30 pm. Dinner in the evening was at 6 pm. We needed to keep well by having a good diet and rest as we dealt with infectious diseases every day.

STAFF PROBLEMS – TIME FOR TEARS

The administration was a headache for Dr Leeser with her heavy medical workload, and it was something I felt I could do. We had some troublemakers among our male staff, and the situation became very stressful. Thousands of rupees were handled by certain clerks, which proved a great temptation. It was almost impossible to dismiss staff, and we had to learn this the hard way. Therefore I kept records of the written warnings given to a staff member. No one could be dismissed unless three warnings had been submitted and signed. We knew of one clerk with his hand in the till, but we couldn't catch him in the act. Sylvia felt led to confront him by saying, 'I will come on Monday and see how you handle this responsibility.' He was so frightened that he didn't turn up for work on Monday. He didn't come for a few days. Therefore we could dismiss him. He had built himself a brick house with hospital money.

The Business Manager became a thorn in Rene's side. Rene graciously gave him and his assistant office space in a side room in our bungalow. After some time, I sensed that this nearness was causing Rene added stress. I prayed and thought earnestly about how this situation could change. After carefully thinking it through, I discussed my solution with Rene. She agreed to what I suggested. I said to the manager and his assistant, 'We have arranged for your office to be in the corner of the new building – now the Paediatric Ward. There will be a blocked-off area to keep your motorbikes in a safe place, and the staff will be able to access the area easily to collect their wages.' My office was on the other corner of the same building. A hospital clerk, Anandarazu, became an inpatient clerk to assist me. The move went smoothly. One drawback of the new location was that it was nearer to the labour ward. The manager finally left under a cloud. Later, I drew up plans for erecting another building near the Outpatient department, incorporating a business manager's office, his assistant, and a recording room. The second-floor rooms provided accommodation for the Business Manager and his wife.

The following may have occurred while I was home on furlough, for I cannot remember this happening. On this occasion, Rene had asked that the wages be paid only when she was there. Contrary to Rene's request, wages were paid, with the troublemakers demanding that the female staff give money so that they could start a Labour Union. Then they sought out the Labour Union representative in Amalapuram, seven kilometres from Ambajipeta, to establish this for them. The Labour Officer came and was highhanded and offensive. He reduced Rene to tears. Sylvia spoke up and told him what she felt about all of this. 'Here is Dr Leeser trying to help your people, and here you are trying to disrupt and get all the money you can on this case.' Benny, working in our bookshop, said that the Labour Officer had a heart attack on the way home. He never burdened us again. Perhaps he became aware of a far Higher Power on our side.

Similar staff problems were occurring in our mission hospitals in West Godavari. When I first arrived in 1971 in the Godavari District, twenty-eight missionaries were associated with the Open Brethren Churches, serving in various ministries. We called ourselves the Godavari Family or Godavari Delta Mission. We met every six weeks to support each other, pray about our problems, and report how God answered our prayers. These were encouraging times of fellowship.

Chapter 9

Thresholds of Opportunity

You will be blessed when you come in
and blessed when you go out.
Deuteronomy 28:6

MY VISIT TO PAPUA NEW GUINEA

In 1975 I received an aerogramme from my mother informing me that my father had a stroke. This was a shock and I felt so far away. As I was due for furlough, I thought I should go home to see how they were managing in Rockhampton. I departed India on 30th April and was pleased to see my parents and help in various ways. My dad recovered but was left with some residual paralysis. Most of my family gathered to celebrate my parent's 50th wedding anniversary in December 1975.

As my sister Gweneth could not attend the anniversary, I wanted to visit Gweneth and Russell, so I flew to Port Moresby and onto the West Sepik where they were stationed. When flying in the little MAF plane, I looked out the window and saw the mountainous terrain and little villages tucked away among the trees. It was a joy to see them and their ministry.

One day when Russell, Gweneth and I were driving along a lonely road visiting mission stations, a woman stopped us. She was a Roman Catholic nun and nursing sister in a small clinic. She asked, "Would either of you be a midwife?" How amazing! I replied, "Yes, I am." She then asked me to look at a pregnant woman in labour and give my opinion on whether the woman should be flown out to a hospital. I saw the young woman, examined her and said I thought she would be fine.

We continued to a village that Russell had intended to visit. The local Christian men needed help discerning the source of recent unusual events. A spiritual revival had swept through the Highlands and many miraculous things happened. At such times Satan is known to perform counterfeit wonders. He appears as an angel of light (2 Cor 11:14). He deceives so that men claim the visions are from God. He raises up false prophets and teachers.

When entering their settlement, we were greeted by a joyous group of women and men. Russell went off with the men while Gweneth and I sat down with the women, joining in with their singing in Pidgin English. We listened to their story and felt convinced God was working amongst them. Their story went something like this. When they were gathered in their primitive church building, a shaft of light came through the roof, and they felt the presence of the Holy God in their midst. Immediately, they were smitten with a terrible sense of guilt and shame. They started to confess their sin of adultery, theft, jealousy, and malicious thoughts against fellow Christians. They wept and confessed their sin to each other and God. This went on for some time. Gradually, their sorrow was replaced by tremendous joy.

Before we left, we joined in their celebrations with a mu-mu, a feast cooked when the food was wrapped in banana leaves and buried under hot coals. Being part of that moment and sharing in their joy was one of the highlights of my visit.

After visiting various villages in the Sepik, we went to the Southern Highlands to attend the C.L.T.C. (Christian Leaders Training College) Conference. Russell attended as a mission representative, and Gweneth was responsible for catering. Early one morning when walking down an incline, Gweneth slipped on the wet grass and landed heavily into a sitting position. As she did, she heard the vertebrae in her back crack. She lay back and found it difficult to breathe. She had sustained indirect fractures to her thoracic spine. Such an injury requires an X-ray and immediate help from an orthopaedic doctor. And marvellously, one was visiting the Kudjip Nazarene Hospital in the highlands. Transporting Gweneth there, and later by a little plane back to her home in Anguganak, was no easy task. This injury caused Gweneth trouble for many years. Because I was due to leave from Port Moresby,I felt unhappy not being able to help Gweneth in any way.

I arrived in India on January 4, 1976. When I returned to the Ambajipeta Hospital, everything was going as usual. The workload was just as heavy, yet we received the strength to meet the challenges. We were conscious that many on the home front were praying for us, and we sought to keep in touch. We wrote letters in the evenings if the hospital was quiet.

Dr Leeser went on furlough and was due to return at the end of July. May was a hot month and we longed to be released from the grip of the fierce heat. The power cuts had caused much trouble and discomfort. We looked forward to installing a large generator, a gift from the Deepdene Assembly in Melbourne. The council finally commissioned a narrow strip of bitumen laid on the road from the village centre to the hospital. Before this, the roughness of the road almost caused the pregnant women to deliver before they reached us.

In March 1977 a telegram arrived from home saying my father had another stroke – this one severe. My sister Gweneth flew from PNG, and my dad died aged 72 on the 18th of March. My father had a simple faith in God and I knew he was safely Home with Jesus. When the ambulance came to take my dad to the hospital he said to my sister, Margaret, 'I am in safe Hands.' A few days later my mother let me know of my dad's death by an aerogramme. I spent some time alone to grieve and thanked God that He gave me a good dad. I had many good memories of my dad to warm my heart. Hope that I will see him again did away with the heaviness of my grief.

I prayed earnestly about what I was to do about my mum. She would need some support until she adjusted to living alone. I discussed my concerns with Rene and Sylvia, and we prayed together. Mum needed me so I flew home on the 21st of April 1977. I was able to hug Mum and grieve with her. As it happened, I didn't return to India until January 1979. This was made possible by being given a six-month extension on my N.O.T.R. – permission to return to India on a missionary visa.

HOME AGAIN IN ROCKHAMPTON (1977-1978)

I felt blessed to be able to care for my mum at this time, but I also wanted to serve the Lord in some way. I was in fellowship at the Rockhampton Kent Street Gospel Hall. An opportunity arose to run a girls' class in Mrs Scott's home. Besides this, I was interested in spending time with the teenage girls from the South Sea Island Community at Joskeleigh. I approached the elders and asked their permission to meet with the girls on a Saturday. They agreed that I, and another Christian friend who attended Kent Street Gospel Hall, should become involved.

These girls were part of today's Australian South Sea Islanders (SSI) community which has a special place in Queensland's cultural diversity and history. They are the descendants of South Sea Islanders brought to Queensland from 1863 to 1904 from eighty Melanesian islands to work in the State's cotton and sugar plantations. They helped to boost the Queensland economy. In 2000 the Queensland Government recognised them as a distinct ethnic and cultural Australian group.

A small community came together at Joskeleigh, also known as the Sand Hills, 40 minutes from Rockhampton. Many years before this the brethren in Kent Street Assembly in Rockhampton started a ministry amongst them. In time a small church building was erected to hold a Sunday school and church service.

In 1950 William Biddle and his wife, Lillian, came to serve in the South Sea Island community. Before this Mr and Mrs Biddle had been in Fiji as missionaries for a few years. Joskeleigh was in a rural area. To obtain supplies one needed to travel to Rockhampton. Summer days were scorching and Mr Biddle's car was unreliable. The battery was often flat. When winter came, the nights and mornings were shivering cold yet they kept going, longing to see the gospel penetrate to change lives and give hope. They praised God for those who responded.

Mr Biddle found that women usually looked after their extended families while men travelled to work as stockmen, on the railways, at meatworks, or fruit picking. When young folk became Christians, it was hard to follow them up when they were away for months at a time. The young Biddle children, Peter and Ethel, attended the local schools. Ethel went to the Joskeleigh State School and the Sand Hills State School, while Peter went to Keppel Sands as there were no suitable classes for him at Joskeleigh. Ethel Biddle, after nursing training, became a missionary. Later on, Ethel married John Orr in Queensland and was a sought-after Bible teacher. Ethel and John now live in the same Retirement Village as I do in Rothwell.

It was a sad day in December 1953 when the Biddle family was farewelled. Goodbyes were said to their many friends among these beautiful people. The Parter, Warcon, Edmunds and Malamoo families and many others came to say goodbye. Everyone was weeping. They said to Mr and Mrs Biddle, 'Never have we known such love and fellowship from white people.'

When I travelled down to Joskeleigh on Saturdays with my friend Beth, I loved visiting the families and being with the young girls. We did a craft together, played games, and I took a Bible study. A Christian young man named Durham Bertram started to come to encourage the boys and took them pig shooting. We ended the day with a BBQ to which everyone was invited.

A few years later, in 1982, I was pleased when I heard that Allan and Shelley Moss had moved to Rockhampton and became interested in the little church in Joskeleigh. They visited and soon developed an amazing love for these South Sea Islander friends as they spent time with them. The Lord encouraged the Christians as Allan and Shelley ministered among them, and some youngsters changed their ways and turned to the Lord. Allan and Shelley left in 1989 as Allan had a promotion with the Main Roads Department on the Gold Coast. This experience in Joskeleigh proved to be good training for their later missionary work in Colombia.

Today the museum, established in 2001, captures and charts the history of these South Sea Islanders. It celebrates their contributions to Queensland, including the sugar industry at Farnborough from 1885, and showcases the unique community that emerged in Joskeleigh.

ROCKHAMPTON SCHOOL OF NURSING

Needing to be financially independent, I obtained the position as the midwifery nurse educator at the Rockhampton Base Hospital. I started at the School of Nursing with educators Kate Hoare, Ann Williams, Jane Maikin, and Yvonne Kelly. The Director of Nursing was Miss West.

Pauline with Nurse Educators and Miss West

I created a complete Midwifery Curriculum and enjoyed teaching. Later, the Director of Nursing, Miss West, asked me to attend the planning committee meeting at Rockhampton University to discuss nursing training moving from hospital-based to university.

I came to realise there was a need for expectant mums and dads to have antenatal classes to educate them about pregnancy, labour, the birth process and care of the newborn. I ran my ideas past Miss West and found the support I needed. When I rang an obstetrician, physiotherapist, and others to participate, I was met with a positive response. They did it voluntarily, so I did not need to charge the expectant parents. More than thirty expectant parents attended the first session of eight classes, which meant we were meeting a need. I was also asked to go through the birth process and immediate care of the newborn with a group of men from the Ambulance Services. These days, their training is more advanced beyond the basics I taught.

Dr Bevan and Beth Walker, along with Col Krueger and Glen Wix, started a Sunday School in the Frenchville suburb of Rockhampton. Their vision was to start a church on the north side of Rockhampton. They bought eight acres of land and had it developed, and Mobile Mission Maintenance constructed a church building on the remaining three acres that were not sold for development. Bevan said they would like me to consider working full-time in pastoral care, supported by the church. However, as I prayed, my commitment to Ambajipeta was still an important consideration, as both Dr Leeser and Sylvia needed the opportunity to go on leave.

The months went by. I loved teaching in the School of Nursing, but spiritually I felt I was in a valley of dry bones. I know God sometimes sends dryness of the soul as a discipline to create a thirst to know and experience Christ more.

As the deer pants for streams of water,
So my soul pants for you, my God.
My soul thirsts for God, for the living God.
When can I go and meet with God? Psalm 42

Feeling the need for life-giving Bible teaching I did several courses with the Emmaus Correspondence School based in Sydney to enrich my spiritual life. Mr James Savage of the Bethany Home, Norman Park, marked these Emmaus courses. When he marked my essays, he became a real source of encouragement. I was thirsty to experience God in a fresh way and spent many hours in God's Word. I believed that God could use this season of weariness to bring me into a deeper relationship with Jesus, who promises to quench our thirst. (John 7:37-38). I missed the ministry in India where I lived my life on a different plane.

My prayers and thoughts were very much with my colleagues in Ambajipeta. I was praying about returning so that Sylvia Wright could go on furlough. If this eventuated, I planned to travel via England to visit Mary Miller and Muriel Pitts, my nursing colleagues from my time in Kerala. My passport arrived with an endorsement for one year. Mum seemed more settled. It was time to say goodbye to her once again. She knew I was a faithful homing pigeon.

MY VISIT TO ENGLAND

By November 1979 I was in Colchester, England. The mission in London has a helpful system of caring for missionaries on leave by fitting them out with winter clothes. I needed them as the weather was cold. However, I thoroughly enjoyed my stay with Muriel Pitts and Mary Miller, retired missionaries I worked with in the hospital in Thiruvalla, Kerala State. They lived in Mrs Pitt's home in Colchester so Muriel could care for her mum. Colchester in Essex occupies the site of the first major city in Roman Britain and was its first capital. It was a magical experience touching a stone wall the Romans built before Christ's birth.

My soul welcomed the sights. Frozen grass was sparkling in the sun. Drifting autumn leaves of gold and orange fell like gondolas to cover the moss-laden ground. Bare tree branches reaching upwards formed lace-like patterns against the sky. This was all new to me, coming from the tropics. One day I saw two donkeys, one grey and obviously male. He tried to nibble my boots and coat as I balanced on the iron gate. They wouldn't keep still and pose for me. I would have the ears of one and the rump of another

– the head of one and no head on the other. Mrs Pitts, who was bedridden, eagerly awaited my return from my walks to hear about what I had seen and experienced. She had a good laugh about the donkeys.

The English folk speak in complete sentences. Unlike some Aussies who finish half a sentence with 'you know.' In November in England, night shadows begin to fall at about 4.30 p.m. I used to take Mary's dog to Friday Woods for a walk. Don't you love the sound of that – 'Friday Woods'? When I went to church with Mary and Muriel in Colchester, I showed my slides and found the women friendly and interested. I sadly said goodbye to Mary, Muriel, and Mrs. Pitts and took the last breath of English air. I connected with my flight to India.

BACK IN INDIA

By December 6th 1979 I was back in Ambajipeta. When I arrived, Sylvia went on furlough to NZ until June 30th, and Rene had a short break in the Nilgiri Hills. While they were away, I also helped see patients in the Outpatient Department. Patients attending often buy Bibles or portions of Scripture. There is such a need for God's truth to dispel spiritual darkness.

My stay expired on my missionary visa by July 1980, meaning I had to return to Australia, but I was granted a NOTR (No Objection to Return) when I went to Kakinada. The next day our Godavari family came for the Day of Prayer, and I was blessed by Dr Walkley's message. Dr Walkley was superintendent of the Bethesda Leprosy Hospital in Narsapur. He said God uses distress to discipline and train his children. He encouraged us to sing praises to God.

Hear me when I call, O God of my righteousness;
thou hast enlarged me when I was in distress; have

mercy upon me, and hear my prayer. Psalm 4:1.
But I will sing of your strength in the morning;
I will sing of your love, for you are my fortress,
my refuge in times of trouble. Psalm 59:16.

Singing reduces stress levels when endorphins are released from the brain. We relax and feel a sense of well-being. Singing praises to God aids God's Word to dwell in us richly.

BACK IN ROCKHAMPTON

I flew into Sydney in July 1980 and then onto Rockhampton. My mum had acquired a little dog to keep her company, and I was pleased to see what a difference Tina made to my mum's well-being. It is strange having two homes, one in India and one in Rockhampton. I guess home is where one feels safe and happy emotionally.

This time I felt led to attend the new Frenchville Assembly in North Rockhampton as my home church and received a warm welcome. The young men from Annerley Assembly, Brisbane, Kevin and Colin Bray, Ian and Garth Grant and Graham Poulsen, built me a room on the side of Mum's house at ground level. Others helped to make the space more functional. All this was gratefully appreciated.

O LORD, I know that the way of man is not in
himself; it is not in man that walks to direct his steps.

My diaries contain scripture verses and poems God has used to nourish and challenge my faith, including the following – partly quoted.

What has stripped the seeming beauty
From the idols of the earth?
Not a sense of right or duty.
But the sight of peerless worth.

Not the crushing of those idols
With its bitter void and smart;
But the beaming of His beauty
The unveiling of His heart.

This poet talks about the unveiling of God's heart. We could ask the question. 'How has God unveiled His heart?' Indeed at Calvary, when Jesus died on the cross. We see God's heart of love for sinners such as you and me. As God incarnate, Jesus flawlessly reflected his Father's nature and ministered compassionately to the morally weak and spiritually blind. Jesus drew children to himself and wept at the grave of his friend, Lazarus. He commanded the widows to be treated with dignity and kindness. We can read about these events in the four gospels. Throughout life, God unveils his heart to those who wait in his presence.

The next significant event in my family needed us to see our God as compassionate and good. The reason was soon revealed in November 1980. I have my eldest sister, Margaret, in Rockhampton, her husband, Eric, and their son and daughter. Gary was living with his parents. Their daughter Laurel married Maxie Trathen in 1973 and had two sons, Guy and Brendan. Laurel was awaiting the birth of her third child.

Laurel was admitted to the hospital for delivery, and Zoe was born on November 5th 1980. We all went to the hospital to meet her. We were unprepared to meet this special child God had chosen to give to our family. Zoe's head was significantly smaller than other newborn babies, resulting in less than average brain function. But God had put within Zoe a beautiful spirit, given her a wicked sense of humour, a magical smile, and a mass of black curls. The family rallied around Maxie and Laurel, supporting them as they adjusted to this life-long challenge of caring for Zoe. The grandparents, Margaret and Eric, gave valuable assistance, sometimes having Zoe on the weekends to provide Laurel and Maxie a break. Through Zoe, we have learnt invaluable lessons – the value of human life and the way to love authentically. The family loved Zoe, and she knew it.

There are medical reasons why some birth anomalies occur. In the absence of known medical reasons, the story of the blind man resonates with me. Jesus' disciples asked, "Why was he born blind?" Jesus answered, "*…that the works of God might be displayed in him.*" (John 9:3). There is a higher purpose in many things, and I felt this was so in Zoe's case. Zoe was in God's care, and He spoke through her to teach us many lessons. I cannot claim to know the reason, but I do know that Zoe drew us closer to the kind of love God has for us.

I returned to Ambajipeta in January 1981 for two years, enabling Rene and Sylvia to go home on furlough.

VISITORS TO AMBAJIPETA WOMEN'S HOSPITAL

What a joy it is to have visitors. I enjoyed meeting Colin Tilsley who came to visit his sister, Joy, but also visited us in Ambajipeta. Colin and Joy Tilsley were born in India, and their parents were missionaries in the Godavari Region. After gaining her master's Degree at Oxford, Joy was called to serve among the young people of Narsapur in the Godavari in 1956. The Lord gave Colin a passion to reach the many who were not evangelised. He was a man of vision and started Gospel Literature Outreach (GLO) in 1965, a worthwhile venture of faith. Sadly, he was diagnosed with Motor Neurone Disease and passed away in Sydney in 1981. He went Home to his reward.

From 1975 to 1981, a few Doctors from the UK and Australia came to gain medical experience and stayed for about three months. One visiting doctor was from Wales and I loved how she prayed in Welsh during our prayer times.

In November 1981 my thirteen-year-old niece, Julie Pearce, travelled to India with an Australian doctor and had a marvellous experience. I introduced Julie to one of our doctors, who had a daughter the same age as Julie. Julie and I visited them in Amalapuram, a nearby village, and I have a photo of Julie wearing an exotic Indian outfit. Our friends hired a horse and carriage to take us back to Ambajipeta. I will never forget that ride home, a distance of seven kilometres. The full moon turned the coconut fronds to shimming silver and settled gently on the rice fields. Little bells tied around the horse's neck set the enchanting scene to music.

When I was able to leave the hospital for a couple of weeks, I set out to show Julie the land I love. We visited Kerala and then rode the Nilgiri Mountain train that travels partway on cogs (a rack and pinion system) up to Ootacamund (Ooty), a height of 7228 feet. The scenery caused us to catch our breath in wonder. Small waterfalls, dense forests with monkeys swinging from trees, and coffee and tea plantations could be seen through the train window. After a few days of looking around Ooty, we travelled down the other side of the mountain into Mysore State, where we visited the Mysore Zoo.

Everywhere I took Julie, folk loved to look at her dressed in an Indian churidar – a long top and trousers. I mostly travelled in a long dress of heavy Indian cotton. This attraction to Julie opened the door to the zoo's nursery, which is not usually open to visitors. We saw baby monkeys being cared for. They were so cute. We saw the elephants being hosed and lots of other animals. A Maharajah of Mysore started the zoo in 1892, and it is certainly worth seeing.

The next adventure was to see wildlife. For this we travelled by a crowded bus from Mysore to meet our guide, who was to take us to a lodge deep in the forest. We were awakened at 3 a.m. and mounted on tame elephants from a raised platform. Told to be very quiet, we rolled along, swaying with the movement of the softly treading elephants. We saw monkeys, peacocks and wild elephants in the distance. As wild elephants can be dangerous, the guides took a safe path.

India is the most colourful, fascinating, and emotionally challenging country. From slums to palaces, from mountains to vast plains sweltering in the heat, India's onslaught leaves the emotions raw. Julie and I now travelled north by train to Delhi to see the Taj Mahal, a breathtaking structure, and the imposing Delhi Red Fort.

Julie and Pauline

We travelled around the sprawling city of Delhi in a horse-drawn cart, facing the road we had just travelled on. I didn't feel very secure as we had a nerve-racking view of different modes of traffic buzzing around us! Julie and I travelled by train to Ambajipeta to connect with the Australian doctor who would safely take her back to Australia.

The hospital remained busy in Sylvia's absence, and I worked in outpatients and the wards. Later, in 1982, I developed a serious medical problem and realised that I would need to go home and see a specialist. My visa also expired in early 1983.

Chapter 10

Living in the Moment

For from his fullness, we have all
received grace upon grace.
John 1:16

My 1983 diary chronicles a strange record of facts. It starts with, 'I need to go home for urgent surgery' and ends with an entry in December, 'Still home but glad to be in His will.'

I left India on February 11, 1983, with God's promise, '*I will be a father to you.*' I knew that I needed major surgery. God would guide, protect, and help me in every challenge. The Ambajipeta Hospital staff bid me farewell in a programme they arranged with precious promises from God's Word. Indira spoke on behalf of the ayahs, Bhagyam for the nurses, and Raju for the men. It was challenging to obtain flights home. Because I was so ill, Dr Leeser travelled with me to the Madras airport.

1983 proved to be a stressful year for my health, but it was also a fantastic year of opportunities to touch others with God's love.

Dr Ivor Thomas at the Royal Brisbane and Women's Hospital was not pleased to see me as I had returned to India against his advice in 1981. I soon discovered that I was not the only one needing surgery. My mother in

Rockhampton had intermittent claudication due to blockage in the arteries in her leg. Consequently, we both needed surgery in Brisbane. My being home meant that I could support her. God's timing is perfect. Our family friend, Dr Bevan Walker, smoothed the way for us both by ringing the specialists needed.

I was admitted to the Brisbane Women's Hospital for surgery. Thankfully the tumour was not cancerous, but it had adhered to abdominal organs. Sister West, not the Rockhampton Miss West, was in charge of the ward I was in post-operatively. I had incredible opportunities to speak into people's lives during my hospitalisation.

I discovered that Sister West had lived for some time in northern India; in fact, her ancestors were in India, serving in the British army from 1820. Her ex-husband had climbed with Sir Edmund Hillary. We discussed my experiences in India.

I drew alongside the patient near me called Ruth. Ruth had converted to Roman Catholicism and underwent training to become a nun. Disillusioned, she quit and went to live in Thailand. She listened attentively to me as I explained the Good News and seemed touched. Another patient, Mrs C, noticed my visitors praying with me and asked if I was religious. This patient had cancer of the larynx. I shared with her from Psalm 139 how intimately God loves and cares. She seemed comforted when I prayed with her. The following day Mrs C said she felt relieved that she could now tell her friends, 'I have cancer.' Knowing that God cared gave her fresh courage. Sister West brought another patient to me: a dear woman called June from Morayfield. She was at the end of her tether because of the stress of coping with her nine-year-old child. We talked for some time, and I prayed for her son, Christopher.

Because of the after-effects of the delayed surgery, I visited many doctors for the rest of 1983 and was admitted to hospitals in Brisbane and Sydney. The stress of all of this exacerbated a muscle problem. I underwent muscle electromyograms and a muscle biopsy to diagnose my muscle problem, revealing myopathic changes in the muscle tissue. The report said, 'This patient will require close monitoring.' If I returned to India, I would need to return within a year to undergo more tests.

But God – don't you love that little phrase? But God was with me, and I kept moving forward. I settled back to life in Rockhampton. Knowing I would benefit from hydrotherapy, I was admitted to a program at the Blue Care Community Centre in Gracemere. The program included exercises in a heated pool, art classes, physiotherapy and a meal. I found that I could paint in oils! This boosted my confidence and gave me much joy because I have always enjoyed drawing. All of these sessions cost me three dollars!

When able, I travelled to many places sharing about the ministry in Ambajipeta. Many friends supported and prayed for me. Peter Brandon, a gifted Bible teacher, was visiting Brisbane and through him, the Lord was strengthening me as I listened to God's Word.

By August I was back in Sydney, where I spent time with Fiona Kelaher, a trained nurse interested in visiting Ambajipeta. Her help would be appreciated in my absence. I had several meetings planned. My sister Janice always welcomed me to her home in Beverly Hills, where I often stayed. Everywhere I went God's people were generous in their giving. Some gave knitted baby clothes and money towards building a new Paediatric Ward. MMM (Mobile Mission Maintenance) was geared to help in this project.

In September, Professor Murnaghan, a urodynamics specialist, admitted me to the Prince Henry Hospital and eased some of my distressing pain. Though I had been functioning at a surface level, deep within I struggled with all the uncertainties that pain and suffering brought. When a feeling of panic arose, I called out to my Heavenly Father.

I trusted the Lord to keep me in his will and purpose. I called to mind the words by Andrew Murray that I needed to say to myself in times of trouble. "God brought me here; It is by his will I am in this strait place. In that, I rest. He will keep me in his love and give me grace in this trial to behave as his child. He will bless the trial, teaching me lessons He intends me to learn. And working in me the grace He means to bestow. He can bring me out again in His good time, how and when He knows. I am here by God's appointment, in His keeping, under His training, for His time."

In 1983, I contacted Gordon Blowers of Mobile Mission Maintenance to see whether MMM could spearhead the construction of the paediatric ward in our hospital in Ambajipeta. I had drawn up plans for this building and made known the need via the AMT magazine, and the Lord's people gave generously. The team arrived on January 3rd 1984, and helped with this project until February 23rd. I was sorry that I could not be there to welcome them.

The MMM team consisted of John de Boer, Ross Miller, Wes Bates, and Geoff Reeves, a team put together by Leigh Minehan. They worked alongside the local labourers, who were intrigued by the foreign trowels and levels and amazed at the Aussies doing such menial tasks. The caste system in India has a rigid social grouping of people by occupation and social status.

Sylvia wrote: "It has been a real eye-opener to the locals to see these men do the most menial tasks, even taking orders from a younger team member.

Leigh Minehan wrote:

> "Some of the highlights of the team's time in Ambajipeta were the bridges of friendships they established with the local labourers. They visited the villages on Sundays and witnessed the baptism of believers. The work done by the MMM Team cannot be measured by the number of bricks laid or iron rods bent. The impact of their attitude to work and toward

> each other will have driven home the truths of the Christian message. We anticipated spiritual blessing from their labour of love."

While with Rene and Sylvia, the MMM team had many speaking engagements in the evenings. Ross Miller, who was full-time with MMM and a gifted Bible teacher, had about forty speaking engagements on the weekends and evenings during the eight weeks the team was there. They were farewelled at a function in February 1984.

Early in 1984 while caring for my mum in Rockhampton, I drew up plans to build an extension on the back of Mum's little house in Park Avenue. Her house had a flat roof and became a hot box during summer. Mr Lionel Maddocks (MMM) offered to build the large room as a service to the Lord. My brother Raymond worked with Lionel for a couple of weeks as the extension included a carport and fernery. God is so good.

Until I returned to India in August 1984, I was actively engaged in teaching and pastoral care while attending the Frenchville Assembly, now the Christian Community Church. When I went to Biloela for a missionary conference I was asked to speak on 'A Career Missionary', as the invited speaker, Dr Peter Hill, had missed his plane. Not being a stranger to making impromptu speeches, I quickly made notes and felt God enabling me to speak clearly.

Once again I was helping my mum accept that I would return to Ambajipeta. Mum's little chihuahua dog kept her company, and I could see how much comfort this pet gave her. Tina slept with Mum at night, tucked against her chest. During the day Tina sat on Mum's lap. My sister Margaret did not live far away and would often pop in to see Mum.

After hearing about the staff problems in the Ambajipeta hospital, Rob Rae, a hospital administrator from Sydney, documented standards and strategies to mitigate the problems encountered and gave guidelines to improve staff relationships. I posted his documents to Dr Leeser, who intended to visit Sydney to meet with Rob. Dr Leeser arrived in Sydney from England in August 1984. I flew to Sydney to meet her to discuss our administration problems with Rob Rae and Richard Saxby.

We were also invited to speak at the Epping Ladies Missionary Meeting. This was a tough time for me as it was the day of my mum's corrective surgery in Brisbane. Cynthia Tilsley prayed for my mum during the meeting, which was comforting. On the 24th of August Rene and I travelled back to India bearing gifts. However, upon our arrival we were asked to pay a hefty tax on a foetal heart monitor at Customs.

STAFF PROBLEMS

1985 proved to be a stressful year trying to implement the strategies Rob Ray had suggested to solve our staff problems. Mr Satyanarayana, the administrator of our Narsapur Bethesda Hospital, assisted me. He was a godly man with a gentle demeanour.

By March I felt I couldn't struggle any longer with the problems, so I resigned as Nursing Superintendent! I stayed in my room in the bungalow, spending time in prayer. My meditation was in the Psalms. I can laugh now when I read an account of my actions in my diary. For me to have gone to such an extreme, I must have been at the end of my tether. Sometimes we need to come to the end of ourselves to find the treasures stored in God – the mighty power of God to strengthen and the blessings of Christ's sustaining grace to the humble and contrite.

You have done marvellous things. Where is another
God like you? You let me sink deep in desperation,
but You will bring me back to life again.

My health fails, and my spirit droops, yet God remains. He is the strength of my heart.
Psalm 71

Also, I turned to Zechariah where the prophet says,' *Not by might but by my Spirit says the Lord of Hosts.' Zech: 4:6*

I received a timely gift in March in the post from my sister, Gweneth. It was a book entitled '*A Shepherd Looks at Psalm 23'* by Phillip Keller. Timely because I felt like a 'cast' sheep, as described in Keller's book. A cast sheep is a shepherd's term for a sheep lying helplessly on its back and unable to roll over again because of the weight of its wool. It remains with its feet flaying frantically in the air. The cast sheep needs the shepherd to rescue him. Sometimes, even the fattest and strongest sheep can become a casualty. Had I drifted away from the source of my strength – God himself?

In the gospel accounts, we see Jesus' compassion and concern for men and women cast down by the burden of sin and the cares of this world. In chapter thirteen of John's gospel, a woman had been bowed down for eighteen years. Immediately after Jesus touched her, she was healed. This happens to the human soul when Jesus touches us at our point of need. My good Shepherd came near and lifted me up.

After a few days I was back in uniform, committed to trusting God to accomplish his good purposes. Specific steps had been taken to avoid further conflict, and there was nothing else we could do to change the attitude of certain staff members. Only God could do that.

My visa was expiring, and I had a flight booked for the 4th of April from Madras.

Chapter 11

More Events – Some Tragic

The grace of our Lord was poured out … abundantly.
1 Timothy 1:14

HOME AGAIN

By 1985 I considered myself a seasoned traveller as this was my sixth time returning from India. I arrived in Sydney, declared the gifts in my luggage, and spent a few days in Sydney staying with my sister Janice. I met with friends at the AMT (Australian Missionary Tidings) to report how things were progressing at the Ambajipeta Hospital and in the village ministry. Then I caught a flight to Brisbane to meet with praying friends. I travelled by train to Maryborough and then to Rockhampton. I was home in Rockhampton for my mother's 78th birthday on April 20th. I found my mother happier in spirit as she said she had grown spiritually during the last year. This was a real blessing as my mum suffered from periods of depression and was on antidepressant tablets for many years. I once read that depression often comes from lies that we tell ourselves. For no particular reason that I knew, she would start thinking negatively and become depressed. Yet despite this, she never lost her sense of humour. My mum was reserved and rarely, if ever, talked about her troubles.

I was asked to take the studies at the June junior beach camp, where about fifty-five bright youngsters gathered. Guy Trathen, my great-nephew, attended. I had the joy of counselling some children who wanted to accept Jesus as their Lord and Saviour. I was also asked to speak at the Mt Archer Lion's Club and was fired with questions. Many laughed when I told them about the Baby Show I held in Ambajipeta, which was a howling success. They were interested to hear that the Amalapuram Lion's Club supplied gifts for the children. I also attended and spoke at a Rally Camp in Yeppoon. The camp surroundings suited my taste for adventure as I love gum trees, the smell of smoke from the open fire, billy tea and a full moon. Even the primitive shower arrangement added to the bush experience.

Woven into my everyday activities were opportunities to speak about the ministry in the Godavari Delta in hospitals and villages at places like Gympie, Maryborough, and Emerald. When I travel like this my heart is warmed by the interest I find and the fellowship I have experienced.

One day in November, with the deep rumble of thunder, a lightning bolt hit Mum's house in Park Avenue, causing damage. It split the silky oak tree in the front yard and danced over the roof. As the shockwave created by the impact of the lightning strike travelled over the roof, it damaged the nail heads. It was a terrifying experience for Mum and her little dog.

While in Rockhampton I heard about Kerry Voigt, a trained nurse, through a friend called Judy. After finishing her studies at Queensland Theological College, Kerry was looking at serving the Lord as a missionary and enquired about coming to Ambajipeta. I wrote to Rene about Kerry, and she said Kerry would be very welcome. I was planning to take her to India in January 1986. I had more tests on my muscles – a muscle biopsy and electromyography, but there was no further deterioration in muscle tissue.

Whenever I was home, I was on the lookout for designs or procedures to improve how things were done in the Ambajipeta hospital. One problem the nurses had was to heat warm water to bathe babies. The water was heated on a primus stove. This would have become arduous if we had several deliveries in one day. When my dad heard about this, he said, "Why don't you use solar heating?" Dad's idea was to use light tubes and rubber bicycle tubes, and I organised this with some success on the flat roof of the labour ward. Another problem was transporting patients from the operating theatre on the ground floor. Patients, following surgery, were carried up the stairs to the second level by our nurses. While discussing this with Glen Wix, a friend at church, he took me to see a lift powered by water. We had plenty of water on the Godavari Delta. I was excited about this possibility and worked out everything needed for such a project. This project did not happen because I was too busy to organise the finding of the necessary materials. Later, in 2002, a long ramp was built, and the operating theatres were built upstairs on the roof of the labour wards.

The clock was ticking, and I was turning the page of my calendar to January 1986. Kerry and my passports arrived from Canberra with our visas stamped inside our passports. Kerry was granted a three-month visa.

BACK TO INDIA

Kerry and I left Brisbane on January 20th, arriving in Bombay and going through the green channel with nothing to declare. We were to fly to Madras, but I thought it was a domestic flight and only found out in time that it was a flight leaving from the international airport as the plane was going to Singapore via Madras. That wasn't the only plane I almost missed in all my travels. When we finally arrived at the Ambajipeta hospital, the staff welcomed us with garlands. Climbing into bed that night,

I felt at home. We were woken at 4 a.m. by a doctor who had come from Vijayawada for an interview! Yes, I was back in India.

Kerry settled into working in the operating theatres. One evening I took her to meet Dr Uma Devi, our senior doctor who came as a professing Christian. I left her quarters rendered speechless. Dr Uma had been reading a book by a famous Yogi Guru and became full of his teaching. She told Kerry and me that Jesus wasn't divine and the Bible wasn't the inspired Word of God. She said that our staff members were a bunch of hypocrites. The more she said, the more my stomach churned. Finally, I could only say, "Uma, the Bible says if you seek, you will find. But you have to seek truth in the right place. I will pray that you do this." It was a sad moment when I told Sylvia and Rene what Uma had said. Not long after this, Dr Uma handed in her resignation. I pray that Dr Uma will thirst for the truth and find it in Christ.

Throughout India's long history, religion has been an important part of India's culture. I have found it easy to have conversations about religion with fellow travellers on my many train journeys. These conversations usually started with cricket and what I was doing in India and ended up discussing religion. Discoveries among spiritually hungry people alert us to the spiritual warfare being waged for the minds of individuals, no matter what nationality. I don't know whether you have ever read or heard Vishal Mangalwadi, who addresses the subject of *When the New Age Gets Old.* I have read his books and heard him speak at the Mueller Community Church, Redcliffe. Vishal Mangalwadi shows why the New Age Movement has disappointed the hopes of many followers and points to answers to their longings that lie beyond the New Age – in the person of Jesus. So many in the West have sought meaning and purpose in the New Age Movement and become dissatisfied with their experience. Another helpful book is *India's Search for the Unknown Christ* by Paul Pillai. We can only pray that spiritually hungry people will continue seeking until they find the blessing of knowing Christ.

The days continued to be busy and Kerry had many opportunities to see complicated cases. All the beds in the hospital were occupied, so when five nurses left for positions at government hospitals, the new, poorly trained nurses could not cope with all the demands. I could barely keep up with the things I needed to do. A patient was admitted, and she ruptured her Caesarean Section scar before we could operate. So many outside doctors were doing longitudinal incisions instead of the transverse lower segment. It was a beautiful stillbirth little girl. Illegal Ultrasound Clinics to detect the sex of the child meant that many female babies were being aborted. Having a girl required giving a dowry to have her married, which often became a debt that the family could not pay. Dowries have been illegal in India for fifty years, but the custom is entrenched. 'Dowry deaths' occur more often than the recorded eight thousand deaths each year.

Another case was of a dear woman who came for an abdominal hysterectomy and remained ill in the hospital for several weeks. We didn't know why until she returned months later, expelling a dirty linen surgical sponge from a body orifice! How could a surgical sponge be retained for so long, be absorbed by the bowel and then expelled? It seemed an impossibility. I still shiver at the thought. The theatre nurses had not done a correct sponge count at the time of her surgery. When this patient was in hospital, her daughter cared for her mother. The daughter had a little girl aged about one year. One day the daughter came running into the nursery where I was sitting, with her child not breathing. I was able to resuscitate her and send for Dr Leeser. The child probably had meningitis. That was the second meningitis case I had done mouth-to-mouth resuscitation on! We treated the little girl and she became healthy again. But because of the extended hospital stay, the girl's father-in-law came with an axe when his daughter-in-law was home and killed her. It was over a dowry debt and her long absence from home.

Another married girl aged fourteen had petrol poured over her and was set alight. I wept when I saw her. Even though we sterilised the bed linen, we could not nurse her appropriately. I kept saying to her, 'Jesus is the God who loves us. He loves you so much. This evil thing should not have been done. Tell Jesus you will trust him to take you to a beautiful place called heaven.' I prayed that the Lord would take her gently to himself. I often wonder how many of these dear ones I will meet in heaven. One day, I watched a patient who needed an operation die because Rene could not come to help. The woman lay there, and I watched her die.

And just as it is appointed for man to die
once, and after that comes judgment.
Hebrews 9:27

Shall not the Judge of all the earth do right by
executing just and righteous judgment?

Dan Roberts quoted: Grace is when God
gives us what we don't deserve. Mercy is when
God doesn't give us what we do deserve.

Kerry, the Australian nurse, helped in various ways. She accompanied Sylvia or Rene on the visits to the villages. This was an essential part of our ministry. She went with me when I was asked to speak at the Nurses' Graduation Ceremony at Narsapur Christian Hospital. I used a lump of clay and talked about God wanting to mould us into professional nurses and Christians who honoured Christ. While in Narsapur I went with Enid Wagland and bought a quantity of lace. Narsapur is prominently known for its lace-making artisans. Later in Brisbane, when I showed this beautiful Godavari lace to Margo Heyburn and her mother, Mrs Chase, they started a small business selling Indian lace in Australia.

In April it was time for Kerry to fly home. On the 16th I took her to the Madras airport, then caught a train to Coimbatore, where I met Phyllis Treasure and travelled up to the Nilgiri Hills on the little mountain train. I wanted to see this beautiful part of India once again before I left India. I never tire of looking out over the hills covered with tea plantations. After a few days I travelled back to Trichur with Phyllis, intending to see an orthopaedic specialist at the Roman Catholic Hospital about my neck problem.

I was admitted to the orthopaedic ward. The specialist arranged for me to sleep in a harness! This harness business with weights was a terrible experience, and I had doubts about this form of treatment. I had known for some time that I had a narrowing in the cervical spine with some encroachment. I travelled back by train to Ambajipeta in a neck brace.

In August 1986 I couldn't manage my muscle problems and the neck brace in the heat. It was 40 degrees. I was trying to put up an IV infusion on babies with sweat running into my eyes. Then I had a nasty fall because I missed a step. The time had come to return to Australia. I didn't count on my departure taking place during a flood crisis. However, I knew my mum in Rockhampton needed me.

I felt guilty about leaving Rene and Sylvia with extra hospital work. Even though they understood and had seen me struggling. I left India without a proper closure. With no de-briefing on my return, I continued in my grief and a sense of loss. God helped me make some wise decisions, which I will discuss later. Not until 2007 did I have a good closure that proved such a blessing.

THE GODAVARI FLOOD 1986

Heavy rain fell during the rainy season in 1986 and the Godavari River broke its banks. On the 16th of August, we received the first warning that the thirty-foot-high levee bank was breaking, and water had started to pour into the East Godavari district. When the water reached Ambajipeta, our church building was flooded. Consequently, we had the worship meeting in our bungalow.

Suddenly a message came that another levee bank had burst open. We only had one hour to prepare. My emotions went on high alert. I sent a 'help' prayer to the Throne above. I walked around giving orders in all directions. We had to move about 100 patients from the ground floor. We needed to take over a private hospital room on level one as an operation theatre and shift sterile equipment upstairs. A labour ward was set up in the storeroom upstairs near the toilets.

Because the outside kitchens would go under, I asked two men to gather all the wood from the kitchens and put it on the labour ward flat roof. Men were sent to the village to buy rice, lentils, and oil. While I was doing this, Rene and Sylvia were in the Outpatient section trying to make preparations. But then, the outpatient buildings were inundated. We lost thousands of rupees worth of medical supplies. The nurses accommodated downstairs in the nurses' home moved up to the top floor. The doctors did the same.

The dirty water did not reach our bungalow, which was built on an elevated compound area. Rene, Sylvia and I moved into two bedrooms upstairs, making the bottom rooms and the wide upstairs veranda available for staff members whose houses were flooded. Other staff moved onto the Outpatient's flat roof. Rene waded through the water and slept in one of the hospital rooms to be available for the night staff. Two feet of water ran through all the downstairs buildings, including the operating theatres.

We made coffee, cooked rice, and lentils for the patients on the top of the Labour Ward. The patients all cooperated wonderfully although many were worried about their families. The news told of the loss of four hundred thousand acres of rice crops.

Dogs sitting on roofs cried pitifully day and night with no one to rescue them. People died. Many little churches lost their buildings. Some patients arrived in boats as we were the only hospital open for miles around. Dr Leeser did a Caesarean Section in the patient's bedroom we had prepared, and the patient survived. I did a forceps delivery on a trolley with wheels. When I pulled on the forceps, the nurses needed to pull the trolley in the opposite direction! Every day we waded to the hospital from the bungalow.

Within four to five days the water started to recede. We could see the awful mess left behind. Thousands of medicine bottles lay with the labels washed off in the Medical Stores. Every ward had to be thoroughly cleaned. We killed a viper near our car shed. Because some of our staff houses had fallen down, we needed to provide a place for them. Two families moved into the car shed while others stayed on the Outpatients' flat roof.

Rene and Sylvia moved around, assessing the damage done to our village church communities. I had already booked my train travel to Chennai (Madras) for my flight home. Before leaving the Godavari District, I needed to obtain my Income Tax Clearance and an N.O.T.R. (No Objection To Return). It was hard leaving them all, especially Dr Leeser and Sylvia. This is not how I wanted to leave the place and the people I loved.

On the way to Rajahmundry to catch the train to Madras – an overnight journey, the devastation caused by the flood was still evident, with large fields of rice and mud houses flattened. When the train reached Nidadavolu Station, a missionary friend, Joyce Harding, was there to wave goodbye to me. Joyce and a few of her hostel girls had been sitting on the flat roof of the Girls' Home for several days without enough drinking water. The dirty water had overflowed into their wells. My tears flowed freely when I heard their stories.

The hospital clerk had bought a first-class ticket for me, and I was sitting in a plush cabin all to myself with the service of an attendant. Never had I travelled that way before. I felt so sad and unworthy. One time when travelling in Kashmir, my two friends and I were parked in a corridor as no seats were available. All night people were climbing over us when they wanted to pass. Another time water from the toilets flowed under my feet as the train went around bends. The worst may have been when I was locked in for the night with three men. People lock their cabin doors to prevent belongings from being stolen. My choice was to travel second class in a cabin with women. Then we had the crying babies and little children, but I loved it.

While waiting in the Chennai terminal for my Singapore flight to Brisbane, I talked to an Australian Art Teacher from Melbourne who was on a spiritual quest and thought he would find some truth in Hinduism. He was feeling very disillusioned and couldn't leave India fast enough. I asked him if he had ever sought the truth in Christianity. Then I explained how salvation and forgiveness are found in Christ Jesus. He listened attentively and took the Gospel of John that I gave him. His name was Tony.

I arrived in Rockhampton on September 16th, and my mum was waiting with her little dog, Tina. A new chapter in my life began: caring for my mum, working part-time as a Nurse Educator in the Rockhampton Base Hospital, and pastoral care with the Frenchville Community Church.

Chapter 12

Settling on Home Soil
(1986 -1990)

Let us then approach God's throne of grace with confidence so that we may receive mercy and find grace to help us in our time of need.
Hebrews 4:16

Besides travelling to Sydney for medical tests and Maryborough to see family and take meetings, I settled into life in Rockhampton. This included continuing with my health regime and caring for my mum. I asked my sister Janice for titles of books that would help me understand the present church culture and assist me in a ministry to women. I bought several books like *Encouragement – the Key to Caring* by Larry Crabb and *Yet Will I Trust Him* by Peg Rankin. I didn't want to sink into a void of non-expectancy. God had not changed. The gospel and God's Word were still powerful. The spiritual encounters would be different from the spiritual darkness in India. However, the needs were the same: people needed to come to the saving knowledge of Jesus Christ and the power of the Holy Spirit to live a life pleasing to God.

I knew I would carry memories and images of India for the rest of my life. I was left wondering how I could use this in God's Kingdom. I did not want to forget the lessons I learned on the mission field or God's gracious dealings with me. I knew there would be a period of adjusting. Even shopping was a challenge. Goods and clothes seemed so expensive. Buying stuff seemed a waste of good money. I often thought, 'In India, I could buy so many Bibles for this amount I am spending on clothes.'

From everyone who has been given
much, much will be required;
and for the one who has been entrusted with much,
much more will be asked. Luke 12:48

Some Indian mannerisms would need to go. Indians wobble their heads to say 'okay', tilting their heads slightly from left to right in a quick motion. It also means 'yes'. That head wobble would need to go. Then there is the quick hand movement, which says, 'I don't know.' I used these two sign languages in India and other hand mannerisms.

Mum was pleased to have me home, and I loved caring for my mum. Her garden was full of daylilies, colourful bushes and ferns. However, I found watering the plants in Rockhampton's hot summer a trial at night because I'm not too fond of cane toads – ranidaphobia, to be exact. It may seem like an irrational fear to some, but I previously had several close encounters like putting my foot into a gumboot and squelching a large green frog. On Dad's farm the kitchen was downstairs, so we had to access upstairs by the back stairway every night. This meant ducking under a place crowded with green frogs.

I applied to teach in the School of Nursing at the Rockhampton Base Hospital and happily settled back into the role I loved back in 1979 as

Midwifery Nurse Educator. Yvonne Kelly, Ann Williams, and Jane Makin were still there as Nurse Educators. I mainly taught midwifery subjects with odd lectures here and there, such as the disease rabies from being bitten by a rabid dog. I treasured the many nursing friends I worked with.

Steve Turner was the acting pastor of the Frenchville church. He also had responsibilities in the ministry of Cornerstone. In 1988 he asked me to consider working full-time in pastoral care. The church fellowship was asked to respond to this appointment, and all members reacted positively. After careful consideration, I resigned from my position at the Rockhampton Hospital and was sad to terminate my thirty-year nursing career. This had been a difficult decision to make. My mum was not happy about me giving up my nursing position. In my role of service with the church, I worked with Margaret Bangay and had several contacts I regularly visited. Margaret and her husband, Peter, had served the Lord for many years at Doomadgee Mission.

A faithful group of ladies at the Frenchville church supported the outreach programs, such as Friends Alive, when fifty ladies enjoyed a lively program. We also started an annual Women's Retreat, seeking to attract women from townships west of Rockhampton. These Retreats were well attended. Es Morse had many contacts with people on properties in his ministry as he flew around the Australian Outback. I gave him brochures to distribute. The Retreat was held on the Neerkol property, once St Joseph's Orphanage, until 1975. The nuns cooked our meals. It was a quiet place to gather for Bible Study. One year we celebrated the Jewish Passover and found this a meaningful experience as we thought of Jesus as the Lamb of God, his shed blood on the cross and the freedom we now have from slavery to sin.

It so happened that Steve and I did encounter demonic activity in the life of a young girl coming to our fellowship. We prayed earnestly and put on

God's armour before we visited her. I call to mind the verses in 2 Corinthians chapter 10, verse 4. *"The weapons we fight with are not the weapons of the world. On the contrary, they have divine power to demolish strongholds. Verse 5. We demolish arguments and every pretension that sets itself up against the knowledge of God, and we take captive every thought to make it obedient to Christ."*

When we entered her home, our coming caused a dramatic reaction in the young girl. She acted like she was coming from a dark place into a dazzling bright light. I never want to think about the stuff that came out of her defiled mind. I asked several questions to determine whether the devil had gained a foothold in her life. Questions such as, 'Have you used an Ouija board to contact the spirits?' All this may seem strange to some readers, but just as there are forces for good, there are forces for evil. Even anger or bitterness can give the devil a foothold in our lives. Once the devil gains a foothold, he can set up a stronghold of deception.

Years later I received a letter from this girl pleading for help. She said that she had lied. She had dabbled in all sorts of occult practices. The Apostle Paul instructs us in the book of Ephesians chapter five, *"Walk as children of light – for the fruit of the Spirit is in goodness and righteousness and truth… And do not have fellowship with the unfruitful works of darkness; instead, expose them."* I sought help from an elder at the Mueller Church and was advised that unless the person repented and sincerely desired to be free, release from demonic oppression would not happen.

Our Rockhampton church fellowship was concerned about the nightclubs in our city, so we targeted two of these with warfare praying. What happened next was astonishing, almost unbelievable. One nightclub was closed because of an arson attack on October 16th 1989. The bomb squad was called in and found twenty-nine unexploded sticks of gelignite wired to timing devices! The second nightclub was bombed in June 1990! Those responsible for the bombings have never been apprehended.

Another answer to prayer was less dramatic but still so needed. The newborn baby of one of our church members contracted the herpes simplex virus, which can have devastating effects. The infection can reach the brain. A group of us prayed around the baby's crib, asking God to heal the child, and God did.

As I relate this story, I know God does not always answer in this positive way. God has built an excellent healing mechanism into our bodies, but what happens if our defences break down? When a health crisis occurs, what is the role of faith in God? Peg Rankin says in her book that 'man's faith will cause healing to happen only if God has planned for it to happen. If healing is not in God's plan, no amount of faith will make it happen.' Our sovereign yet loving God has some higher purpose, and he will work in it for good. We will not fret if we pray with a heart like Martin Luther, who wrote, "Prayer is not overcoming God's reluctance. It is laying hold of his willingness." I would add to this, "Thy will be done."

I was asked to take the studies at the 1989 Pialba Ladies' House Party. Mum was with me for the weekend and enjoyed my antics on Saturday's fun night when I acted out the story of the Chewing Gum. This skit was a bit of a shock for those who did not know me. Consequently, when the clapping stopped, and a little elderly lady stood up, apprehension gripped some. But my mum, the little elderly lady, did not miss a beat. She said, 'How can a mother like me have a daughter like that!' Everyone joined in the laughter, some with relief.

With the resurfacing of this memory comes another. Gweneth and I learned dancing from age ten for a few years, while Janice learned the piano. When the family visited, Mum would ask us to perform. Cheesed off about this one time, we decided to turn a beautiful minuet into a comedy act. I resurrected Long Johns, belonging to my grandfather, and did up the front with a series of large safety pins. Gweneth also dressed up. On the piano,

Janice played the introduction, and we waltzed in. I thoroughly enjoyed the laughter and clapping as we carried out comic manoeuvres.

When talking to Joy Lund, a nursing friend, about my experiences in India, I wondered whether I could take a group of nurses to experience India. There was so much for them to see in this fascinating land. In January 1989 I wrote to the Ambajipeta Hospital about returning with a group of nurses from October to February 1990. The response was positive. A warm welcome awaited us.

Chapter 13

Not 'Goodbye' to India, after all

And without faith, it is impossible to please God,
because anyone who comes to him must believe that he
exists and that he rewards those who earnestly seek him.
Hebrews 11:6

THE FIRST THREE-MONTH MISSION TRIP (OCTOBER 1989 – JANUARY 1990)

I thought I had said 'goodbye' to this needy land, but India was in my blood. I saw the value of nurses going on a short-term mission trip. I have mentioned that Fiona Kelaher came to Ambajipeta for several months while Sylvia was in New Zealand and was a great help. Kerry Voight travelled back with me in 1986. After her time in India, Kerry worked with The Leprosy Mission in Indonesia.

I wanted others to experience this land of India, for it pulsates with life, a life fascinating to Westerners because of its unique features. From the towering Himalayas in the north to the meetings of the three seas lapping the walls of a Hindu temple at Cape Comorin in the south, an ancient civilisation slips into the electronic age without a stir. More than one billion people, descendants of the Dravidians, Aryan invaders and the tribal folk, the indigenous people groups of India, continue their customs and religions, bringing a sense of timelessness to this country. India is also a land of great beauty where human tragedy, deprivation, and tears are wrapped in colour and tradition.

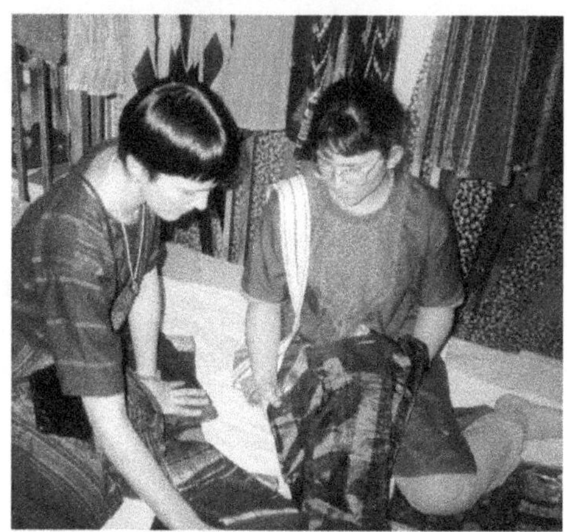

Mandy and Joy choosing Indian clothes to wear

When nursing friends heard I was considering visiting the Ambajipeta hospital, Joy Lund, my Rockhampton nursing friend, was the first to put up her hand. Two other nurses, Mandy Walker and Sarina Ewings also expressed interest, and my sister, Janice, intended to join us in this adventure. I needed someone to stay with Mum as she was having more falls. Elizabeth Bangay was willing to keep Mum company for the three months I was away. Our visas arrived and we eagerly packed our bags.

In 1989 we flew to India via Singapore on October 31st, arriving in Madras to the usual chaotic road conditions. However, we made it to our accommodation at the YWCA. Two days later we shopped for Indian clothes and left on the Howrah Mail for the overnight train journey to Rajahmundry.

What a welcome we received. The three nurses worked shifts in the hospital and visited the villages with Rene, Sylvia and me on Sundays. Joy Lund was in her element in the labour wards. Mandy mainly worked in the nurseries and was encouraged to see improvement in some of the frail babies. Sarina tackled the operating theatres. The idea was for them to supervise our Indian staff and increase the staff's skills in areas needing correction. I taught in Telugu, and they followed up with practical demonstrations. They also worked in all areas to gain experience. They had many unique experiences and saw God answering prayer. We had lots of laughs and good companionship.

Having my sister Janice visit India was very special. While at the hospital, she spent time with Dr Mitta and Prema's children. Janice told Bible stories and sought to help their son adjust to his separation anxiety about attending the mission boarding school in Ootacamund on the Nilgiri Hills. Janice wrote little Bible verses of encouragement and pinned them to my pillow, and I know she prayed for me. She was aware that I was struggling with some administrative issues. Her quiet and humble service was much appreciated.

Janice - Village Sunday Schools

Sylvia provided opportunities to see the evangelistic work in the villages, so off came the uniform and on came the sari. The Aussies learned how to wind six metres of material around them securely. Eating curries and rice with their fingers was simpler but messier. They needed to see this aspect of the work, which was why the medical work was commenced. Seeing women in their domestic cultural setting gave identity to the patient on the bed and the need to hear about the Lord Jesus.

Janice loved visiting the village Sunday schools when we gave out prizes for their yearly celebrations. Sylvia bought reams of material which she cut up into lengths needed for a boy's shirt and a girl's long skirt or blouse. The children came from poorer Hindu communities. We presented a Telugu Bible or New Testament for the first and second prizes. The Sunday School ministry was vital to spreading the Good News and commencing local fellowships. We visited dozens of Sunday schools during the year. The children were delightful. When each child was called to the front to receive their prize they said a Bible verse in Telugu. On one occasion, one said, 'Behold, I have come quickly.' Another, 'The Lord is my shepherd; I am not going to get anything.' We had a good laugh at that one. It reminds me of a verse in a hospital nursery. 'We shall not all sleep, but we shall all be changed.' Thank you to all on the home front who generously gave, enabling us to carry on this vital work. Dozens of church fellowships grew out of the Sunday school work.

Like true Aussies, Joy, Mandy, and Sarina packed their bags and went on a ten-day walkabout. They travelled to Bangalore and Mysore and then into the jungle, where they rode elephants to view the wild animals.

Janice and I headed down to Kerala State by train. This trip to the Rehoboth Orphanage was a treat for Janice, who loved children.

When our train stopped at Coimbatore station on our way south, we were suddenly informed that we had to change trains. I said to Janice, "I will need to find a coolie to help with our luggage." We had many gifts for the orphanage. There was no platform where our carriage stopped. I left Janice perched high on the carriage's steps while getting a coolie. Suddenly, the train pulled out and I watched my sister disappear into the distance! I couldn't speak Tamil and couldn't make anyone understand me. Oh no, what now? After about two kilometres, that part of the train shunted back onto another track. Still sitting precariously in the doorway, Janice waved, and the knot in my stomach undid. I had my sister back. Even though I knew not to eat food at the railway stations as it wasn't safe, I gobbled an omelette to satisfy my gastric juices. Our carriage was later picked up by another train heading to Trichur, Kerala State, our destination.

The Indian Rail System is incredible. It is the fourth most extensive network globally and covers 122,000 kilometres of track. Travelling by rail offers a truly unique experience. My longest journey took three days, from the northern region of Kashmir in the Himalayas back down to Kerala.

Janice and I arrived at the Rehoboth Orphanage on the 19th of December. Phyllis Treasure from NZ has been a wonderful mommy to hundreds of girls under her care and has done this for many years at the orphanage. Previously on my visits to Kerala, some of the girls had crept into my heart. I loved young Lali, who later became a nurse like Pauly Aunty. I was there in 1966 when a beautiful baby was given into Phyllis's care. As Phyllis wasn't well I cared for the little one, giving her condensed milk until I could buy buffalo milk. The first nappy she wore was a food parcel calico wrap from NZ! Shoba, Joy and Tina played together as babies. Before Shoba's arrival, babies were not admitted to the orphanage. Joy now lives in Ireland with her daughter and husband and is a faithful daughter to Phyllis.

The children knew that when I visited I often brought gifts. One year I was woken to see little faces peering through the door wire screen. They spotted the bicycles I bought for them stored under my bed.

The Rehoboth property was first purchased very cheaply by a German missionary, Mr Volbrecht Nagel. The orphanage was commenced in 1905. Phyllis arrived in India in 1957 and is still the resident missionary there. In 2023, she turned ninety.

After Mr and Mrs Mc Naught retired, Edith Wallace and Phyllis took over caring for the girls and managing the large compound. Edith spoke a form of colloquial Malayalam fluently and moved around freely among the village folk. When Edith retired, Phyllis prayerfully took over the care of the expanding ministry at Rehoboth. Edith Catherine Wallace, from New Zealand, died in 1993 in New Zealand at age eighty-five.

Phyllis felt the need to care for older people, so a small complex was built on the property. The Rehoboth International School, an English-medium school, has been functioning on the spacious compound for many years. Sarah Simpson from New Zealand cares for that part of the ministry. The Rehoboth Theological Institute commenced in 2002 and now offers degree courses.

A lot of hard work and prayer keeps the Orphanage, filled with children, ticking over. Every day, clotheslines are full of washing, firewood is chopped to cook food, and coconuts and bananas are collected. Over one hundred children need to be helped with their homework. From age five, some children study in an English-medium school in three languages: Malayalam, English and Hindi. Two matrons help, one in charge of the senior girls, and one cares for the younger girls. Senior girls look after a younger 'sister' assigned to them. Often this forms a strong bond between the two. Six older girls look after the under-three-year-olds. Thirty workers, some from outside, see to milking the cows, digging, weeding, harvesting, and caring for the gardens and yards.

Rehoboth is the children's home in every sense of the word. When new children arrive, they are given names that rhyme. A group of 'Annes' came, so were called one by one – Grace-Anne, Debbie-Anne, Sherry-Anne and Paulianne! They receive a good education and university studies if academically inclined. Some go on to become nurses or teachers. One has become a lawyer. Phyllis arranges marriages for her girls, sometimes with Hindu converts serving the Lord. These pastors find it difficult to find a wife to marry.

Janice and I were excited about our trip to the Nilgiri Hills. I was keen for Janice to see this beautiful part of India. We commenced our journey, longing to feel the coolness of the mountain air. The humidity in Kerala is high all year round. The trip takes us through rice fields, a couple of large towns, and then up the winding Ghat Highway to Coonoor, about two hundred kilometres. As we climbed up and up in the bus, recent heavy rain filled the tumbling waterfalls. The air was filled with the rich smell of sodden earth. There is so much to see in the changing scenery. Coffee grows at five thousand feet, and tea at six thousand feet. Inquisitive monkeys watched the bus negotiate the twenty-hairpin bends.

We met up with Joy, Mandy and Sarina in the Nilgiris at the Coonoor Brookland's Rest Home, which we used as a base for four days while we looked at the sights. While there, Phyllis, Janice, and I visited one of Phyllis's girls, Susheela and her family. They lived in a hut comprising one room, which must have been difficult with four children. Susheela's son Philip later served on the ship *Doulos* as a radio officer. He married a Hindu convert, Shakila, and is now an evangelist serving in Tamil Nādu. So many blessings have flowed out of the Rehoboth Girls' Orphanage ministry.

We met an attractive Danish couple, Tony and Jytte. They had bought a property and decked it out beautifully to take in unwanted children. We also had an interesting conversation with a group of richly dressed Bengali folk travelling with their servants. We seek to minister God's love and grace in these contacts.

On our return trip to Rehoboth Orphanage, the car stopped in the middle of a village. Phyllis secretly met a woman with a new baby to give Phyllis. She handed the baby into the car, to Janice's delight. There was great excitement among the children when we arrived with a new little brother.

Our stay in Rehoboth did not disappoint. Janice interacted with the younger children and used her visual aids to tell Bible stories to them. Mandy Walker sewed play clothes for the children, and Joy kept busy making interesting contacts. They had many opportunities to share their testimonies at Women's meetings.

The one hundred orphan girls and a few little boys eagerly wanted our attention. We had so much fun with them. Every day the Aussies found new things to see on the orphanage compound of about sixty acres. It was mango season, and the crops harvested produced big, delicious mangoes. Peppercorn vines ran up the jack fruit trees. Tapioca, a root vegetable widely used in Kerala, was grown on the compound. When boiled and seasoned, it makes a delicious meal.

However, real dangers lurked on the compound. Rats would dig down to eat the tapioca roots, and snakes would go after them. These were very dangerous snakes—Russell vipers, king cobras, and kraits. A Russell viper can kill twenty-two people with one bite. Only a foolish person would put a foot to the ground at night without first shining a torch.

Because of its long coastline, Kerala has been exposed to foreign influences that have impacted its culture. Kerala is known primarily for the spice trade. According to historians, Jewish traders came to Kerala during the reign of King Solomon. Very few Jews are now living in Kerala. We caught a train to Ernakulum to visit the Jewish Synagogue constructed in 1568 and the ancient Portuguese-Dutch church in Cochin. This all adds to Kerala's charm and the uniqueness of the Malayali culture.

Kerala's diverse natural environment is home to an extraordinary array of wildlife. Elephants, tigers, and leopards inhabit the rainforests. Trained elephants are used in the teak forests, and one often passed the orphanage on his way home with the mahout sitting on top. These elephants were dressed with bells around their necks and sometimes chains. The children would call out "ആന" (ahna) and run to the front gate to view one of their favourite animals.

These three months went quickly, and the 'hellos' and 'goodbyes' were too close together for me. Again I was faced with departing a land and people I loved. I did not return for another visit until 2003, thirteen years later. We said goodbye to our friends, hot curries, unique smells, and many images that would remain with us for many years. Janice, Mandy, Sarina and I flew back to Brisbane, arriving on the 30th of January 1990.

Joy Lund obtained an extension on her visa and stayed another three months working in the hospital with Dr Leeser and Sylvia at Ambajipeta. On her return to Queensland, Joy married Peter Newman. She gained her pilot's licence and flew within her community work in Longreach. Later on, Peter and Joy settled on a cattle property near Longreach. Mandy Walker married John Murrell and now works in Community Health. I lost contact with Sarina Ewings from Melbourne. Janice returned to her ministry as the Outreach Deaconess with Mortdale Baptist Church in Sydney.

Chapter 14

Being There When Needed

Lord, be gracious to us; we long for you.
Be our strength every morning,
our salvation in times of distress. Isaiah 33:2

HOME IN ROCKHAMPTON 1990

Life in Rockhampton is taxing during the hot summer months, but the winter days are often glorious. Residents of Rocky need to conscientiously protect against skin cancer as there is an average of 300 days of sunshine a year. My sister's family has a beach house at Emu Park, which allows us occasionally to enjoy the sea breezes and escape Rocky's hot summers. Also, the sea is safe to swim in and the water is warm.

On my return from Emu Park one time in February, I received an interesting parcel in the post. It was a book entitled *Life with Maree – Our Down's Syndrome Daughter*, by Terry and Jackie Flanagan. Jackie's daughter was born with Down's Syndrome. An enclosed letter explained how one of Terry and Jackie's daughters had seen my name on a brochure advertising the Ladies Fellowship Weekend at Burleigh Heads, where I was asked to take the studies in May 1990. From this brochure, they acquired my address.

When I opened the book they had written, I read, 'When Pauline Hodgkinson, a nursing sister, heard about Maree, she visited Jackie in the postnatal ward. She gave her a book, *Angel Unawares,* by Dale Evans, wife of Roy Rogers. They had a mongoloid child who died when she was two years of age, and they told their story in their book.'

This contact with Jackie happened in 1964 when I was undergoing midwifery training in Brisbane. When I heard that Jackie's baby girl was born with Down syndrome, I bought a copy of Dale Evans's book. I wrote in the book, 'To Dear Mrs Flanagan. With the sincere prayer that God will richly bless you and your little one as you travel through this scene together.' I went to see Jackie and gave her the book. She was deeply touched as certain friends had suggested she admit the baby to an institution. They said in the enclosed letter that Jackie treasured the book I gave her and the words I wrote. They mentioned that they would like to see me in May when I was on the Gold Coast. I enjoyed reading the delightful story of Maree, who enjoyed life beyond all expectations. I looked forward to meeting them again.

After the Ladies' Camp, I visited Terry and Jackie in Tugun, taking an oil painting of a garden scene I painted for Maree. We talked about life's experiences, and I shared that salvation was by grace alone, by simple faith in Christ's sacrifice. Terry had been a detective in the Police Force, and Jackie was president of the Ladies Guild in their local parish. They attended the new St Joan of Arc Catholic Church at Herston. I didn't see Maree because she lived in a Mobility Home and worked in a laundrette. However, Maree responded by letter, 'Dear Auntie Pauline, thank you for the painting for me. It is very lovely. I hope you have a lovely weekend.' Maree's sister said that Maree was also responsible for the chocolate cake smudges on the paper.

Not often do we hear when we have blessed someone. So, my dear readers, we never know how one small kindness can have a ripple effect and open doors for God to bless.

The months rolled by and then in September, my Sydney family informed me that my sister Janice had been severely injured while walking along a footpath. A speeding car mounted the kerb, struck her, and pushed her into the chemist's shop window. She sustained several fractures and was hospitalised in the St George Hospital, Kogarah. When we received the phone call, my Rocky family was visiting my mum at her home on Face Street, and my brother-in-law Eric generously gave me money to fly to Sydney and care for her.

MIRACLES DO HAPPEN

So many miracles happened while Janice was a patient. One day an intensive care nurse visiting her mother noticed that Janice was not breathing. She quickly sounded the alarm and the staff successfully resuscitated her. A fat embolism had become lodged in the pulmonary artery. The formation of a fat embolism is a complication of multiple fractures, especially fractures of long bones. Janice had sustained a fractured head of the femur, tibial plate, pelvis, and wrist. Her church family put out a prayer request and many were praying.

I flew to Sydney and went early the following morning to be with her as they transported her on her bed to Radiology. They transported Janice this way to prevent unnecessary movement. The bed got stuck in the doorway, and there was only a slight Asian technician to help. I prayed, 'Lord, please help us.' Along came four burly workmen wearing shorts and singlets. They were working on a hospital extension. I said, 'Can you please help? My sister has a clot, and we must lift her carefully onto that table. Can you do that?' In typical fashion, they nodded, swooped in, picked Janice up, kept her body level and placed her gently on the table. God's timing is always perfect. God answered our prayers.

Though previous tests were positive, that morning scan was negative. No clot was detected! God had answered prayer. Janice had a gruelling time in the hospital with the loud noises from the building site and an intense heat wave without air conditioning.

I wanted everything to look fresh when Janice returned to her Beverly Hills house. I arranged for her bedroom to be painted, bought a new mattress and bed linen, and hung new curtains. Throughout her life Janice has suffered much. She was twenty-two months older than I. Whenever in distress, I was the warrior who swooped in to help. Janice told me of an incident that happened at school. Some boys were calling her 'goggle eyes.' Janice had strabismus, a squint that wasn't corrected until she was fourteen. My eight-year-old face became red, and with hands on my hips, I called out, 'She's my sister, and I love her.' With that, my fist flew out and connected with a nose.

Following Janice's hospitalisation, I was with her in Sydney until I felt she could manage.

The Lord gave Janice the heart of an evangelist. She was quiet, gentle, and humble, with a tenuous hold on the Lord during the tough times – and there were plenty of those. She raised three gifted children and was a foster mum to many needy children. After training in the U.S.A., she served with CEF, Child Evangelistic Fellowship, for seventeen years.

Early in 1991 after recovering from the accident, Janice felt led to open a centre to reach needy women in the Mortdale shopping complex. The JAM (Jesus At Mortdale) Centre was opened in November 1992, and fifteen women from Mortdale Baptist Church helped. They served a cuppa and scone and provided a library of Christian books and free pre-loved clothing. The Lord blessed the ministry with many opportunities to have meaningful conversations with women, some of whom were from Middle Eastern countries.

Janice continued this ministry until December 1997, when she was diagnosed with a malignant butterfly brain tumour following a brain haemorrhage. The next few months were harrowing as we walked with her through her crucible of suffering.

We would need grace to endure what lay ahead; this was our heart cry. This would be a challenging and incredibly difficult time for Janice's two daughters and all those close to her. I prayed that God's grace would bring peace, comfort and the strength to endure. It helps to draw upon the Bible promises stored in our hearts at such times.

Throughout many years of walking with the Lord, I've listened to gifted Bible teachers, who have greatly enriched my Christian experience. Gifted Bible teachers come to the Mt Tamborine Conventions held each year. My friendship with Jill Bembrick, who lived on Mt Tamborine, opened doors to the Capernwray Ministry on Mt Tamborine.

Chapter 15

More Riches to Experience

However, I consider my life worth nothing to me; my only aim is to finish the race and complete the task the Lord Jesus has given me – the task of testifying to the good news of God's grace. Acts 20:24

MT TAMBORINE

Jill Bembrick was a retired cross-cultural missionary with Wycliffe Bible Translators. On her avocado property on Mt Tamborine, she also kept Arabian horses. Previously when visiting Jill, I found that my friend had a Bedouin-like love for her horses. Her fridge was full of horse medicine, not food. When visiting one time I offered to cook a curry and rice meal because Jill had been in India. It smelt great however, when we put the loaded spoon in our mouths – ugh. Instead of oil I used horse liniment that Jill kept in an oil bottle!

In 1991 Jill wanted to fly to the U.S.A. for the Wycliffe Conference. She rang me in April and asked me to be in her home during her absence over the Christmas and New Year holidays. As I intended to be at the Capernwray Convention, I readily agreed.

I had just returned to Rockhampton from the Pialba Missionary Weekend. I asked Mum if she would like to go with me to Mt Tamborine. I didn't want to leave her alone for an extended period. She seemed okay but by this time, she was on Digoxin for her heart and Lasix. Her eyesight had become cloudy because of macular degeneration. I was not only looking after Mum but also after her large garden, and this was becoming increasingly difficult. I wondered how I could best manage my commitments. When she seemed happy about my suggestion I breathed a sigh of relief. During the conference I was to look after Chris and Bonnie Thomas, Cliff Burrows' daughter, who would be staying in Jill's home. They were coming from the U.S.A. for the Capernwray Conference week.

In December Mum and I travelled to Mt Tamborine and settled into one of the bedrooms. Before Jill departed for the U.S.A., she gave me instructions on how to care for the valuable Arabian horses. The horses had established a pecking order and knew which horse was boss. Jill emphasised that I had to feed them in a specific order and show them I was the boss. If one tried to bite me, I was to use my elbow to block its advance or give a quick tap on its nose.

I think Mum enjoyed watching the horses as much as I did. When she was sitting on the veranda enjoying her morning porridge, the little foal, Radi, came and put her nose into Mum's porridge plate and made great slurping noises as she enjoyed her treat.

Have you ever been entranced, absolutely enthralled by an image dancing before your eyes? I have. The vision I saw was different from the mesmerising grandeur of the Grand Canyon or the breathtaking spectacle of Victoria Falls. Nor was it the gentle image of a field filled with bluebells or the loftiness of the towering Rockies in Canada. No, it was the vision of an Arabian foal running joyously free across a grass-filled paddock. I felt so inspired that I wrote a poem!

Radi, on what dunes did your ancestors prance?
Tell me, Radi, before you frolic and dance,
Do you rejoice in their strength or feel their battle fire?
Or quiver with the urge to hunt, not willing to tire?
Come, run with the wind Arabian wonder of Wild Rose;
Vision of the past and present – our Radiant Rose.

I invited my family to spend Christmas in Jill's home on beautiful Mt Tamborine, which sits on the edge of an escarpment and commands stunning views.

Gweneth and Russell, with their young daughter Robyn, were booked on a Qantas flight to return to PNG on December 31st 1991, to serve the Lord, this time in Green River. Russell was to build the High School and teachers' houses. I was pleased that my brother and his wife came to Mt Tamborine to take Mum and me down to wave goodbye to Gweneth and Russell. Robyn's friends were there to see her off on her first adventure. Mum has needed to say 'goodbye' to her children often, and it does not get any easier. Still, I was thankful that she seemed to be coping okay. After seeing them off, the way back to Mt Tamborine was through a storm, and there was a problem with my brother's car. The radiator was boiling. My brother went in his wife's car to get help, and Mum and I were left locked in his car. It was late by the time Mum and I thankfully fell into bed.

Chris and Bonnie Thomas arrived on January 2nd and were warmly welcomed. I was way out of my comfort zone but willing to serve in whatever way was needed. Looking after the horses was challenging, and my muscles spasmed because of all the travelling around.

Richard and Glenys Drew also moved into Jill's home as there was no vacancy in Capernwray. There was much coming and going. I was trying to entertain young Ben Thomas by talking about the Australian bush and catching redback spiders! There were plenty of those around. It was his first visit to Australia.

I attended as many of the sessions as possible, and the messages were thought-provoking.

However, I found myself really challenged when Gayle Erwin was the speaker at the previous year's convention. His messages had a profound effect on me. He spoke of the nature of Jesus and said that God's Kingdom was an upside-down kingdom, for the Lord of Glory came as a servant to humbly serve. And we are to be like Him – humble, honest, transparent, and non-threatening so that children are attracted to Jesus.

Gayle's second session spoke of Christians as pilgrims passing through. Therefore, travelling light and focusing on Jesus was the way to go. Jesus made himself of no reputation. *As the Father has sent Me, so I send you.* John 20:21. Gayle spoke of the heroes of faith from Hebrews chapter eleven and the 'but others' who refused to turn from God and were tortured. The world was not worthy of them.

In the Gospel of Mathew 12:20, we see a picture of Jesus, God's chosen servant. *A bruised reed he will not break, and a smouldering wick he will not snuff out.* This speaks of Jesus' extreme gentleness.

So many people around us are like bruised reeds, bruised and broken by the weight of sorrow, stress, or sin. Jesus sought to bind up and strengthen. He reached out in compassion to pour in the oil of His gracious Spirit to revive those with doubts and fears.

I liked the poem Gayle used in his sermon entitled The Porcupine Debate:

Two porcupine friends named Willie and Bill
Were talking one day of porcupine ills,
Said Willie to Bill with a sorrowful moan,
'isn't it sad that we live all alone?
The animals shun us. I have not one friend
Please tell me, Bill, what is our sin?'

'Don't sweat it, my friend,' said Porcupine Bill,
'It isn't your sin. It's just your sharp quills.
We live all alone, for that's just how it goes
For no one wants quills in the end of his nose.'

'I've got it,' said Willie, 'the answer I know,
I'd rather have friends, so my quills must go.'
But Bill exclaimed, 'It doesn't make sense.
Without your sharp quills, you'll have no defence.'

Willie thought, and he thought, but he couldn't decide
Should he give up his quills or save his own hide?
Then, in a flash, he decided with glee
I'll put out my quills on the trunk of a tree.
With all of his might, he ran at the trunk
And into the bark went his quills with a thunk!

'Free to be eaten,' said Bill in disgust.
You'll find out soon there's none you can trust.'
But Willie said firmly, 'I must leave my cage or
I'll risk friendship, then die of old age.'

Far into the night, they debated the matter
Live safely alone or make someone fatter!
The porcupine question remains to this day
Is it outreach or safety – which one do you say?

Christ Jesus sets believers free of self-concern. I have found that it takes courage to look squarely at the strategies I use to protect myself. We don't want to get hurt. However, the life of Jesus and the cross of Christ teach us that love for God and others is God's purpose for us. Not being involved with others can become our way of staying out of pain. It is not God's way.

There was something restful about Gayle's teaching. It reminded me of the hymn:

Drop thy still dews of quietness,
Till all our strivings cease;
Take from our souls the strain and stress,
And let our ordered lives confess
The beauty of thy peace.

At last, the busy days of the 1992 New Year Convention were over. At one stage, five cars were parked outside, and eleven were sleeping over. And I burnt the custard!

When Mum and I arrived back in Rockhampton the garden was in a mess because of a lack of watering. The people who were house-sitting had not read my letter about watering the garden, so the arrangements I had made hadn't worked out. My heart sank to my boots, knowing how this would affect my mother. However, Mum's little dog Tina gave Mum a royal welcome, which helped.

Chapter 16

The Seasons of Life

But the plans of the LORD stand firm forever,
the purposes of his heart through all generations
Psalm 33:11

MY MOTHER'S ON-GOING CARE

Mum was injured in a fall and admitted to hospital in 1992. She was having more frequent falls. This highlighted the need for Mum to go to some Care Facility. According to my research, there were three places with suitable hostel accommodation – one in Rockhampton, one in Maryborough and Bethany Home in Brisbane. I called in an estate agent, Mr Gary Cooper, who said Mum's house was worth about eighty-five thousand dollars. Even the thought of all this – finding hostel accommodation and selling Mum's house was stressful.

I was still being asked to speak at various gatherings and was organising a twenty-four-hour Retreat for twenty women from our Frenchville Christian Community Church. This proved to be a good time for making meaningful connections. I usually use life experiences and sometimes funny illustrations to emphasise an important point of my messages. At the Retreat, one sentence in my message was very challenging. 'Holiness means experiencing the baptismal pattern as one's life of faith.' Identifying with Christ in his crucifixion and resurrection gives us spiritual release from our old life.

I illustrated this truth with the story I once read about Michael Landon. The family was going away for the weekend and just before they left, their white rabbit died. Michael asked his neighbours to keep an eye on things. The neighbour's dog came in the next day carrying a dead white rabbit. 'Oh, no. Our dog has killed Michael's rabbit,' Chuck exclaimed. They shampooed the rabbit, gave it a blow dry, and put it back in the pen. The Landon family return only to find the rabbit back in its pen! Michael scratches his head and explains to his neighbour, 'Funny thing has happened, Chuck. Our rabbit died before we left; we buried it, but now it is back in its pen.' How foolish to unearth old buried hurts and grudges, hold them up, blow dry them and put them back in our hearts to simmer again? It's best if we deal with them and leave them buried! The Lord gives us new life to be lived in resurrection power.

It is hard to look at the uncertain future with courage. What would happen to me when Mum sold her house? I didn't have any money to set myself up. All this anxiety affected my muscle problems. I found hydrotherapy and massage, along with prescribed anti-inflammatory tablets, helpful.

The uncertainty wasn't because I thought God would fail me. I couldn't see how it would all work out. The truths of God's faithfulness stored in my head had to take root in my heart. '*The purposes of a person's heart are deep waters, but one who has insights draws them out.*' Proverbs 20:5. The Lord needed to guide me, and I needed to dwell upon His faithfulness to me in the past.

Stories in the life of God's prophet, Elijah, have often helped me deal with life's uncertainties. Elijah had his moment of human weakness when he was deeply discouraged. In 1 Kings chapter nineteen he reached the bottom of his endurance and prayed that he might die, 'I have had enough, LORD.' God graciously came alongside and met his most profound need, which was more than courage and physical sustenance. I have found that these times of waiting on the Lord to meet every contingency can lead to greater intimacy with the Lord. '*But the plans of the LORD stand firm forever, the purposes of his heart through all generations.*' Psalm 33:11. The Lord would unfold the plans of his Father's heart to his struggling child. I needed to wait in expectancy. Little did I know how precious those plans would be, nor how God would need to heal my broken heart. Our late Queen Elizabeth said, 'Grief is the price we pay for love.'

I like the Living Bible's translation of Zephaniah chapter three, verse seventeen, '*For the LORD your God is living among you. He is a mighty saviour. He will take delight in you with gladness. With his love, he will calm all your fears. He will rejoice over you with joyful songs.*' What a beautiful picture of God our Saviour.

My sister Janice intended to visit Rockhampton in April. When she arrived, we talked and laughed together. Then on Saturday afternoon when Mum and I were in the front garden, three boys entered Mum's house through the back door and stole our purses. I had just withdrawn money from the ATM. Mum's dog tied to the letter box warned us, but the boys took off over our neighbour's fence. Later, the Police returned with two boys from Lauga Street, but I could not identify them as the culprits. The church fellowship gave Mum and me more than four hundred dollars. Though Mum was upset, this gift showed that others cared and that God was faithful to his children. The two boys from Lauga Street named the three boys who stole our purses. I don't know how the Police dealt with the juveniles.

It was time for our church to have an all-night prayer vigil on top of Mt Archer. At two thousand feet, Mt Archer National Park is easily accessible.

Flasks of hot coffee kept us warm and alert. I stayed for about two hours, then made my way down, appreciating the light from the full moon. I certainly needed guidance about our future. Having my sister Janice with me meant we could pray about a way forward.

THE SURPRISING PHONE CALL

The timing of the next event was so remarkable. Mum, Janice, and I were sitting on the couch together, and I had Mum's file on my lap as we looked at the three places offering hostel accommodation. The phone rang. It was Mr Malcolm Arnold from Bethany Home in Norman Park, Brisbane, an institute with three levels of care. He rang to say that a unit was becoming available for $56,000 as the present occupant was moving into the hostel section. He asked if we were interested. I said to Mum, 'Mum, we can afford a unit at Bethany. If we take it, I could continue looking after you.' I indicated we were interested and put down the phone. I sat there stunned. This was the answer to the prayer for guidance we needed, and Mum seemed happy and relieved. Malcolm indicated it would take two or three months to refurbish the unit. I rang him back, saying I would visit Brisbane to see the unit and complex.

With my stress levels rising and the enormity of what I needed to do almost overwhelming me, I was pleased when my friend Jill Bembrick rang. I asked for prayer, particularly about Mum's little dog, as no dogs were allowed at Bethany. Understandably, my sister Margaret in Rockhampton was upset about us moving to Brisbane to live. Now, we had so little time left with her and our Rocky family.

Mum used to say to Margaret, 'I am not going to die until you become a Christian.' My Rocky family and I enjoyed holidays together, especially when we went to Woodgate, a sleepy little seaside spot in the Bundaberg region. We had much in common and had lots of laughs together.

So many friends were offering to help. Lila, a dear friend who came every week to clean Mum's house, offered to help. I asked Lila if she understood the Good News of God's salvation and found her eager to hear. She said she believed when I explained how much God loved her and what Jesus had done to secure her salvation. I gave her a copy of the gospel of John, and we hugged.

My brother flew from Brisbane to help, and I hoped this would comfort Mum. I knew she was thinking about her little dog, which slept cuddled against her every night. We had a garage sale in May, which was an exhausting experience. The house on the outside was painted, the garden tidied, and a buyer had made an acceptable offer. Those few words summarise much hard work and unpleasantness on the part of a solicitor and the buyer. I was left traumatised and it was not over yet.

Mum struggled emotionally and I needed to protect her from what was happening. To make matters worse she fell backwards down the steps and received a nasty head wound. She also hurt her back in the fall. Our doctor arranged admission to St Andrew's Hospital.

We will miss all our friends. Several called in to say goodbye. The Kahl sisters, Muriel and Avriel from Pink Lily in the 1940s, and several others came to say goodbye. Friends in the Frenchville church gave us a warm farewell with words of love and appreciation.

Mum decided to have her twelve-year-old chihuahua put to sleep. 'Tina will only fret without me.' I was feeling her pain. I went to my niece's place and asked Laurel if we could bury Tina under their poinciana tree. We cried together, and during the following days Mum and I cried ourselves to sleep. Estelle Watson offered to take Tina and me to the Vet. I had rung him beforehand. The Vet came out and took Tina wrapped in Mum's cardigan.

My heart broke with sorrow when he gave her back to me, this now lifeless little dog that had given Mum such comfort and joy. This was one of the hardest things I have ever had to do, and I needed to experience the reality of God's comfort.

I was deeply thankful to those who journeyed with us during these busy and stressful days. Gordon and Estelle Watson drove my car to Brisbane as I realised Mum needed me to be with her on the flight to Brisbane. She needed my support as she said goodbye to Margaret, who was very upset at our leaving. As the Flight Centre had accidentally booked three for the flight instead of two, we were not charged excess on our seven pieces of luggage!

BETHANY IN BRISBANE

We moved into our unit at Bethany on the 6th of July 1992. The views of the river, Story Bridge, and river traffic were spectacular. We could enjoy a million-dollar view for a few thousand dollars. In the beginning Mum could not appreciate it, for she was locked up in her grief. She wanted to feel different, for she appreciated all the kindness shown to us. It was hard watching her trying to adjust to all the changes. I hoped that some of her pain would soon go away. I had prayed for guidance and the Lord answered, so I needed to trust that this move was God's will. Even though I cared about Mum's feelings, I could not live in her world.

I presented not a blank page to the Lord, for I saw life as a treasure chest to explore, packed with God's promises and blessings. God is a good and gracious God. As someone said, 'Whatever waits for us around the corner, God is already there.'

I joined Forum, an organisation that encourages public speaking and meetings in small, friendly groups. This allowed me to put my thoughts into words and testify to my relationship with God. It was exciting to enter a contest and have my speech on the *Seasons of Life* chosen as the best speech in the Forum organisation.

On a beautiful spring morning, Mum and I were enjoying a cuppa when we received a phone call saying Brendan was bringing his grandma for a visit during the September holidays. Knowing that my sister Margaret was coming to visit changed Mum immediately. Mum said, 'I never thought she would come.' We had such a happy time together. Other Brisbane relatives were visiting Mum, so I hoped she would soon settle.

We even had a Family Reunion in January 1993 when nineteen members from Sydney, Rockhampton and Brisbane celebrated with Mum. Her five children, Margaret, Janice, Pauline, Gweneth, and Raymond were together for the first time in thirty years. After lunch I shared snippets from the family tree, Janice shared memories of Mum, Julie recited, Russell, Gweneth and Robyn sang in Pidgeon, and Vicki and Julie sang a beautiful duet. Mum looked around and said, 'It is good to see the fruit of my labours!'

I bought Mum a canary and continued praying that she would see the positives of being at Bethany. On beautiful sunny days, we caught the ferry to Southbank and had coffee while watching the river traffic. There were so many places to visit, and I was determined to find my way around. One day in the city when I was hopelessly lost, I said to Mum, 'Mum, see that little red car in front. I am going to follow it.' And that little red car went the way I wanted to go!

Becoming aware of the need for some women to have a Bible Study together, I thought we could commence having KYB (Know Your Bible) at Bethany. I was dumbfounded and saddened that this suggestion caused such an irrational reaction among some residents. I prayed for the grace to understand and that these rebuffs would not steal my enthusiasm. I often prayed with Edna Ramage, whose spiritual life spoke volumes of the richness of her relationship with God. Finally, with permission from Malcolm Arnold, keen ladies met once a week in the library for a precious time together. Besides this, I received invitations to speak at missionary gatherings, women's retreats, two studies at the Hervey Bay Ladies Weekend and other ladies' groups.

In his book *Future Grace*, John Piper gives much food for thought. He speaks of future grace as the grace promised to sustain us in future experiences. I like his thoughts on the promise in Romans 8:28. He writes that '… nothing will ever enter your experience as God's child that, by God's sovereign grace, will not turn out to be a benefit to you. This is what it means for God to be God and for God to be for you, and for God to freely give you all things with Christ.' He says, 'You must believe this to thrive. There is so much pain, many setbacks and discouragements, and many personal failures and pressures. God is taking these, stripping them of their destructive power, and making them work to enlarge our joy in God and our compassion for others.'

In the past I have not handled conflicts very well. My nervous system seems to go on high alert and I fail to interpret what is happening correctly. I feel very insecure. I can trace some of this back to my childhood when my mother would go away for a while. I did not know where she was. Later, I discovered that she went to relatives in Gladstone when she felt overwhelmed. Also, I had those other encounters that I mentioned previously. Besides this, as a young child, I had difficulty saying some combinations of sounds and was sent out of my class to a large room for remedial help. This caused me anxiety and I overcompensated my feelings by acting up in the playground. As children we absorb similar thinking and behavioural patterns from our parents and family members. I thank God for the grace and strength He now pours into my life so I can live to enjoy his blessings.

In one of my messages at the Pialba Ladies Camp, I shared a story I love to tell and think about. It goes like this.

A young red Indian boy in America found an egg from an eagle's nest. He took it to his camp and put it under a prairie chicken to hatch. When the eaglet hatched, the eaglet thought he was a prairie chicken. He did everything that a prairie chicken did. He scratched around in the tall grass, finding insects and seeds to eat. Every day was the same. He scratched around. He clucked and cackled and fluffed his feathers.

One day, he was captured by an extraordinary sight. High above soared an eagle, gliding effortlessly on a thermal current. He asked another prairie chicken, 'How can that bird fly so high while we scratch around down here?' His friend answered, 'He is an eagle, born to fly high in the sky. We are only chickens born to scratch around in the dirt.' How sad if that eaglet died thinking he was nothing but a chicken.

The moral of the story is that Christians are born to fly, to soar with God's power as we depend on the currents of God's Spirit, to leave behind the encumbrances of sinful desires and earthly ambitions, to enjoy and explore the 'heavenlies' – the spiritual blessings in Christ. I have often quoted this saying: 'The truest thing about you is what God says about you.'

I was preparing for the Burleigh Heads Ladies weekend in May 1995, where I was asked to speak about the benefits and drawbacks of being single on the mission field. You can imagine my surprise when, on February 8th 1995 I received a phone call from Fred Robins asking me out for lunch. But this story deserves a new chapter. The providential care of a loving God was ready to reveal the next chapter in my life.

Chapter 17

A Life-Changing Event

(1995)

For I know the plans I have for you," declares the LORD, "plans to prosper you and not to harm you, plans to give you hope and a future.
Jeremiah 29:11

We don't hear sermons often about the providential care of our loving God. Millard J. Erickson writes, 'Providence in certain ways is central to the conduct of the Christian life. It means that we can live with the assurance that God is present and active in our lives. Therefore, we are in his care and can face the future confidently, knowing things are not happening merely by chance. We can pray, knowing that God hears and acts upon our prayers.'

I will never forget that day in February 1995 that was to change my life. I was about to have breakfast when the phone rang. I picked up the receiver, saying, 'Hello. Pauline here.' 'Hello. This is Fred Robins. Would you like to have lunch with me?' Those few words opened doors to what God had planned for me to experience next. I responded rather shakily,

'That would be nice.' After making a time to meet in front of the Bethany complex, I put down the phone and sat there stunned.

I knew the Robins family primarily through my long friendship with Bill and Hazel Hutcheon when I first became a Christian in Rockhampton. Gwen Robins, Fred's deceased wife, was Hazel's older sister. Gwen had been called home to Glory in November 1993, and I had attended her funeral. I knew that Fred and Gwen's daughter, Jennifer, attended the Acacia Ridge Assembly, and their younger daughter, Leonie, served the Lord in Kazakhstan. I did not know their son, Mark, but had seen him at gatherings. Nor did I know Fred.

What preceded that phone call was also remarkable. On Tuesday, the day before Fred rang, I visited Hazel and Bill Hutcheon on my way back from a Forum Speakers' gathering. I mentioned to Hazel that I needed a friend. That very night, Fred rang them, saying he was lonely. Hazel said, 'Fred, what you need is a friend.' He responded, 'Like who?' Hazel said, 'How about Pauline Hodgkinson?' Fred said he was already praying about the matter. This was because his daughter, Jennifer, and daughter-in-law, Helen, had made up a list of suitable companions for their dad, and my name was on the list. Priceless!

The day after that phone call, Fred called for me in his new Eunos car and took me to that popular restaurant on the corner of Beams and Gympie Road, which was not far from his house at Carseldine. I could not relax but must have said something that made him laugh, for I thought, 'I like his laugh.'

The weeks rolled by, with Fred organising picnics and taking me to concerts. In other words, he courted me. It wasn't long before interested observers noted that things were becoming serious. Though aged fifty-seven, I had never been in love like this before. By May, Fred and I had decided to marry. I had no doubts that the Lord had brought us together.

At the Ladies' May weekend, where I was asked to speak of the benefits of being single on the mission field, I did so with Fred in the recording room listening to me and probably chuckling. Fred designed an engagement ring that his jeweller made. Wanting to have a memorable event, we went to a lovely spot at a restaurant in Yandina on the Sunshine Coast, where Fred officially asked me to marry him. We announced our engagement in July at the Wynnum Church. I felt that we needed to give Fred's family time to adjust to the changing situation in their dad's life. Also, in December, Leonie, Fred's daughter, would be home in Australia from Kazakhstan. We decided on December 2nd as the wedding date. Fred's other daughter, Jennifer, was with her husband, Neville Brown, and family serving the Lord in the Christian campsite in Rockingham, WA. Fred arranged for their flights from Perth to attend the wedding.

Fred and I seemed to have much in common, except that he was much quieter. At our wedding, Bill Hutcheon said Fred was like a steadily flowing river, and I was like a cascading waterfall! We both liked classical music and enjoyed going to concerts. Teaching Scripture was another gift we shared.

My mum was watching our friendship with some misgivings. She was making a concerted effort to manage without me by going to devotions alone and on day trips with the residents. I wanted my mum to know that we would continue looking after her welfare, but I did have deep concerns that I shared with no one. Fred and I drove to Rockhampton for him to meet my Rocky family. We saw Beris, a friend of mine in Bundaberg, on the way up about having my wedding dress made from a Vogue pattern.

Fred was putting in a heated spa pool for me as he knows how much pain I experience and how hydrotherapy helps me, especially now that I had developed shin splints and was suffering the excruciating treatment of 'crushing' the inflamed muscles.

I struggled to stay calm about the wedding, which was only a few weeks away in early December. There seemed to be so much to do. All my family intended to join in the wedding celebrations. I wrote a poem and printed it on the table placemats for the reception.

Thank you, God, for sending Fred to me
For letting me experience this love so free,
My soul is enriched, and my heart sings
For you have given such beautiful things,
Like fun and laughter and loving and sharing,
Mending hurts, forgiving and bearing
Life's heavy burdens by together praying,
Contentment in silence and music and saying
What echoes in one's heart and enters one's mind
What a miracle of grace, what a treasure to find
A friend and lover all wrapped up in one,
Thank you, God, for all you have done.

As December drew near, we waited to welcome Leonie from Istanbul and Jennifer, Neville and their family from Perth. I was pleased that Fred's mum had accepted me, asking me to call her Lal, a pet name her sister had given her. I felt honoured to have my mum and Mrs Robins, both aged eighty-eight, at my wedding. So many helped in various ways to bless us.

The morning of our wedding dawned at last on the 2nd of December 1995. I was thrilled with my beautiful wedding dress and the jewellery Fred gave me. For my bridal party I chose my nieces, Vicki Gibson and Robyn Todd, and Fred's two young granddaughters, Melissa Robins and Tamara Brown. They looked beautiful dressed in blue and enjoyed the ride in the stretched limo before the driver drove to Shangri-la Gardens at Wynnum for the ceremony. Mark Robins, the best man, stood smiling with his dad at the end of the avenue of flowering bushes as I walked up to join them. Fred and I then walked to the musical sound of flutes playing to where Neville Brown, the celebrant, stood in the alcove. Laughter rippled through the guests when Neville asked, 'Who is giving Pauline away?' My brother stood, and my family called out, 'About time.'

Fred and I went to Hervey Bay for our honeymoon. After a delicious dinner at the Kingfisher Resort and a moonlight cruise, I said, 'This is the best honeymoon I have ever had!' Like Esther the Jewess, I felt God had brought Fred and me together 'for such a time as this.' I wanted to be a blessing in this new family and fulfil God's purpose for bringing us together. I marvelled at God's grace; His gracious favour showered upon us. How can it be that I have been so blessed?

Everything was working out as our families adjusted. In January, Fred and I had a wonderful holiday in Tasmania. Mildred Simpson, from Lutanda Home days in 1957-8, took us on a pleasant drive to Boat Harbour Beach. We also called in on Jean Campbell, who had served the Lord in Goa, India. When we visited beautiful Bicheno, my artist friend, Joanne Stronach, and her husband, David, welcomed us. They had an Art Gallery displaying beautiful woodwork and paintings.

Such a funny but embarrassing incident happened at Camp Clayton, Ulverston. It was St Valentine's Day, and Fred and I didn't get away with it because our friends had resurrected a lost custom and tin-kettled us. Fred and I had retired after a pleasant evening. At first, a sound like a gum nut falling on the roof stirred me. Then, the sound of a squirrel scampering across the roof. This was followed by a cacophony of noise from whistles, banging tin cans, crackers, and balloons popping. I opened the door to find a sea of smiling faces. Mine was bright red, but it was hilarious and good fun. Fred remarked, 'You married late, but you haven't missed out on anything.' Fred, who had retired early as the senior radar supervisor in Civil Aviation at the Brisbane airport, was eager to cook delicious meals, so we began entertaining friends on a Saturday evening. And so, I started to live life as Mrs Robins.

Fred and Pauline 1995

Chapter 18

The Grief of Saying Goodbye

(1996-2000)

He heals the broken-hearted and
binds up their wounds.
Psalm 147:3

As I recall memories and walk a sometimes-difficult path during these next five years, I am cast once again into the loving arms of my Father God. His grace entered through my brokenness when I said goodbye to my mother, sister and husband, all within a short time. I retrace the providential care of God and rest in the truth of His divine character as a loving, compassionate God as revealed in the Bible.

What richer gift can we offer each other than our stories – of finding a loving God and the God-given courage and grace that sustains us on the journey? What more can we want than telling our story and knowing we are heard? We pass the bowl of tears, shed some of our own, and perhaps, in the naming of that sorrow, secure in a sacred place the healing slowly begins.

Although my life with Fred brought me such happiness, I was concerned that Mum was not managing in her unit and needed supervised care in the Hostel section of Bethany. She was looking so frail, missing her little dog, and seeing her grief pulled at my heartstrings. The enemy of our souls is ruthless. He strikes down those who are weak and vulnerable. This has always been his spiteful way. Mum was in grief and distress of soul. I prayed to El Shaddai, the Almighty God, the enough God, to show compassion and mercy. Periodically I stayed with Mum, and Edna Ramage a resident in the Village, was a good friend, helping when necessary. The Assessment Team made an appointment to assess Mum. I was juggling my commitments as usual. Janice came from Sydney and spent time with Mum. Mum had a few days with Gweneth and then with Fred and me in Carseldine. When room 202 became available in the Bethany Hostel in March-April 1996, our family united to move Mum into a safer place of care.

This was another step that I found emotionally tough. I gave Mum's care to those unaware of her deep needs and who did not know Amy as a faithful wife and mother proud of her five children: Amy with dancing eyes, a loving heart, and a love for her garden. Knowing how much Mum loved flowers, Gweneth arrived at Bethany with a potted chrysanthemum. But this was no ordinary plant. It had one single, very large white flower. Mum was so impressed that she carried it around for others to see.

During the rest of 1996, Mum struggled. Depression was robbing her of so much. She did not see herself as God sees her, as his beloved daughter, nor did she believe that God loved her unconditionally. Distorted thoughts blinded her to the reality that her family loved her dearly. As Fred and I visited family in Western Australia during September and October 1996, Gweneth saw to Mum's well-being. We were all suffering with Mum, and her heart was failing to support her physical needs. She was hospitalised and received treatment. God was merciful, and Mum was responding to us. We had our mum back.

On Christmas Day 1996, Fred and I called in at Bethany Home and took Mum to meet with family members in Russell and Gweneth's home in Parkinson. On our return to Carseldine, I nursed Mum propped up in a lounge chair as her lungs were full of fluid. I slept in the same room. On Boxing Day, she watched cricket on TV, and then I said, 'Mum, we need to take you to the hospital, for your old heart is worn out.' I think she was relieved that her struggles were almost over. Her words, 'Thank you for looking after me,' grabbed my heart and signalled acceptance of the approaching end. I rang the hospital and said my mum had severe congestive heart failure and needed admission. My Mother-Dear was admitted to a three-bedded ward. The hospital staff at the Princess Alexandra Hospital was marvellous.

Gweneth was also anxious as her daughter-in-law, Merryl, suffered serious complications following major surgery. Gweneth cared for baby Caleb during Merryl's hospitalisation. Jeffrey and Merryl had introduced Caleb to his great-grandma Amy during their welcome visit to Bethany. Mum was delighted with these visits, and the blessing was reciprocated. Sadly, Merryl was unable to attend Mum's funeral.

God was gathering the loose threads and weaving them into His chosen pattern. Our family stayed with Mum around the clock, and my brother, Raymond, rang the Rocky family. Margaret, Gary and Laurel arrived and stayed with Fred and me. Mum was on continuous oxygen but knew everyone. Suddenly she said, 'Where is Eric? I want to hug him.' Eric is my sister Margaret's husband. I stayed the night until Laurel and Gary arrived early in the morning. On the 30th of December Mum wasn't responding. Later, becoming more aware, she felt loved when young Robyn curled up on the bed beside her. We were all loving mum into Heaven. She lifted her oxygen mask and said to Raymond and me, 'He's looking at me.' 'Who is looking at you?' I asked. 'The Lord Jesus.' She whispered. I eagerly asked, 'What does He look like?' 'He has beautiful wavy hair.'

1996 ended, and as 1997 New Year's Day dawned, I believe the Lord sent his angel to accompany Mum into the Lord's presence in Glory. (Luke 16:22; Psalm 91:11). The hospital staff rang at 5 a.m., and I opened my bedroom door, saying to my Rocky family, 'She's gone, and I was not with her.'

The timing was such that most of our family members could attend the funeral and spend time together. We arranged for the flowers on Mum's coffin to be a simple cross made of red flowers surrounded by white carnations.

At the service in Wynnum, my sister Janice recited her daughter Julie's poem, 'Always There.' Gweneth, Amy's fourth daughter, said she appreciated the visible work of God's grace in her mum's life after she became a Christian late in life. At a stage when change is difficult, Amy's willingness to let the Lord have his way was an inspiration to Gweneth. Even when her Mum struggled with depression, her wonderful sense of humour was rarely dampened.

Robyn Todd, Gweneth's fifteen-year-old daughter, shared some cherished memories of her grandma.

> 'Grandma was always very special to me, not only because she was the only grandparent alive during my lifetime, but also because she was always so loving towards everyone. There was not one person whom she did not love. Even Tina, the dog, was so loved that it used to sleep in the bed with her every night.
>
> I remember when I was young, I used to love visiting her, Aunty Pauline, and Tina, the chihuahua, in Rockhampton. Some mornings when I was really young, I would wake up disappointed that I was in my own bed in Maryborough because I had just had a dream that I was visiting Grandma in Rocky. I remember sitting on her lap as she told many sto-

ries, like the one about Grandpa and his pig that won a prize and her chooks. I remember when I was really little, I didn't realise that the word 'Grandma' was just another name for one of our parent's mothers. I thought it was a person who turned up one day and called herself 'Grandma' and gave you gifts and told you stories just like Santa Claus, I suppose, and I used to think I was lucky to get a nice one.

Grandma's gardens were her pride and joy; she spent hours labouring to get them looking just right! I always found Grandma lots of fun. Her great sense of humour meant lots of laughs when you were ever around her. When I was little, I wanted to play games that must have been stupid to her. However, she still played them with me. I remember I used to test her on her colours, and she used to pretend (I think) that yellow was black or blue was green, and I would correct her. She must have found it boring, but she still had time to play with me.

I loved telling her everything that I did, even up until the day she left us. Because no matter how weak she was, you knew that she wanted to listen, and she had a smile ready for everything funny. Grandma was a really special person to me and still is and always will be. And if I could ever be half as loving as her, I would be happy. I will miss having her as my special Grandma and definitely by far my favourite! I will always love her, and I guess the one thing that makes this easier is that I will see her in heaven.'

Fred read out the eulogy I wrote. The funeral hearse left the church building with us, singing:

Onward to the prize before us!
Soon His beauty we'll behold;
Soon the pearly gates will open;
We shall tread the streets of gold.

During the following weeks, I coped by writing it all out in my diary, writing poetry and finally committing Mum to God's care. Losing her severed a tangible link in the indefinable bond between mother and daughter. It is an irreplaceable loss. My siblings felt as I did. But I had cared for Mum for more than ten years and sought to keep her safe and happy. She told me her secrets, which I have not shared with anyone.

Several weeks later when I was walking the dog, God said to me, 'You don't have to feel her pain anymore.' Those words caused a shift in my grieving, taking it into a place where healing began. I recited the words from the book of Hebrews again, which I shared in my eulogy, '*Mother-Dear, you have come* to *Mount Zion, to the heavenly Jerusalem, the city of the living God. You have come to thousands upon thousands of angels in joyful assembly, to the church of the firstborn, whose name is written in heaven. You have come to God, the judge of all men, to the spirits of the righteous made perfect, to Jesus, the mediator of the new covenant.*'

My mum had come to love and trust God, and now her perfectionist heart is at peace. I have often turned to Amy Carmichael's poems. This one fits the moment.

Before the winds that blow do cease,
Teach me to dwell within Thy calm.
Before the pain has passed in peace,
Give me, my God, to sing a psalm.
Let me not lose the chance to prove
The fullness of enabling grace,

O Love of God, do this for me,
Maintain a constant victory.

In February another family member suffered a loss. My brother Raymond, who had been working as a medical orderly for many years, first in Rockhampton's Base Hospital's operating theatres, then at the P A Hospital, was made redundant as most medical orderlies were being phased out of the Health System. He had gained many nursing skills and knowledge and now needed to try his hand at some other trade. He had learned many hands-on skills from my dad, a jack of all trades. Raymond gained employment at a new school as a janitor and groundsman, a role he managed responsibility for many years.

In April 1997 Fred and I were asked to run an over-50s Camp and I enjoyed working with him. I was also preparing four studies in the book of Philippians for the May Ladies weekend. On my return from the camp, Fred welcomed his granddaughter Melanie, who was born on the 25th of May. I felt special when Leonie called in with Melanie and said, 'Here's Grandma.' Prayer was being answered. I was being accepted as part of the family.

Not long after this, I became concerned about Fred's health and his mother's ongoing care. Fred had lymphoma, and we noticed that the lymph nodes in his groin had become larger. We went to see Dr Eliades, but he felt that there was no need for chemotherapy. I did not fully understand Fred's medical condition, and my concern remained. Fred's mum had been hospitalised, and we needed to consider her ongoing care. She stayed with us for two weeks before agreeing to enter a Care Facility. Woven in and out of these worrying events were family gatherings and birthdays, including my sixtieth in July, when Fred secretly invited family and friends to celebrate. John Webb, who had spoken at our wedding, said to Fred, 'Pauline looks radiant.' Why wouldn't I feel happy when my husband told me that he loved me every day? Fred and I also had a happy holiday with family in Cairns, where I went snorkelling. It was a magical experience.

Meanwhile, as the months passed, Janice my sister in Sydney was feeling strange symptoms that her GP dismissed as psychological. In November, because I was concerned, Fred and I travelled to Sydney towing our Camper Trailer. On the way through Grafton, we enjoyed the feast of colour as we drove through avenues of jacaranda trees and flowering gum. We found that Janice was very ill and I stayed with her while tests using isotopes were being done at St George's Hospital. Because Janice felt so ill, we went from the hospital to Dr Joy Mowbray's surgery, Janice's G.P. By this time I was feeling desperate. I knew my sister well, yet even her GP was not listening as Janice described her symptoms. Dr Joy Mowbray was assessing that it was all in Janice's head, her imagination, or possibly from stress. I noticed that Janice was using a book by Charles Swindoll for her daily reading. Entitled *The Finishing Touch,* the devotional readings centred around God's touches of grace that strengthen when we struggle with life's trials.

While in Sydney, apart from feeling helpless regarding Janice's welfare, Fred and I spent precious time with Janice's two daughters, Vicki and Julie, and their little ones. Vicki had six-month-old Dean, and Julie had three-year-old Naomi and one-year-old Rayana. Leaving them all was hard, but Fred and I needed to head back to Brisbane.

We were busy emptying Fred's mum's unit at the Golden Downs complex in Fitzgibbon with help from friends to put it on the market. I occasionally rang India, but all my family commitments eclipsed that part of my life. I still felt the grief of my mother leaving us.

When I rang Janice on Christmas day, Janice had trouble putting words together. I rang Gweneth about my concern. I rang Vicki, who wasn't home. Later, the family in Sydney rang to say that Janice had been admitted to St George Hospital. On New Year's Day, a CT scan revealed a large tumour covering the frontal section of her brain. The top surgeon wanted permission to operate. After months when Janice knew something was wrong, the reason for her distressing symptoms was finally revealed. Many were praying as we waited. It was not good news. The pathology report showed that the malignant tumour was a butterfly glioma tumour. The surgeon was not able to remove it all. Dr Kwok had previously dealt with this type of aggressive tumour and considered that radium therapy would be of no use in dealing with the portion he did not remove during surgery.

We contacted family members and my siblings were considering flying to Sydney. How could I say goodbye to Janice? Janice's broad smile came directly from her loving spirit. We will all miss her gentle ways and her prayers for us. She persevered despite hard knocks and lived a purposeful life serving others.

My thoughts as recorded in my diary were not questioning God's goodness, nor were my emotions bereft of His comfort. God was feeling our pain. A beautiful hymn asks this question: *'Does Jesus care when my heart is pained too deeply for mirth and song; As the burdens press, and the cares distress, and the way grows weary and long?'* And the refrain says, *'Yes, Jesus cares. I know he cares.'* We needed expressions of God's loving care during the following distressing days and weeks.

I flew down to Sydney with my sister Margaret and later, along with my siblings, Gweneth and Raymond, stood around Janice's bed. Looking into Janice's eyes was like looking into her very soul. It was a truly harrowing experience. I think she thought she was dying and, thankfully, didn't know all the suffering that lay ahead. She looked at me and said, 'No more battles.' Then, a pause as she gathered her thoughts, 'Can you be a surrogate grandmother to the little ones?' It was almost too much, and my heart was breaking.

Dr Graham came and assessed Janice's eligibility for Radiation Therapy. He summarised the benefits as giving her more time and maintaining some quality of life during her last months. But how would we endure being with Janice in this crucible of suffering?

I expressed my concerns about Janice's ongoing care. How would Janice manage if she was discharged to her home? Who would care for her? Her husband Graham could not give the level of care needed. As a family we all shared our thoughts and shed tears together. We had to cling to the Lord, knowing that brain tumours cause personality changes and sudden mood swings. Janice's 'control panel' in her brain's frontal lobe was damaged. Her anxiety levels increased and her cognitive abilities diminished. Those attending her needed to make allowances for these changes and come fortified with empathy.

I felt for my nieces, Vicki and Julie, having to see their mother like this. Fred and I visited Sydney four times, caring for Janice in her home and visiting her later in an Aged Care Facility. Fred was a wonderful support and helped in many ways. And so, the months of caring for Janice and supporting each other gave way to Janice's admission to the Calvary Hospital for the terminally ill early in July.

Julie was admitted to St George Hospital and gave birth to her third daughter on the 17th of July. Fred and I slept in Nabil and Julie's Sydney home to care for the toddlers, Naomi and Rayana. To complicate matters further, eighteen-month-old Rayana was admitted to a hospital with gastroenteritis, so Fred and I rushed off to sit with her to enable Nabil to be with Julie for the birth of Elina. Young Rayana was shy, and I wondered how she would react to us at 3 a.m., but she looked up and said, 'Uncle Fred', with a delightful lisp on the 'F'.

Knowing Janice's condition, the hospital staff arranged for Julie to visit her mother to show this new grandchild. Janice then slipped into a coma.

When visiting her a few days later, I noticed changes in Janice's breathing and alerted the family, who gathered around her bed, singing hymns of faith in our gracious God. I didn't go to be with Janice as I was not coping with my grief. I stayed in Julie's home with baby Elina Jane, holding her while I said goodbye to my sister. Then Nabil came and took baby Elina to be with her Nanna for that final hour. As they sang, the Lord mercifully sent his angels to escort Janice into His Kingdom where there is no more suffering, tears or death. Janice had kept the faith.

When your work is all completed
He will gently call you home
Oh, the rapture of that meeting
Oh, the joy to see you come.

These are sacred moments when we are suspended between heaven and earth; when earth's sorrows give way to the joys of heaven; when our earthly tears fall and are gathered by God in 'a bottle' (Psalm 56:8) to be kept as a memorial of our grief until all sorrows are forgotten. Our tender-hearted Heavenly Father takes note of our distress and suffers with us. Death is our enemy, but because Jesus defeated the power of death through his death and resurrection, death has become a gateway to God's kingdom's glory for little ones and those who love Jesus.

Julie returned so joyously thankful that her mum died surrounded by her family. Nabil rang his mother in Lebanon, and as I listened, I heard him say, 'Mama. Mama. Julie's mum has died.' It sounded so pregnant with grief in Arabic.

Fred was not with me. He had left for Brisbane for a medical appointment and was helping his son, Mark. On his return to Sydney, I felt comforted. I sat on Janice's bed in her house and read some of the poems and quotes that Janice had penned in her Bible. Images of Janice came to mind. Her quiet calm, the way she was tuned into spiritual things and lovingly held her Bible. Her love of fresh buns and tidying her kitchen. Her courage as she faced all the disappointments. Her joy in the flowering violets on the windowsill. Often, I tried to take care of her when she was in need. We were like two peas in a pod. I felt that when she needed prayer, she would also know when I needed it. At last, Janice was safe. She was in the place in God's abode that Jesus had prepared for her not because she was 'good' but because she had asked for forgiveness and had been brought into the saving knowledge of Jesus as Lord of her life.

At Janice's funeral on the 3rd of August, the service was very moving, with tributes from several. In my part of the eulogy, I wrote:

> 'While many of us protect ourselves by not becoming involved, Janice absorbed into herself the pain felt by others. Such was her empathy. Janice went on doggedly despite her weaknesses. She had a go at whatever confronted her, showing a tenacity of spirit, which she needed as life dealt some hard blows. Having experienced the richness of God's grace herself, Janice was willing to be a channel of God's love and grace to others. This empathy, this forgetfulness of self, and this intimate knowledge of emotional pain enabled Janice to touch many lives. She encouraged the timid, the disheartened, the lonely, the hurting and thus modelled Jesus.'

Fred and I stayed for a few more days in Sydney. We caught two trains to Eastwood to meet with Richard and Rosemary Morton to discuss overseas mission concerns. I took their advice when I shared my idea of writing a Ladies' Devotional, which would be included in the monthly AMT correspondence. This developed later into a Devotional, covering the disciplines of life that help us mature spiritually in our walk with God. I had ten trials/disciplines of life, starting with 'D', the first being the Discipline of Disturbance – the eagle stirs up her nest (Deut: 32:11). The A4 document incorporated scriptural outlines that could be used in ministry. With the business of missionary life, finding time for preparation can be unmanageable.

When we arrived back in Brisbane, life continued to be busy. When preparing the first two Devotionals, my own missionary experience came alive. There were things I would like to erase from the landscape of my life. But I wanted to share what God had taught me. There were also moments when I experienced God in a special way. I would share these times to encourage. I sent my first one to the AMT office for the October issue to be sent to the Queensland lady missionaries.

Fred prepared the camper trailer for our trip north to attend the October Missionary Expo in Pialba, then onto Rockhampton to spend time with the family. A vertigo attack left me bedridden until it eased with medication. I also had a ringing sound in my right ear. Although Fred seemed very tired, we planned a trip to Norfolk Island to celebrate three years of marriage. Fred's mum was admitted to the Prince Charles Hospital with congestive cardiac failure. While with her, she said she was afraid to die. This allowed me to share the good news of God's love and forgiveness offered through faith in Jesus, God's Son. Trusting Jesus lessens our fears because he has promised eternal life in God's abode. She listened and seemed more at peace.

Fred had a health check with his specialist and received a good report. At last, Saturday the 28th of November dawned, and we boarded the plane for Norfolk Island. God has graced this little rocky island, jutting out of the sea with tall pine trees and gentle hills surrounding it with a deep blue ocean. It was a special time together. The seven days included tours, and we found the old historic St Barnabas Church, where there was a morning service with children performing. I loved hearing about the history of settlements and seeing historical buildings.

Back in Brisbane by the 5th of December, I was thankful for the heated Spa Pool to deal with all the muscle spasms. We contacted the family and went to see Fred's mum, who had fallen out of bed. Her speech was slightly slurred. She said a funny thing. 'My father lived till 92. He got to 92 without someone saying that he had fallen out of bed.'

It soon became obvious that Fred was really ill, as some abnormalities alerted me that he needed to see his GP. We made an appointment for the following Monday, the 14th. I rang his son, Mark, and Neville, Fred's son-in-law, and said that I was very concerned about their father and that we would visit them on Sunday. After seeing the GP, Fred was admitted to the hospital, and a laparoscope investigation and CT scan revealed a tumour on the bile duct. Fred was scheduled for immediate surgery. A successful outcome depended on whether the cancer had spread. This couldn't be happening again, could it? My heart was crying out to God.

The night before major surgery on the 17th of December, the staff gave Fred a single room so we could spend time around Fred's bed as a family. The grandchildren did not realise that they were saying goodbye to their granddad.

The following day, before they wheeled Fred into the operating theatre, he said one simple word to me, 'Thank you'. Family and friends like John Hockey and Russell Hockaday waited until Dr Fielding came out of the theatre. Our hearts sank when we heard that the surgeon had to remove three-quarters of the liver. Jennifer supported me as we went in to see Fred.

He looked so pale like death warmed up. 'Lord, spare him for me, but you know best.' Gweneth gave me a comforting thought, 'When we feel the stress of the storm, it is then we prove the strength of the anchor.'

Following surgery, Fred was very restless. I thought he looked hypoxic; later, the doctor ran blood gases. So many were supporting us in prayer. On the 22nd, the hospital rang me as Fred was so restless and wanted me, but by the time I arrived, Fred was having a seizure. Family members came, but Fred was not aware of us. The following day, my phone rang at 6 am. It was Fred. He cried, 'Pauline, I need you; I love you, Pauline. Please come.' He was so distressed, but again, when I arrived, he was not responding. But what he said has been written indelibly on my heart.

At no time was Fred rational enough to communicate, which deeply hurt his loved ones. His children could not say,' You were a great Dad. We love you, Dad' I couldn't say, 'You made me so happy. I thank God for the loving man you have been to me.' My darling Fred was called home early on the morning of the 27th of December 1998. My loving sister, Gweneth, stayed with me and could take the many phone calls. I spoke with Fred's mum. 'You have lost a loving son, and I have lost a wonderful husband.'

Fred had a council library book on his bedside table in the hospital. I found that he had put a bookmark in place so that I could read his last words to me. It was a farewell poem by Anne Bronte entitled *Farewell to thee. But not Farewell.* He had a premonition that he would not survive. The poem's last lines speak of Heaven, where joy replaces anguish and smiles tears.

I'd lost something irreplaceable. I longed for something irretrievable. I kept repeating, *'God is my refuge and strength.'* At the funeral service, Mark Robins said words that comforted me. 'Pauline, you made Dad very happy. Now that you are marked with the name 'Robins,' even though my father is not here, you are still part of our family.' This loving acceptance would have made Fred proud of them.

I wrote in lipstick on the bathroom mirror. 'You are my hero'. Fred was a mentor in many ways and I deeply felt the loss of his wise counsel. As I prepared Bible sermons I ran my thoughts past him. The devotional for the missionaries I was working on for January was the Discipline of Disappointment. This was before I knew Fred was gravely ill. In the introduction, I had written, 'Our Heavenly Father often washes our eyes with tears so that we can see.' I was experiencing the greatest disappointment in my life, but I was proving the truth of this saying. Grief gives us a new perspective on life and the things we value most, and grief also changes us. I wanted that change to be God-honouring.

Weeks later, I changed the writing in the mirror to a happy, smiling face. I would stand in front of it until my expression changed. There was so much to be thankful for, so many reasons to praise God. In God's providence, my marriage to Fred brought healing to my inner being. Along with that change came joyous freedom. Out of these blessings I wanted to minister comfort and wise counsel to others.

Tom McNabb sent me a poem he had written. Before it arrived, my heart cried, 'He is not here. Fred is not here.' After reading Tom's poem, I cried, 'Yes, he is there. Fred is there.'

I have gone and left my body
Through the door called 'death' by you,
While you all will mourn and miss me
I can see a different view.

Here, a golden dawn is breaking
Bringing in eternal day

And the light has so much beauty
Every cloud is swept away.

So, my faith is no more needed
Now I see Him face to face,
Oh, the wondrous joy of meeting
He who showed me so much grace.
No more sorrow – no more parting
Just reunions I will see
When the Lord calls home His people
All together, we will be.

A poem sent by Jill Bembrick was as if Fred was speaking to me:

And He came Himself to meet me
In that way so hard to tread
And Jesus' arm to lean on
Could I have one doubt or dread?

Then you must not grieve so sorely
For I love you dearly, still
Try to look beyond earth's shadow
Pray to trust our Father's will.

God's grace entered my life through my brokenness. When broken, we are open and vulnerable, allowing God's grace to enter our lives fully. We experience our limitations and recognise that we cannot handle everything on our own. Turning to God for strength, we are thankful for his grace to sustain us. We become more compassionate towards others and thus are enabled to share God's love more realistically. We draw upon God's power and seek His loving presence hungrily in our brokenness. As we do, we experience that we are never alone in our pain.

Chapter 19

Life Goes On

(1999)

Let your conversation be always full of grace …
Colossians 4:6

FINDING RICHNESS IN RELATIONSHIPS

Despite the drastic changes in my circumstances because of the death of my loved ones, life continued to unfold, and I faced the inevitability of moving forward and facing new challenges without my husband. At the same time I wanted to share how Christ had impacted my life, for personal experiences are often the most compelling and I have gained much from other Christians sharing their experiences.

The Lord gave me a friend in my next-door neighbour, Adrina. She invited me to the Bald Hills Know Your Bible study (KYB), which she attended. Studying the Word of God with these ladies in my friend Lyn Harrison's home became a real blessing. Both Lyn and Adrina were great friends to have. Sometimes Adrina would call, saying, 'Let's go out for breakfast.' She knew how much I was missing Fred. I was still on an emotional roller coaster. Sometimes I was quiet. Other times my heart cried, 'I want him back.' I longed for the emotions of grief to be recycled into memories I could cope with.

FAMILY TIES

Family is important to me. There are many ways to promote strong family ties, including spending meaningful time together. When my sister Janice was dying, she asked me to care for her two daughters, Vicki and Julie and their little children. By 1999, Vicki and Malcolm had young Dean, and Julie and Nabil had young Naomi, Rayana, and Elina. I packed my suitcase and flew to Sydney in July to celebrate my 'surrogate' grandchildren's birthdays. Elina turned one, and Dean turned two. Raymonde, Nabil's mother, was visiting from Lebanon. We shared a long hug, which communicated a lot despite the language barrier. It was heart-warming to hear young Naomi sing about God, and I was impressed by her thoughts and sentence structure. Not having been surrounded by toddlers before, I was fascinated by these little ones. They were little persons wrapped up in a child's body. Julie said young Rayana looked at a photo of Fred and said, 'My best friend'. Fred had undoubtedly made an impression on her. It's so sad; Fred would have been such a friend and help to his family and my 'surrogate' grandchildren.

Rayana is a compassionate little soul. When Julie asked what she would do when she got older, she said, 'When people cry, I will get the tissue box.' Rayana is now a doctor working at the Royal Brisbane Hospital. I hope she always sees that her patients are scared and need compassion. Julie, my niece, has a fantastic cognitive memory and finds learning languages relatively easy. She taught her little girls some of the mysteries of idiomatic language. One day Rayana leaned over and said to her sobbing two-year-old sister, 'Elina, take it on the chin!'

In October 1999, Julie asked me to join her family on their trip to Los Angeles to spend time at Disneyland. We were seeking to inject some joy into our lives after the times of family grief. The three girls were young, but they had some great experiences. I captured fun times with my camera, including Elina sitting on one of the stars embedded in the sidewalk on Hollywood Boulevard. The stars on the Walk of Fame are a historical monument to famous actors. Fifteen-month-old Elina looks so cute in the photo.

MINISTRY OPPORTUNITIES

I started a young ladies' class named Friendship Encounter. My idea was to provide a place where young Christian women could meet to nurture friendships and study the Bible together. The course I chose was *The Challenge of Being a Woman.* About six girls aged between eighteen and twenty-three would arrive at my home at 8 p.m. for a Friday night sleepover and to spend Saturday together. I made no rules about lights out but occasionally hid treats for a midnight snack. The following morning at eight o'clock we cooked breakfast, playing the part of ladies using butter knives and jam spoons! This was followed by the girls going through the excellent teaching in the handbook on the *Challenge of Being a Woman.* Instead of a leaden silence, the house became full of chatter and laughter. I taught the art of folding serviettes and floral arrangements as we set the table for the Dinner Party that night. The girls had previously made the invitations and I posted them to the ten selected guests. We cooked a three-course meal which was later served beautifully to our guests. Amy from next door, worked in a hotel and knew how to cook delicious desserts. After a meal of the leftovers the girls went home, knowing that our guests felt blessed. Mealtimes have changed in the last twenty-five years. Will we ever recapture the dignity and grace of dining around the table as in former days?

Another ministry which was close to my heart was sharing God's Word. Rosemary Morton in the Australian Mission Tidings (AMT) Sydney office said that the NZ Global Connections in Mission office staff had asked for a copy of my Devotionals and wanted permission to send them to their NZ missionaries. Writing these Devotionals kept me in God's Word. There is so much to learn. The writings of Stuart Briscoe have corrected my theology in one area, an error absorbed from other sources. I like how he shares about living by the Spirit.

> The fruit of the Holy Spirit, love, joy, peace, forbearance, kindness, goodness and faithfulness (Galatians 5:22), is the result of the inner workings of God but is also the result of our response and understanding. It comes from obedience as well as dependence. All of us desire to exhibit these qualities in our lives. It will rest on our obedience and reliance on Christ's life within. (John's Gospel Ch 15).

After I wrote the Devotionals about the disciplines that help us mature in Christ, I wrote studies on the book of Philippians with the key thought of joy. This was when my heart was heavy with grief, but the Lord had spoken to me through Psalm 84. Verses five to seven speak of those who set their heart on pilgrimage. *Blessed are those whose strength is in you, whose hearts are set on pilgrimage. As they pass through the Valley of Baka (Tears), they make it a place of springs; the autumn rains also cover it with pools. They go from strength to strength till each appears before God in Zion.* I chose to be busy making the valley a place of springs of refreshment not only for myself but also for others.

There is a vital ministry that every Christian needs to be involved in: the ministry of caring and encouragement. Each of us is especially called to care for our families. Fred's mum was in a Care Facility and had fallen out of bed again, so Helen Robins and I decided to visit her. As Fred would have been seventy on the 6th of October 1999, I knew Mrs Robins would be sad remembering that Fred was no longer with us. We chose that day to visit and found her very ill and distressed. She was confused but knew us and responded by clasping our hands. Mrs Robins and some of Fred's relatives were in the Masonic Lodge. Helen and I asked Mrs Robins what hymn she wanted us to sing, for I had seen my grandfather's Mason books with hymns. Masons believe in a Supreme Being they address as 'The Great Architect of the Universe'. Surprisingly, Mrs Robins said, *Blessed Assurance, Jesus is Mine.* Becoming aware of her critical condition, I looked at Helen and mouthed, 'She's dying.' I read John 14:1- 6 and explained again simply what it meant. It was remarkable that the Lord had put into our hearts to visit that day, for a few hours later, I received a phone call from her son, Arthur, who informed me that Mrs Robins had passed away. I rang her family members and wrote to Margaret Price in England, who invited me to visit, but I declined as nothing would have been the same without Fred. How small is that little dash between our birth date and the year of our death, yet it represents all the time spent on earth? We either use this time productively to bless others or waste it. I know that Fred used his time well.

Another family needing encouragement and care was my eldest sister Margaret's family in Rockhampton. I caught the Tilt Train to visit for her granddaughter Zoe's birthday. After having two robust boys, Laurel, Margaret's daughter and her husband Maxie had a much-loved daughter, Zoe, who was born with a small head (microcephaly), which led to cerebral palsy. Zoe, however, was also born with a delightful sense of humour and a beautiful spirit. I was Zoe's godmother, and I often drew close and whispered, 'Zoe, you have a Heavenly Father who loves you dearly.' Zoe turned eighteen on November 5th, and she enjoyed her birthday celebrations. Her smiles did our hearts good.

When Zoe went to be with her Heavenly Father in 2021, her brother Guy estimated that Zoe's parents and her brother, Brendan, had lifted Zoe 220,000 times throughout her lifetime. God had entrusted Zoe to a family that gave exemplary love and care.

On the 2nd of December 1999 I thought about my marriage to Fred. It was over and the grief was still there, but I was comforted by God's love. I played the beautiful hymn on my CD recorder.

Loved with everlasting love,
Led by grace that love to know;
Spirit, breathing from above,
Thou hast taught me it is so.
Oh, this full and perfect peace!
Oh, this transport, all divine!
In a love which cannot cease,
I am His, and He is mine.

C.S. Lewis, the renowned author of the much-loved Narnia stories and other books, also married late in life. After three years of marriage, he lost his dear wife, Joy, as I lost my Fred. He echoed my feelings when he wrote about his three years married to Joy.

I don't want to go back and be happy in that way again. It frightens me that a mere going back should even be

> *possible. For this fate would seem to me the worst fall; to reach a state in which my years of love and marriage should appear in retrospect a charming episode – like a holiday that briefly interrupted my interminable life and returned me to normal, unchanged. And then it would come to seem unreal, something so foreign to the usual texture of my history that I could almost believe it had happened to someone else.*

Fred was no longer with us, but I wanted to be a blessing to his children and cherished the times I spent with them. I refer to Fred's children as my second family. Fred's son Mark married Helen. Jennifer, Fred's daughter, married Neville and Fred's last daughter Leonie married Vladik. Vladik was serving in the Australian Army in Wodonga. I was pleased I was included in a trip to Wodonga, leaving on December 18th. We had not seen Leonie's twin boys, who had been safely born in June.

On the way to Wodonga we stopped at Dubbo, staying with Beth and Dr Bevan Walker, who was involved in the Cornerstone Ministry and had a visitors' wing at the Cornerstone Centre. I was well acquainted with Beth and Bevan from our time together in Rockhampton. We also wanted to spend a few days in Canberra. Leonie had invited me to stay with them and I looked forward to being with the three children, Melanie, Lochlan, and Denzel. We all had a happy time with the cousins having fun together. Young Melanie called her Uncle Mark 'Murk' and me 'Grandma'. One night when I sang Lachlan to sleep, he chuckled in the way that Fred used to chuckle. Leonie and Vladik planned to stay with me on their way north to Vladik's new army posting in Townsville in February 2000.

Time and effort must be invested in our relationships to enrich the lives of those around us. I had much to learn about making meaningful connections and needed to improve my listening skills. I longed to be a blessing in all my relationships.

I thus ended the year 1999 with all its comings and goings. What lay ahead in the year 2000? When I heard Graham Kendrick's song "For This, I Have Jesus," I thought, what a helpful mindset and attitude-adjusting fact to take into this New Year.

For the joys and for the sorrows
For the best and worst of times
For this moment, for tomorrow, and all that lies behind
For fears that crowd around me
For the failure of my plans
For the dreams of all I hoped to be
And the truth of what I am
For THIS, I have Jesus.

Chapter 20

Extending Grace to Others

(2000-2001)

Accept one another, then, just as Christ accepted you, in order to bring praise to God. Romans 15:7

In early 2000 a heat wave in Brisbane ended with a storm and a rainbow of burnished light. As the last faint colour drained from the scene, it left me with a sense of peace. I thought of that verse in Nahum chapter one: *The LORD has his way in the whirlwind and the storm, and the clouds are the dust of His feet.*

I have always enjoyed Phillip Keller's books. They challenge the quality of our relationships. A quote from *Salt for Society* is worth sharing as it highlights the virtues needed to relate successfully with others. He relates to extending grace to others.

> *Mercy is to care, and to care very deeply about one another. It is to care to the point where we are prepared to be involved with the suffering and adversities of others. It implies that I am prepared to put myself in the*

> *other person's place. It means I shall try to understand why they behave as they do, even though it hurts me. I am willing to walk in the other man's moccasins before I criticise his conduct. It is the extension of goodwill, help, forgiveness, compassion, and kindness to one who may not deserve it.*

Living, as Phillip Keller describes, is very challenging. However, I do desire to respond to life and people in a way that models the grace of the Lord Jesus. For this I need the enabling of the Holy Spirit. I have had so many different kinds of relationships to practise responding graciously! What are your thoughts on this? Have you experienced a situation where extending grace made a significant difference?

Sometimes I wonder about what it really means to extend grace to others. Someone once said it means to offer kindness, compassion, and understanding, even when it might not be deserved or expected. It involves patience, forgiveness, and generosity, especially when someone has made a mistake, hurt you, or is struggling. Extending grace is about giving others the benefit of the doubt, allowing room for their imperfections, and treating them with empathy and mercy, much like how one might hope to be treated in return. Over the years I have been very thankful for the many who have extended grace to me.

OPPORTUNITIES TO EXTEND GRACE

In June-July of 2000 I was planning to see Leonie, my stepdaughter, in Townsville, and I asked her sister Jennifer if her fifteen-year-old Tamara would like to travel with me. Both Leonie and Tamara were excited about the venture. Before the trip, I went to Neville and Jennifer's home in

Forestdale to be with their family while they had a night away. Tamara and I discussed our train trip north, leaving on the 9th of July, and what we hoped to do together. Our holiday was a happy time and it pleased me to see Tamara enjoying herself. One thrilling experience was sitting in the IMAX Theatre for the screening of *Antarctica*. It gave me goosebumps being surrounded by the dome screen and music and watching the visual display. Tamara and I went snorkelling together and saw lots of colourful fish. We also saw a whale breach and a school of dolphins. Tamara loved being with Leonie's children. Young Melanie was a quaint little soul; the twin boys were delightful. They smiled and chuckled a lot and were inseparable. All good things come to an end. Back in Brisbane the weather heralded the coldest day in sixty years. We shivered as the temperature struggled to reach twelve degrees during the day.

On another occasion when Vladik had been posted to East Timor, and Leonie was alone with the three little ones in Darwin, I asked her if she would like some company. I flew to Darwin and spent a few weeks with them. I have lost that diary, but I know I enjoyed being with the three children. The twins were so funny. They would sit watching a video and act out the characters' antics without making a sound.

My niece Julie was expecting her fourth child. This time, a boy after three girls. When they phoned, I was ready to fly to Sydney and had a plane ticket. George William was born on September 26th 2000 and I welcomed my next 'surrogate grandchild.' This happened during Sydney's Olympic Games, so his birth occurred during the 'best Olympic Games ever.' One day when George was crying unhappily, young Rayana commented, 'Baby George sounds stressed out.' I stayed with this little family until the 21st of October.

Nabil, Julie's husband, encouraged me to look for a house in Brisbane for them, and I found a five-bedroom home in Carseldine. It also had an office downstairs and three bathrooms. My neighbours, Adrina and John, said it was a good buy at the asking price. By early 2001 Nabil and Julie were owners of this big, solid house in Carseldine. I flew to Sydney to help Julie pack as George was still a baby in her arms. Raymonde, this quiet Lebanese mother-in-law to Julie, said as I was leaving Sydney, 'Pauline, I love you.' Such remarks warm the heart.

The family planned to be with me until the house was ready, but I was soon exhausted because of all the activity. I keep saying to myself, 'For this, I have Jesus.' I don't think Julie felt any better because baby George was not settling. My concern also was for the three little girls in strange surroundings. When I settled them in their beds, I told them a story and said goodnight, kissing each one and spraying perfume on their tummies. Making happy memories that children look back on is crucial to tightening family bonds. It is said that memory is essentially a unit of experience, and every experience shapes the brain in meaningful ways. Demonstrations of genuine love can positively impact even a very young child's brain.

By early April 2001, Nabil, Julie and the little ones were settling into their new two-storey home, centrally situated near the corner of Beams Road and Gympie Road. The children would be going to the Northside Christian College at Everton Park. Because Julie liked Mueller College best for the children, I had rung Robyn Heazlewood but discovered that there wasn't a spot for Naomi. Northside Christian College could take Naomi and by 19th March, Naomi and her younger sister, Rayana, started school.

The Carseldine house had a pool, so the children soon learned to swim and cool off during the warmer weather. It was not an easy transition with four little children. Much prayer was needed, and Julie needed encouragement as George was not a happy baby because of a breathing problem. What a roller-coaster ride that was. Being with the little girls and hearing their endearing expressions and cute sayings made it all worthwhile. They were now safer than they were previously.

During that time, I was busy preparing Bible studies for the Pialba Ladies Weekend in March and was pleased that Joy Woodfield was the other speaker. I also had my sister Gweneth's prayerful presence with me for the weekend. I shared the poem 'For *this, I have Jesus*', a thought that kept me going during the last busy weeks. For many years, friends of these churches in the Hervey Bay region had been an encouragement and blessing. They had given generously to help in the ministry at the Women's Hospital in Ambajipeta. One year, the Ambajipeta Hospital became their missionary project and I was able to equip the new children's ward with beds and rubber-covered mattresses with the money I received. They also knitted little outfits for premature babies.

Soon after that I needed to fly to Sydney for the National Missionary Advisory Council (MAC) and Australian Missionary Tidings (AMT) Conference so I gathered my resolve, caught a flight and ended up enjoying the fellowship of like-minded Christians seeking to extend God's Kingdom. We recognise today that the degree of hyper-connectedness in our world is changing even how missions do ministry. The Western cultural shifts are changing so rapidly, but the powerful message of the Gospel is still the same and must be central to all our efforts.

THE HOLIDAY IN CANADA

In May 2001 my friend Beris asked me to go on a tour of Canada with her. I thought, 'That will be different.' And it was. At the last moment, Beris pulled out and gave the tour as a gift to Eleanor Sheen. Eleanor's husband Noel served in the Emmaus Correspondence School and prison ministry for many years.

Beris had upgraded our flight tickets to Business Class. Eleanor and I sat like ladies enjoying this surprising step up in the world. After we recovered from jet lag, we had the best holiday ever. We saw a wild bear coming out of the forest on our first day, and cars full of excited tourists caused what is referred to as a 'bear jam'. Canada's nature scenery is all-encompassing, and I truly enjoyed the part I saw of this vast land. I felt small when engulfed by the majestic fir trees that stood as sentinels throughout the wilderness, guarding the untouched wonders of nature.

On some of the tours, our world became white with snow. The Globus tours booked us into first-class hotels. Swims in the heated pools removed the stiffness of travelling in the coaches. In Vancouver I arranged to meet Eleanor Shaw, a missionary to Kerala, India. That was special.

The Butchart Gardens on the Island of Vancouver had a marvellous display of colourful flowers landscaped to show off the flowering bushes to perfection. It surpassed any display I have ever seen.

The Globus Tours took us as far as Banff, Alberta. Lake Louise was frozen so we could not go on the scheduled boat trip. The culmination of this Canadian adventure was white-water rafting, and I have a photo to prove I did it! Eleanor and I had the best holiday ever. On the flight home, a short stopover in Japan allowed me to say, 'I have been to Japan!'

When I arrived home and was tucked up in bed, images of black bears and turbulent waters rushing over rocks and snow-capped mountains flashed through my mind. However, I decided I loved my sunburnt country best.

Chapter 21

God's Providential Care

Even to your old age and gray hair I am he, I am he who will sustain you. I have made you and I will carry you; I will sustain you and I will rescue you.
Isaiah 46:4

MOVING TO PENINSULA PALMS (2002)

God's children are to find comfort in knowing God cares for them and guides them according to his purposes. I needed God's guidance about whether to move out of the big house in Carseldine, where I felt cut off from my neighbours and friends because the house was surrounded by high fences. I acquired a miniature poodle dog for company, but this didn't solve the problem of being alone in a big house. I have always lived with people. Consequently, I seriously considered moving into a unit in the Retirement Village at Rothwell. This would give me the security and fellowship I needed. Also, Mueller Church had a Bible College, Mueller Collage of Ministries, on the same campus as the Retirement Village, and I longed to improve my overall knowledge of the Bible. Mueller College ran a Home Stay Program for Japanese and Chinese students, which I wanted to be part of. I discussed the idea with Fred's family and prayed that the Lord would show me the way forward.

The move into the Peninsula Psalms Retirement Village in Rothwell in September 2002 seemed miraculous and providential. For weeks, the beautiful house in Carseldine was not selling. The village administrator, Malcolm Arnold, graciously gave me an extension on the occupancy date. On Thursday evening, a group of village residents came to pray with me in the lounge room. The very next day, a buyer walked in. God answered their prayer, and willing helpers made the move to Rothwell less stressful.

I was starting a new chapter, fortified by God's faithfulness and the strength of his sustaining grace. This was the first time I had a little space of my 'own'. Up till now I have lived under someone else's roof. I dedicated my new home to the Lord and have since practised hospitality and opened the door to all in need. In the mornings, I started like this. I'd sit in my mum's big brown chair and feel the air still, for the strong wind had not woken up yet. I'd have a nice cup of tea beside me in Mum's 'Grandma' cup. I'd say 'hello' to Fred and lift my heart to the Lord in thankfulness. I'd practise spiritual breathing, taking in God's blessings, owning His presence, and confessing my sinful thoughts and actions as I breathed out. I'd ask God to help me see with His eyes and feel with His heart. I so needed this time with Him to transform me. I often feel so needy.

Before coming to the unit in Rothwell, I fellowshipped at Grovely and Wynnum Assemblies. Now I am settled into the Mueller Community Church (MCC) and forming new friendships. Phil Ware, who attends MCC, took a friend and me up in a little plane for a joy ride, and I had a great view of Redcliffe and Bribie Island. I was surprised to see how close the Village is to the ocean. We departed from the Rothwell airport, an airstrip owned by the Council for commercial planes and helicopters.

The teaching sessions from the Bible at MCC are inspirational and challenging. Years ago I remember Ivan Bowden speaking at Mueller Church on Titus 2: 11-15.

> *For the grace of God has appeared that offers salvation to all people. It teaches us to say "No" to ungodliness and worldly passions and to live self-controlled, upright and godly lives in this present age, while we wait for the blessed hope – the appearing of the glory of our great God and Savior, Jesus Christ, who gave himself for us to redeem us from all wickedness and to purify for himself a people that are his very own, eager to do what is good. These, then, are the things you should teach. Encourage and rebuke with all authority. Do not let anyone despise you.*

These verses teach one important aspect of grace that I haven't covered in previous chapters. God is not only gracious, but also holy, and we are to treat him as such. The Bible is the Sword of the Spirit, and this verse cuts deep into my conscience. I haven't always said 'No' when tempted. My self-life takes charge, and I ignore the power of the Holy Spirit to set me free. This is why I desperately need God's grace to strengthen me. This need will continue until Jesus Christ returns to take me home or death takes me into his presence. The desire to be good and do good is a desire God has planted in my heart. But a greater motivation is that Christ redeemed me with his precious blood. I am now bound to my Liberator, who frees me from my old life. The closer I draw to my Lord, the more aware I become of His saving grace and the more the Holy Spirit transforms me.

One ministry that older Christians can engage in is prayer intercession. I have written a prayer book that I use. It contains many prayers from the Scriptures, prayers by saints of old, and prayers I have written. Using these prayers helps me remain focused. As I pray, I am mindful of Martin Luther's words: *Prayer is not overcoming God's reluctance. It is laying hold of His willingness.* I have an entry in my prayer journal that I will share.

> *O Father God, begin a new work of authenticity within me, for I see the self-life often dwelling unrebuked amidst my world of orthodoxy. Lord Jesus, only you can deliver me. I invite the cross to do its deadly work within the deep recesses of my being, where self-sufficiency, self-pity, self-righteousness, and self-promotion are part of who I am in the flesh. I cannot fix this sickness. Only you can. O good Physician, continue to bring me to wholeness.*

My library contains several books on prayer. In his book, Philip Yancey wrote that, *more than anything, God wants your authentic self.* The author, Rees Howells, shared three secrets on intercessory prayer that are worth considering.

> *We are to identify with those needing prayer – to feel their pain and confusion. Like Christ and the Holy Spirit, we are to 'groan' – some praying requires agony in praying. (Hebrews 5:7; Romans 8:26). We are to pray with authority, for we stand bathed with prayer in the presence of God, holding onto and claiming God's promises. We pray in Jesus' name for His glory.*

Often, I cry out to God for my family. Where would we be if we had no recourse through prayer? If we could not ask God to work on our behalf, we would be without confidence, comfort or hope.

Today in our secular world, people seem to function only at a personal ego level of consciousness with minor sensitivity to spiritual realities. Sadly, few traumatised sufferers seek God for healing. Yet his Word says in Psalm 143 that he heals the broken in heart and binds up their wounds. How damaging if we succumb to resentment instead of calling on the grace of God? The author C S Lewis says we cover up hurt with resentment. We choose resentment as it puts us in the driving seat and gives us a feeling of power/control. Instead, we are to master resentment and bitterness with the Lord's help. God cannot forgive those who do not forgive others.

During these past few years, many opportunities to communicate God's liberating messages came through speaking engagements with CWCI (Christian Women Communicating Internationally). I travelled around meeting with groups of ladies to give introductions to the KYB study for the current term. I visited several groups in Brisbane and Bribie Island. I even visited Clay Island. The Introduction to the book of Revelation brought me to a place of worship. Even in the future, when distressful prophecies are being fulfilled on the world stage, God will still show mercy and grace to sinful men and women. However, as the Bible says, *Now is the accepted time. Now is the day of salvation.* Life is so uncertain. We don't know what is around the corner.

MUELLER COLLEGE OF MINISTRIES

I expected 2003 to be very busy, and I was right. The Mueller College of Ministries was offering courses that caught my interest. I enrolled as a credit student for Church History. I have always loved history and can still quote dates and facts learned at school. I also enrolled in the Old Testament Survey with Alan Stanley and the New Testament with John Webb.

While preparing for a Women's Retreat in Rockhampton, Robyn Heazlewood of MCC helped me make the bookmarks I wanted to give out. I was inspired by a talk Ivan Bowden gave about the 'elastic principle of the soul', a phrase coined to describe what needs to happen when our souls are stretched past the usual point of endurance. The bookmark we prepared had an elastic band threaded through the top and the words, 'Bounce back to God', as the principle and with the texts Deut: 33: 27 and Hebrews: 4:16. *Bounce back to God – into his arms to his throne.* That is the place of repair and help in times of need. Always bounce in God's direction.

As I started studying, I felt stretched, preparing five messages for the Women's Retreat and also studying Church History. I thought, 'I should not have taken Church History as a credit student'. There was so much material to cover, but I loved the learning process. I was living out the reality of the sermon I was preparing – of being stretched. Thankfully, I got a credit for one subject and a high distinction for Church History. Alan Stanley was taking us through an exegesis of the book of Romans, and I was learning so much, but I dropped out as a credit student. At the time, I didn't realise what I had learned from the Book of Romans would be used at the Theological Institute in Kerala, India.

I just had too much on my plate. Also, another problem was disturbing my equilibrium. I had discovered a large lump at the top of my hip, and the scan and biopsy came back as a suspicious malignancy. Early in June, the surgeon removed the lump through a large incision and the histology report said, 'no malignancy evident'. I breathed a sigh of relief and a prayer of thanks and then rang my sister Gweneth with the good news.

Gweneth lives in the suburb of Parkinson in South Brisbane and I visit her occasionally. One time we sat in the pergola to chat. I remarked on a beautiful ivy plant she had trained onto a wire stand. Suddenly, she burst into tears. Gweneth is a practical, reserved person, and I had never seen her cry like this before. I put my arms around her and she said, 'It was the ivy off your wedding table, and I was going to give it to you and Fred as a wedding anniversary gift.' It brought back all the sadness. Fred's death before he reached seventy, was a keen loss felt by me and his family in so many ways.

I have been blessed to have such loving siblings. We get on so well together, though we are very different. My eldest sister Margaret had a generous heart and was a hard worker; she rarely talked but was a good listener. She lived sacrificially to help her family. I miss her, for she was called Home in 2023. My sister Janice loved children and telling others about Jesus. She lived her life centred on serving others. She was resilient with a quiet spirit. Called to Glory in 1998, she left a significant gap in the family. My sister Gweneth is thoughtful and gifted at recitation. She is wise, kind and reserved. My brother Raymond learns by listening to others. He is observant and practical and can fix anything. He has a servant's heart. I am in the middle. I love teaching God's Word, drawing and writing stories. I am highly motivated and love allowing young folk to spread their wings. My family's welfare is important to me, and my strong bonds with them have played a crucial role in shaping my identity.

Dear friends, let us continue to love one another,
for love comes from God. Anyone who loves is a
child of God and knows God. But anyone who does
not love does not know God, for God is love.
1 John 4:7-8 NTL

Chapter 22

My Second Mission Trip

(2003-2004)

For with God, nothing is impossible
Luke 1:37

At the 2003 Australian Missionary Tidings (AMT) and National Advisory Council (NAC) weekend in Sydney, I was again enthused by a talk on short-term missions. My last trip to India was from 1989 to 1990, during the cool season, with a group of nurses and my sister Janice. The weather from October to March is a comparatively cooler part of the year in South India. Thus inspired, I rang Phyllis Treasure in Thrissur, Kerala State, to see whether she could accommodate a team of about six and whether we could assist in the ministry at the Rehoboth Orphanage and Theological College. I was thinking this time of a team of teachers. Phyllis responded enthusiastically. Already, I had some teachers in mind.

There was keen interest in the mission trip to Kerala that I was organising and I soon had a team of five: Jill, her daughter Merryn, Tina, Joy, and Tavia. By August, I had booked the seats to fly to India. The tickets and passports were in hand by November and we were issued visas.

Dr Leeser, who left India in 1997, intended to visit at the same time. She wanted to see how the gospel ministry was progressing throughout the East Godavari District. As I would be in India during the same months, I was excited about possibly joining her for a few weeks.

We eagerly packed our suitcases, met other team members, and flew to India via PNG and Singapore, arriving in Cochin (now Kochi) on 19th December 2003. Kochi is about ninety miles from Thrissur in Kerala, and the two-hour road journey would take us through paddy fields and village after village.

The Orphanage where we would be staying was in the city of Thrissur. I was in my second home again, and I knew the team was eagerly looking forward to this adventure. From the airport we travelled by taxi along winding roads that were heavy with traffic. One shaky bridge had a sign: *All traffic except elephants*! There are wild and tamed elephants in Kerala State.

Tucked away in the southwest corner of India, Kerala State was once covered in dense jungle. Rice fields and coconut trees now dominate the landscape. Tamed elephants work in the teak forests but once roamed free. Kerala is very different from other states, and these differences have shaped missionary endeavours. It is progressive, topping other states in human development, mass literacy, economic parity, and harmony of religion. We pray that this harmony will continue.

Finally, we arrived at the Rehoboth Orphanage property where Phyllis Treasure is the resident missionary. Phyllis's love for the little children and girls in her care reaches beyond the orphanage's walls. Some of her girls have married and serve the Lord as pastors' wives. Sarah Simpson, a New Zealand missionary involved in the International School, lives in the same bungalow. Sarah is doing a splendid job in her role and ministry. The Christian witness has continued since Volbrecht Nagel, a leading Brethren German missionary in the Thrissur District, bought the seventy-five acres of land in 1906.

We planned to spend time in Thrissur, where there would be many opportunities to use our gifts in the RTI (Rehoboth Theological Institute), orphanage, and amongst the women in the two Assemblies. Our accommodation was in the long upstairs attic room on an arm of the mission bungalow. We sometimes took meals with the children in the orphanage. The curry and rice meals were delicious.

The team members soon organised themselves and willingly took on responsibilities. Jill Parsonson was willing to teach computer skills in RTI, and her daughter, Merryn, taught those interested in photography. Tina Carter from Brisbane taught Relationship Values and Effective Communication. Joy Brooks tackled Child Evangelism, and Tavia Seymore from the Lutheran College in Redcliffe taught drama. We also taught First Aid. I taught English from the Book of Romans using grammatical markers (linking words in English, for example, 'but' = contrast; 'therefore' = result and 'because' = reason, which helps to connect the ideas in sentences.) We hadn't expected this level of involvement with RTI, but the team rose to the occasion, and we found the students respectful and eager to learn. One of the goals of these lecture times was to expose the students to spoken English. The RTI students were mainly from Kerala: five young women and fifteen young men.

We had funds to buy three new computers for RTI. Since that small beginning, RTI now offers degree courses. A video on YouTube shows the fine buildings of Rehoboth Theological Institute in Thrissur, Kerala, with students and classrooms. God is equipping these young men and women for ministry.

Merryn Joy Tina Pauline Tavia and Jill Parsonson

The Australian team was asked to participate in women's meetings by giving their testimonies and a short devotional. To help with this, I suggested character studies on women in the Bible. This seemed to work well. The team members were undoubtedly stepping out of their comfort zone. We went to the orphanage meeting hall in the evenings, told stories, and used the hand puppets I purchased back home. Christian friends asked us to their homes for delicious Indian meals, which gave the team an insight into the Indian way of life.

Kerala has some fascinating places to visit. The team deserved a break. Jill and Merryn went off to visit Ooty as Merryn had attended the Hebron School when a young girl. With the idea of seeing wild elephants, Phyllis took us on a trip to Silent Valley in the Nilgiri Hills. Mathew Paul, an evangelist working in that area, arranged the transport in an old Land Rover. In some places, there was barely a road. Those riding in the back of the Ute had a rough ride but kept smiling.

Silent Valley is home to the largest population of lion-tailed macaques, an endangered species of primates. We didn't see any wild elephants, but we saw where they had been! Matthew Paul's little church building balances on the side of a steep mountain. Women and young boys sat on mats on the floor. I spoke, and Phyllis translated. It was such a precious time.

Phyllis and Pauline

Later, the six of us and Phyllis enjoyed our stay in a heritage hotel resort on Bolgatty Island out from Fort Kochi. We had a harbour trip and an excursion on the miles of backwaters. Kerala backwaters are a network of brackish lagoons and lakes interconnected by canals, rivers, and inlets. The long canoe we travelled in left a ripple of water. All around was the sound of – silence. We hesitated to speak. Occasionally, folk drew near to the bank to greet us. We watched a man weave coir rope from yarn from the husks of the coconuts.

All good things come to an end. On January 21, 2004, it was time to say goodbye. Jill, Merryn, Tina, Joy, and Tavia left the Cochin International Airport for Brisbane.

I was asked to extend my time to continue teaching English from the book of Romans in the New Testament. I also intended to devote time to the five female students at RTI. But first, I needed to travel by train to Madras to meet with Dr Leeser at the YWCA.

DR LEESER'S VISIT

What a moment that was when Dr Leeser arrived. Mr Thomas Rajan from SAI (Stewards Association of India), Mr Irmiah, the hospital administrator, John Victor, Dr Glory, and her husband welcomed us at the Madras accommodation. That night we caught the train up the coast to Talaku Station, where more hospital staff met us. I was so excited to be back after thirteen years. Ladened down with garlands, we were officially welcomed at the hospital in the beautiful new Bethel Chapel. The three Indian doctors, Dr Prabha, Dr Durga and Dr Betty, watched us while we cut the very creamy cake and tried to eat a piece without making a mess.

Joy Tilsley, caring for the ministry at Holland Wharf Hostel in Narsapur, organised a unique and beautiful welcome. We arrived at the gates and saw two hundred girls lining each side of the path as we entered the compound. Two girls, beautifully dressed, danced backwards, beckoning us on as everyone sang. Joy is the fifth generation of her family to serve in India. She has a real passion for transforming the lives of underprivileged girls.

Since Joy went Home to Glory in 2011, the Girls' Hostel has been managed by Manohara Mani. Mani was a hostel girl trained by Joy, which is evident when one sees how the buildings and grounds are kept spotlessly clean. Mani completed her Master of Arts and Teaching degree. The hostel girls are nurtured in their Christian faith and undergo Bible exams yearly to have excellent Bible knowledge when they leave the Hostel. World Vision sponsored many of these girls until policies changed and support was withdrawn. Individual sponsorship of these beautiful girls now depends on the commitment of people in home churches. Lack of sponsorship has reduced the number of girls receiving the benefits of a healthy lifestyle and Christian and college education.

While in the Narsapur area, I visited the Bethesda Leprosy Hospital and was touched by the needs of these inpatients who received much-needed care. I was moved as I prayed with a patient with AIDS. I took his hands and said, 'Jesus is the one true God. He wants to bless you. He loves you. Reach out to Him. Call on the name of Jesus for salvation.'

Dr Leeser was keen to visit the various churches, and I kept her company. It was a joy to see the village ministry prospering. Pastor Prasad and his wife Krupha welcomed us to their home. When we arrive at our friends' homes, the lady of the house gets us to stand on a brick. She then washes our feet before we step inside. I have named two of Prasad's sons and have supported the family for many years. Some of our young men on the hospital staff minister on Sundays in various villages.

Dr Leeser visited the Eye Hospital to see how it was prospering. This Eye Hospital was constructed in Ambajipeta years ago, and Dr Leeser obtained funds from the Christoffel Blind Society, a German international mission. The hospital provides cost-effective eye care with opportunities to speak God's truth into needy hearts.

I received a message from Phyllis asking me to prepare five one-hour messages for the Kerala Women's Convention in Quilon, Kerala. I needed to extend my time in India, so Phyllis changed my plane ticket to April 22nd. But before this, I prepared three messages for the Women's Conference in Amalapuram on *The Woman Who Pleases God*. Laura and John Peters had a vibrant ministry among the students at the Amalapuram Degree College.

The highlight of this visit to Ambajipeta was meeting Dr Prabha, a skilled obstetrician and gynaecologist. Dr Leeser and I found the hospital alive with activity. A new private ward and a beautiful Prayer Chapel had been constructed. Mr Thomas Rajan of the Stewards Association of India (SAI) was keenly interested in the hospital ministry and channelled funds.

Dr Prabha was a Hindu widow in deep distress after losing her husband when she entered through the hospital gates, not realising that her whole life was about to change. The Lord drew her to Himself and opened her eyes to see Jesus. She met the Lord and devoted herself to prayer and reading God's Word. Soon, village folk heard of her skill and came seeking help for infertility, safe delivery of a live baby, and medical treatment.

In a letter arriving in Brisbane before I left for India, she said, 'I joined here five years back. I was 27 years old, and God blessed me with two children. My husband passed away when my daughter was seventeen days old. He was a paediatrician. I was in deep sadness. God directed me to this wonderful place and started using me as an instrument in his hands. We experienced lots and lots of God's wonderful miracles. Our dear Lord was very gracious and abundantly blessed with this hospital work. Last month, we had 413 deliveries, our highest score so far. This year the deliveries will cross 3,500 – maybe 4,000. He is giving us extra strength.'

Dr Prabha continued in her letter, 'Even the gospel work is going on very well. All the staff sisters are divided into groups, and apart from their nursing duties, they spend one hour in personal evangelism with the patients. We hope and pray for many souls. Dr Leeser said that she might be coming in the cool season. All of us are eagerly waiting for her visit. We hope you can stay with us for quite some time. A Chapel has been constructed in front of the Labour Ward.'

I do not doubt that the Lord brought Dr Prabha to Ambajipeta, so I was deeply distressed when I heard about what happened soon after Dr Leeser and my visit. On all fronts, our enemy seemed to have gained the victory.

Dr Prabha's parents pressured her to marry another Hindu doctor from a hospital in Andhra Pradesh, but I have not been able to arrive at the truth of what happened. This all occurred in 2004. When her new husband visited Ambajipeta, he was deeply hurt by the hospital staff's attitude. Also, the staff was saying bad things about Prabha. In retaliation, her husband had objectionable posters printed and posted around the villages. These posters contained lies about our hospital. In Dr Prabha's letter, she said she felt bad and cried a lot. 'As he is not a Christian, he didn't have a forgiving heart.'

Dr Prabha and I had planned so much for my next mission trip with nurses in the cool session 2004-2005. She was even thinking of starting a

School of Nursing, but I pointed out that this would involve much of her time and take her away from ministry opportunities. I had drawn up basic plans for new staff quarters, but there was still room for erecting a building on the previously used rice field. Building a School of Nursing was too giant a step to take. We were both unaware of future events which would mean her leaving the ministry at Ambajipeta.

On this 2003 visit, I noted that the hospital hadn't made any provision for caring for HIV-positive pregnant women. The laboratory technician said a few women were now testing positive for the virus. I discussed with Rene (Dr Leeser) some possibilities I thought would meet the need. Not that we were finding many cases among the women attending the Ante-Natal Clinic, but our labour ward was not designed to cope with such cases.

In Narsapur the Bethesda Leprosy Hospital, one of our mission hospitals, had empty rooms. Only leprosy patients needing surgery or those with reactions to the prescribed drugs were admitted, so there were empty beds. In 2000, the Lord put the idea of serving HIV/AIDS patients in the minds of Bethesda management. After much prayer, they assigned a ward to admit positive cases.

I contacted the two staff members at Bethesda, Mr Satyanarayana, the administrator, and Mr Paul Raju. I invited them to Ambajipeta to discuss the possibility of sending our HIV-positive pregnant women to Bethesda for antenatal care and delivery. This met with their approval. This would mean we would need to train their doctor and nurses on performing a caesarean section. An elective caesarean section (CS) reduces the risk of HIV transmission to the newborn by half and is becoming the preferred way of delivery. Two of their nurses arrived at our Ambajipeta hospital, and the theatre nurse in charge taught them all they needed to know. The Leprosy Mission is usually well-funded. Bethesda soon had an up-to-date model of an autoclave, a delivery table and instruments for a forceps delivery and

CS. Their Bethesda doctor, who treated only leprosy, was excited to participate in the program.

When I returned on the next mission trip at the end of 2004 with a group of nurses, we visited Bethesda. I was delighted with how they set up the area. They had chosen verses from Isaiah as their text above each patient's door. With no proper cure available, giving comfort and eternal hope to the sufferers is the staff's daily privilege. *'.... to provide for those who grieve in Zion to bestow on them a crown of beauty instead of ashes, the oil of gladness instead of mourning, a mantle of praise instead of a spirit of despair' (Isaiah 61:3).* Today, the maternity section functions well, with Caesarean Sections done on pregnant women and food supplements given to the babies to avoid breastfeeding. Many patients entering the beautifully maintained complex are afraid or grief-stricken. They hear the message about the Lord Jesus and discover Someone who loves them and cares. This ministry impacts many lives, bringing comfort to those suffering discrimination.

My time at Ambajipeta should have been longer, but I left on the 19th of February as I needed to head down to Kerala State. It was hard saying 'goodbye' to Dr Leeser. She was busy visiting the village churches until she left for England on the 13th of March. God granted her the privilege of seeing her vision become a reality. Queen Elizabeth awarded Dr Leeser an MBE on her return from India. She must have received a welcome when the Lord called her name and welcomed her Home in 2017.

I caught the train and reached Thrissur at 5 p.m. on Friday, the 20th of February. That night, tucked into bed in the loft upstairs, I sought refuge under the net, content to wake to the squirrels running around near my bed. There is much I love about the Rehoboth property. The long rows of rubber trees lining the road up to the Bible College (RTI) never cease to delight me. The branches on each side reached over the road to touch the branches on the opposite side, forming an arch. I continued teaching at RTI and preparing the five messages for the Quilon conference. In the evenings I taught English to the five RTI girl students and did fun things like going to the shopping mall and buying them ice cream.

WOMEN'S CONFERENCE IN QUILON

Quilon is an ancient seaport on the Malabar Coast. I travelled there on March 30 2004, to connect with Mrs Joys Mathew of Sodari Bhavan Bible College for Girls. The text given to me to minister on was I Chron 16:11 (KJV): *Seek the LORD and his strength; seek his face continually.* The other speaker was Mrs Ormana Cherian from Tamil Nadu. This was a rich time of fellowship among the five hundred sisters who attended.

My last days in Thrissur were spent teaching English and visiting believers' homes for a meal. I loved all the interaction and was thankful I remembered some Malayalam language studied in 1965-66. Phyllis and Sarah Simpson took me to Kochi to catch my flight back home on the 22nd of April 2004.

I looked out of the plane window at the sea of coconut palms and thanked God for answering prayer, keeping the team healthy, and giving us many opportunities to serve him. I felt I was not saying goodbye to India for good.

Chapter 23

The Changing Face of World Mission

Go into all the world and preach
the Good News to everyone.
Mark 16:15 NTL

Serving in missions has been an important part of my life. We live in a world of rapid change, and I have seen significant changes in mission enterprises because these paradigm shifts are observable. Missionaries are no longer white-skinned. Only a few Western missionaries remain in India. Thousands of evangelical Indians have been mobilised, working in about five hundred agencies, reaching the lost and breaking into the spiritual darkness with the light of the Gospel in this land of diverse faiths. We pray that religious freedom will continue in modern India.

I read once that Blaise Pascal, a seventeenth-century philosopher, alleged that we have a God-shaped vacuum in our hearts that only God can fill. Along with millions of Indian Christians, I believe that true satisfaction will not be found apart from our Creator God and Jesus Christ his Son. He created us to have a relationship with Him.

So, do we have a responsibility to support the national missionaries who form new churches annually? Hopefully, the answer is yes. We can support through prayer, partnership, encouragement, and meeting specific needs. We do this as God directs.

I have visited Colleen Redit in Chennai (Madras), Tamil Nadu State. Colleen and Phyllis Treasure in Kerala State are among the few remaining expatriate missionaries in India. Colleen, an NZ missionary, is the founder and president of the Christian Missions Charitable Trust in Chennai (Madras), Tamil Nadu State, and has been guided by the motto, 'Where there is no vision, the people perish.' Colleen seeks to empower ordinary people by giving them a vision for their future and placing the resources required to accomplish it. CMCT ministry over these many years has included different aspects of care, medical, educational, and occupational, and money is needed to support these twenty or more different ministries.

It is harvest time, and the devil doesn't like it, for we hear that persecution is increasing. The cross of Christ demonstrates the value of every human being to God, and God's call to mission enterprise is still urgent. The problem of ignorance has no excuse in this rapidly connected world, for the world's tragedies come into our living rooms on our TV screens. We are made aware of the broken, suffering world and what our response should be.

While the Western world moves further away from its Christian roots and the reality of a spiritual realm, spiritually hungry souls respond throughout the broader world. They have discovered a God who loves them and cares, a truth that can stand the test, and a hope that is an anchor for the soul.

The ability to travel long distances in a relatively short amount of time, along with other factors, has led to a surge in short-term mission trips. The question remains: will these short-term experiences pave the way for long-term commitment to cross-cultural missions? Only time will reveal if they significantly increase the number of cross-cultural missionaries who persevere. When I started leading small teams on these trips, I aimed not to provide a fleeting experience but to catalyse a transformation in their lives. I yearned for them to grow spiritually and have a profound encounter with God outside their comfort zones.

It's crucial for participants of short-term mission trips to grasp the sacrifices of missionary service, such as the arduous days and months dedicated to language study, the years spent away from family, and the service rendered without immediate visible results. It's easy for them to arrive on the field and make uninformed judgments about the culture or the current challenges in that specific area. However, those who approach the mission with humility and sensitivity can offer invaluable support to the serving missionaries. They can offer prayer support, provide encouragement and assist with assigned projects.

Participants on these mission trips need to realise that they are guests in the mission field and show respect to the serving missionaries and local believers. They should anticipate encountering different customs and remember that they have come to learn. A sincere and humble attitude is the key to being a faithful servant. In essence, they have come to give, not to receive. They represent their home country and the Lord Jesus; their actions can leave a lasting impression on the local community.

Furthermore, participants can ignite a spark in their home churches and beyond through active involvement in this faith-filled venture. Their experiences and stories can inspire others to support the mission enterprise, creating a network of prayer warriors and givers united in their commitment to cross-cultural missions.

MY THIRD MISSION TRIP

There was keen interest in the mission trip to Ambajipeta Hospital in 2004-2005, and I soon found myself putting together another team. The first team went to Ambajipeta and Rehoboth in Kerala in 1989, and the last team of teachers went to Kerala State. This time I planned to take nurses. Jill, an experienced midwife, was eager to come on board. The other four Australian nurses had yet to undergo their midwifery training.

I was aware that there would be many hospital problems I would need to attend to. I had a lot to catch up on. Ruth, another experienced midwife from Victoria, would fill the gap when Jill left with Mandy and Rachel at the end of their six weeks. Renay and Bindi would stay for five months and return to Australia with me.

In October, Renay, Bindi, Mandy, and Rachel attended the Pialba Missionary Rally and shared their desire to go on the mission trip. Jill was unable to attend. We gave copies of our printed brochure and showed a PowerPoint presentation, 'Go light your Candle'. I organised this time with the girls to talk about the Indian culture, spiritual darkness and the need to put on the whole armour of God daily and work as a team. They brought their passports and filled in visa applications so I could apply for visas. I advised them about the vaccinations that their local GP would give them. I discussed what to expect on the journey and what to take in their luggage.

Val Pope of the Retirement Village in Rothwell made winter capes for the fifty female staff with the material she and June McKay bought. I bought shirts for the male staff in Chennai and cardigans for some pastors. The team was excited about this adventure, and interested folk gave generously to enable us to purchase needed equipment for the hospital to improve the standard of care.

I certainly needed the Lord's grace and enabling on this trip. I had no idea that so many dramas lay ahead. Had the hospital recovered after the upset with Dr Prabha? Would the staff truthfully tell me what happened? How will God restore our hospital's good name? Who had replaced Dr Prabha? Was there blessing flowing from the medical services? Would I be able to detect the problems and offer sound advice? Also, there were all the unknowns of the team's dynamics. I was hoping that we shared similar goals. The following verse expressed how I felt:

> *Not that we are adequate in ourselves so as to consider anything as having come from ourselves, but our adequacy is from God, who also made us adequate as servants of a new covenant, not of the letter but of the Spirit; for the letter kills, but the Spirit gives life.*
> *2 Corinthians 3:5,6 (NASB).*

Joy Tisley with the 3rd Mission Team

An excited bunch of six travellers set forth from the Brisbane airport in November. After our stopover on 21st November in Kuala Lumpur, with its vast highways and neat gardens, we arrived at Chennai Airport to see the opposite. India is always a shock to travellers who first experience the ordered chaos when exiting the airport terminal. The noise, smells, splashes of bright colour, and the people – so many people. I can only imagine how the team members felt. I could tell by their expressions that they were excited. The adventure had begun.

Mr Thomas Rajan, SAI (Stewards Association of India), and John Victor from the hospital took us to the YWCA accommodation. The next day we shopped for Indian clothes. We were sitting in the Circar Express train heading north on the overnight journey by Wednesday. We only had two minutes to offload all our luggage at Tanuku railway station, but the hospital staff was there to help us. They piled all our bags into the two vehicles, and off we set. A low mist hung over the channels and paddy fields. I breathed in the moist air and welcomed all the beeping of horns because I was back in my much-loved country.

What a welcome we received. Our Indian friends had worked so hard on the mission bungalow. Everything was freshly whitewashed, and the gardens neatly groomed. After a few hours, I spoke Telugu fairly fluently and enjoyed Indian curries. We had an early night as we were suffering from jetlag.

After attending the staff prayer session the following day, I talked with a staff member. He informed me that no gospel work was being done in the hospital and no nurses' Bible studies. The Christian staff were not going into the villages for the Monday night Jungle Doctor film strip shows – a gospel outreach. This was a cause for grave concern and what I needed to attend to first. How did the spiritual ministry deteriorate so quickly? We unearthed the film strips and flashcards from a filing cabinet. These are needed as visual aids in our village gospel outreach programs when field workers often gather.

A quick inspection of the hospital revealed areas of need. There seemed to be so many sick babies. It was a pleasure meeting Dr Sam, the paediatrician and a Christian. A quick look at the nursery setup revealed an area needing immediate change. Naked electric light bulbs were dangling over the babies to keep them warm! After a few weeks of activity, it was a blessing to buy specialised baby cots, as advised by Dr Sam, and remove all the dangling bulbs.

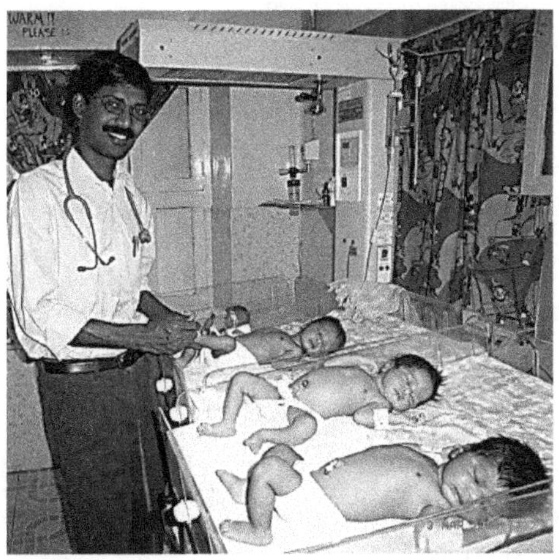

Dr. Sam with the specialised new cots

Jill commenced teaching the Australian nurses midwifery skills, and they were soon delivering babies. The labour wards were busy. I wish I could have seen some of the letters the girls sent home. Renay did share a snippet. She was delighted with her first delivery of a little boy. One time, Mandy delivered a baby with a loop of cord around the baby's neck, and the baby wasn't breathing. Renay quickly started resuscitation, and soon, the baby began to breathe and did well.

Surprisingly, on December 2nd Dr Prabha and her husband came to see us and invited us to visit them in Kakinada at their hospital. They were very brave to return after leaving under such a cloud. I can honestly say that I don't remember what happened – whether I visited them or not. It was so good to see her but awkward as I had received negative stories from the staff about her manner of leaving. I explained to the team what had happened or what I thought had happened. It was all regrettable and I wondered what the Lord thought about our Christian attitudes to one another. Had the devil scored a complete victory, or would the Lord use Dr Prabha another way? Sadly, I have lost contact with her.

The team visited Narsapur for the Christmas Pageant at the Leprosy Hospital and spent time with Joy Tilsley at her hostel for girls. Joy served morning tea from a tea trolley beautifully set up with bone china. It was all traditionally English and introduced life as it was fifty years ago. I spoke twice at their programs.

We set up a games area behind the Ambajipeta missionary bungalow to connect with the village youth and have lots of fun playing volleyball. Even our Indian nurses joined in. These kinds of activities break down barriers.

Pastors were keen for us to visit their church. I loved looking at the congregation's smiling faces and knowing God's truth and love had dramatically changed their lives. Sometimes the planned program went on and on. One time I was asked to speak at 11 p.m. There were days when I was sick with tiredness, but the Lord kept me going. After giving a message, I was often given little bottles of oil and asked to pray for sick relatives. (James 5:14). The relative would anoint the oil on their sick loved one in their home. I wept at some of the stories I heard. God so loves these people. Though poor, they extended to us gracious hospitality. The team enjoyed the curries except when they bit into a hot chilli! Renay, Bindi, and I were given a curry in one village, and were astonished when we recognised what part of the chicken we were eating. A dog sitting nearby was soon licking his chops!

Christmas Day dawned, bringing two days of drama. The Labour Ward was very busy. We delivered twenty-five babies and went to bed exhausted, only to find that a massive earthquake of 9.3 magnitudes had caused a powerful tsunami to affect the Indian coastline on Boxing Day. Though Ambajipeta is in the Delta area of the Godavari River, close to the sea, we seemed safe. We contacted home, knowing that our families would be concerned. East Godavari was damaged along the beach fronts, mainly affecting the fishing communities.

The more I worked with Dr Sam Ebenezer, the more I was encouraged. He and Dr Ramesh treated many sick babies with good results. Dr Sam was highly skilled and rejoiced that we could improve the nurseries with better equipment. Dr Sam, his wife Nancy and baby daughter Ann lived on the hospital compound. Dr Sam is now a Neonatologist Professor working and lecturing at the King Edward Memorial Hospital in Western Australia. He came to Australia after his three-year contract expired in Ambajipeta.

Visitors to India need to be vigilant about personal hygiene, especially washing one's hands with soap before eating and avoiding uncooked food. I instructed the team to drink boiled water and keep themselves well-hydrated. When one team member became ill, Dr Durga sent blood samples to Amalapuram, and the results were negative. We charted her temperature four hourly. Dehydration causes many symptoms, among them an elevation of temperature. I remember an occasion years before when a young English girl arrived at our hospital desperately ill with a high fever. She was a stranger to us. I nursed her in my bedroom and ran the tests Dr Leeser ordered, but every test returned negative. After days of high fevers that did not respond to any medicine Dr Leeser prescribed, she suddenly got well. We had been praying, so this was probably the reason for restored health. There was also another case of an Indian Christian girl who had a high fever for months until she looked like a skeleton. Finally, her parents took her to the prestigious Vellore Medical Hospital, where her health was finally restored. Once, I was sick with a fever and a rash of cause unknown. I sometimes wonder if this was the cause of my muscle problem.

I was encouraged when Mr Thomas Rajan (SAI) visited us and said, 'This is a good thing you have done.' By this, he meant the team's coming proved a blessing. I agreed because healing was taking place, the hospital's good name was being restored, and the community was again coming, knowing they would receive the care they needed. Dr Durga, the senior Indian doctor, worked efficiently and was also keen to see the hospital prosper.

I heard that Jill later said she was blessed to see the faith of the simple village believers. Mandy had been diligently caring for a premature baby belonging to a believer who had lost previous pregnancies. Along with Dr Sam's skill and much prayer ascending to heaven, this little one called Mandy Jyothi lived.

The team had the honour of sharing holy communion with poor believers, having their feet washed by them, and being overwhelmed by their love. This fellowship was precious and received with humility. These services bring blessings that the Lord will note. We had a short debriefing session as Jill, Mandy and Rachel were due to return to Australia.

We welcomed Ruth from Victoria, an experienced midwife to replace Jill, and Renay, Bindi, and I were refreshed and blessed. A little anencephalic baby was born, a condition when the brain, skull, and bones don't form completely. The child was kept in a separate room because the condition was incompatible with life. Ruth went every day and nursed her, singing *Jesus loves you, this I know.* Amazingly, the little one lived for eight days until God sent an angel to carry her to be with Jesus. Another baby died during labour due to four loops of cord around the neck. I was distressed when the grandma said, 'My Hindu family will blame me because I believe in the Lord Jesus.'

Along with nursery equipment we bought a hydraulic operation table, a refrigerator for the nursery and a new Ambulance, as recommended by Mr Irmiah, the hospital administrator. He had no desire to purchase an incinerator costing Rs 650,000 even though I had been to Narsapur to look at the model Joy Tilsley had bought. He thought it wasn't necessary.

Dr Sam invited a professor of pathology from Vellore Medical College in Tamil Nadu to come and advise us on the equipment needed in our laboratory to carry out more detailed examinations of the newborn. This became the next project, and God laid it on the hearts of his people in Australia. God was so wonderfully supplying the funds through his people to improve the hospital's care to the community.

I don't know whether this next drama happened with this team or back in 1990 when my sister Janice visited. Of a certainty, Dr Leeser was not in residence at the time; otherwise, I would have sought her help. A bullock cart pulled up, and the nurses informed me that a woman from a distant village had arrived after local women had tried to help. On examination, we found the case of a retained-dead foetus, probably at about eight months gestation, which had presented as a breech. The village women had tried to extract the body and head. The staff heaved the woman onto the labour bed, and not long after, the dangling body fell into the bucket on the floor, leaving the head still inside! Never had I been confronted with such a difficult case. I explained to the Australian nurses how we should proceed and how difficult it would be. In other words, we needed a miracle. We prayed, gave the woman an ether anaesthetic, and connected an IV infusion. We let the accompanying relative watch. A high forceps delivery was needed to extract the head. I instructed the nurses to hold the head steady abdominally while I applied the forceps. Then, I needed to lock the blades, which could prove tricky. The head was slippery. This was successful, and I began to pull gently, following the direction of the curve of the birth canal. There was a sigh of relief when the head was delivered. I said to our Australian nurses, "Only God could do that."

To complicate matters, a doctor left, and another staff problem came to light, causing another doctor to leave. This meant that we were two doctors short, with every hospital department busy. There was no doctor to cover the Clinics. I asked Renay and Bindi to conduct the clinic in Chakalipalem. Talk about stepping out of one's comfort zone! I sent Mary Ratnam, experienced in outpatient clinics, to translate for them. Mary Ratnam would know what medications to give, and Renay and Bindi could take blood pressure and perform other necessary procedures. One hospital doctor was left to do the Caesarean Sections and Outpatients, and I conducted the forceps deliveries and Hospital Rounds. At the end of the day, we were all exhausted. However, we had experienced the Lord's enabling.

Renay and Bindi were assigned to sort out years of medical records covered in dust and rat dirt. The men built a little record room with cement shelves, and we stored the sorted documents there.

It was time for Renay and Bindi to have a break. They deserved it. They had given me such support. Excited to explore, they caught a train to Kerala State and were welcomed by Sarah in Phyllis's absence. While there, they saw a herd of fifty elephants. What a golden opportunity. They visited the progressive city of Bangalore and arrived back happy after days of travel. I was pleased that they could say that during their experience in India, they had grown spiritually and professionally.

We arranged a staff children's party and gave dozens of children a gift from the parcels from England. There were cotton baby sheets, stuffed toys, talcum powder, toy cars, Snoopy toys, pencils, and much more. The dozens of children thought their Christmases had all arrived at once. It was such fun, and Bindi and Renay organised games and fun activities.

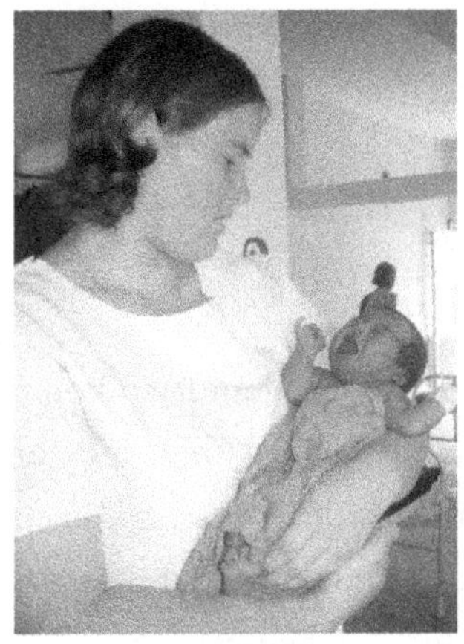

Renay (2005)

Bindi (2005)

Though still busy in the hospital, we visited the village churches. Renay and Bindi took it in turns to accompany me. People still expected me to speak to the women in Telugu, though I had been away for many years. It isn't easy because I have now mixed up the two languages, Malayalam and Telugu. I need to be cleverer and think entirely in one. Our visits encouraged the faithfully serving pastors, and we learned more about their hardships. Everywhere we went, these simple believers asked for prayer. Their needs were significant, but they believed in a great God. As Australian believers living in a land of plenty, we are accountable to God. We will be unable to say, 'I didn't know.' The fields are ripe for harvest, but the labourers are few.

In 2005, I stood again on the wide bungalow veranda, bidding goodbye to my many friends. Knowing there were still significant problems, my heart felt sore for those I was leaving with the burden. When Mr Thomas Rajan took Renay, Bindi and me in a taxi to the Madras airport to catch our flight home, the driver took us into a chaotic traffic confusion far from the airport. I said to Renay and Bindi, 'I think we will miss the plane.' It was a miracle that we made it in time. Our visas were expiring. We needed to be on that flight. Our guardian angels were working overtime.

For He shall give his angels charge over you,
to keep you in all your ways. Psalm 91:11.

A crowd of family and friends welcomed Renay, Bindi and me home at the Brisbane airport. Our pastor, Earle Tonges, thanked the Lord for our safe arrival. A lot happened during this time in India. It had not been an easy five months. I felt drained but, at the same time, thankful to the Lord for his faithfulness. 'Thank you, Lord Jesus, for being my Friend.' Gradually, peace took control of my anxious thoughts as I stepped out of my confusion into His calm, like the calm after a storm when nature settles and breathes in the stillness. Only the Lord knows what is accomplished for His Kingdom from these short-term mission trips.

When we go through hard times, incredible blessings can happen, personally and in the lives of those connected to us. The prophet Isaiah (Ch 40:31) says that waiting upon the Lord will renew our strength. We will soar on wings like eagles; we will run and not be weary; we will walk and not faint. The Hebrew word 'qavah' is translated into English as 'wait'. Qavah means to wait actively with anticipation, hopefully watching for God to act. The root, in its primitive form, also means to bind together. An intertwining occurs between our soul and God's Spirit as we wait upon the Lord. This produces His strength for my weakness. His zeal for my weariness. His serenity for my frazzled striving.

During my walk with God, I discovered that He does not waste anything. He has the right to use anything to transform us from a child being tossed to and fro to a believer mature in Christ Jesus. God's ultimate plan for all believers is for us to be like the Lord Jesus in character. Jesus, in his humanity, lived out the life God intended his created human beings to live, a life of love and service, bringing God glory.

Charles Wesley wrote in his Hymn I know that my Redeemer lives: *He surely will fulfil the counsels of His grace in me.*

Chapter 24

God's Promises

Do not fear, for I am with you; do not be dismayed, for I am your God...
Isaiah 41:10

A LIFE-CHANGING DIAGNOSIS (APRIL 2005)

I felt battle-worn from the last mission trip to India but encouraged when I found two letters in my post box. One was from Phil Thomas of Bundaberg, who said a generous amount had been raised for the laboratory equipment, as more equipment was needed for Dr Sam to treat newborn babies more adequately. The other was from Mr Thomas Rajan SAI, commending the team for their time spent in the Ambajipeta hospital and villages. He knew our service had restored some of the faith village folk had in the hospital after the sudden departure of Dr Prabha.

I settled back into my general routine, not knowing what was around the next corner. However, I was concerned about my hearing. I felt that the hearing in my right ear was not as good as my left ear. I decided to see my GP about the tinnitus and loss of hearing in my right ear. He referred me to Dr. Canty, an ENT specialist who ordered an MRI. Dr Canty rang me on the 27th of April 2005 to tell me the results of the MRI. When I visited his room he showed me the mass sitting next to the brain stem on the computer screen. However, such a tumour, an acoustic neuroma, is non-malignant, which was a praise point.

The operation to remove the tumour was going to be an expensive procedure and I would lose hearing in my right ear. Dr Canty felt that the best course was to wait and use the hearing I presently enjoyed. He indicated the tumour was too large to remove by the usual route.

My natural reaction to the diagnosis was concern about the impact it would have on my life and ministry. However, I did have the assurance that God would be with me. Dr Canty said I could wait six months and have another MRI. The November 2005 MRI showed that the tumour had only grown slightly but was very close to the brain stem. Dr Canty's advice was still to wait and repeat another MRI in 2006. Usually, this type of tumour grows very slowly. At the next visit, Dr Canty recommended surgery in March 2007.

PLANS FOR 2006-2007

During May 2006 I was travelling around the Brisbane region, giving the KYB introduction to the book of Daniel and preparing two studies for the Girls Getaway at Burleigh Heads. On this occasion at Burleigh, for the first time, I shared personal trauma from my childhood and how hard it was to lose my husband, Fred, after three years of marriage. This brought many of the women to tears. I cannot go into these secret places in my heart without feeling grief. However, I have sought to act honouring God, believing that my Heavenly Father washes my eyes with tears so that I can see. He gives me an eternal perspective. In conversation later on, two women came to me and said they had been sexually abused as children. Hiltrud Adams, the other speaker, had previously served the Lord in Pakistan. She was forthright and admitted that her message was 'close to the bone'. The Lord Jesus' teaching often made his listeners uncomfortable. God's truth does strip away facades and is alive and active, sharper than a double-edged sword. It hurts sometimes to hear the truth, but God desires truth in our innermost being (Psalm 51:6).

Requests for me to speak kept coming in. The message I prepared for the ladies at St Barnabas KYB group spoke first to my heart. The message was entitled "Reasons why we should not Worry." I like one whimsical but valid reason – if we worry, we treat ourselves less than birds! Jesus said, *"Look at the birds. Your Heavenly Father feeds them."* When we continue to worry, we question our Heavenly Father's care. This spoke to my heart as I thought of the tumour sitting near my brain stem.

Occasionally I listen to Chuck Swindoll on the radio in the evening. In one program he said, 'Tucked away in a quiet corner of every life are wounds and scars. If they were not there, we would not need a physician. Nor would we need one another.' Since this is God's world, God, our physician, may be discovered in the most unexpected places. We can seek Him in our prisons, our disappointments and tears, our grief and anxieties. If we seek Him in these experiences, we will indeed find Him.

I flew to Melbourne to attend the AMT/MAC Mission Conference, through which I am blessed as we focus on the needs of the missionaries and mission fields. This brought to the surface again my concerns about the future of the Ambajipeta Women's Hospital. Unless a committed Christian Medical Superintendent was on staff to maintain the standard of healthcare needed, unsupervised staff would lack accountability. It isn't easy to attract dedicated and professionally efficient staff to work in villages. Doctors need reputable schools for their children, not just little village schools. If the hospital did not have a good reputation, patients would not come, and wages could not be paid.

I wanted to return to Ambajipeta to finish some projects I had started, especially to attend the opening of the beautiful nurses' quarters. I felt that the hospital would only survive if the preaching of the gospel remained central. That is why Dr Leeser started the hospital: to rescue those trapped in spiritual darkness. I asked my friend Lyn Harrison if she was interested in seeing the work in India and whether we could plan to visit. I was pleased Lyn was prepared to be my companion. Lyn was hostess at the KYB group meeting at Bald Hills. When Brendan Trathen, my nephew, was with me in August, he helped Lyn and me book our trip to India online. We booked from November 12th to January 29th, 2007, flying into Hyderabad, the capital of Andhra Pradesh State. A friend in my Retirement Village generously gave me one thousand dollars to help with the fare.

My friends John and Ethel Orr said, 'If you return to India in the cool season, let it be to see friends, and for a closure, a letting go to move forward.' Until now there had not been closure, for my emotions were still restless as if I had read a book with a disquieting ending.

I kept myself busy and involved. Two Chinese students attending Mueller College were coming to stay with me for two weeks. Communicating with these students was not easy. However, there were strategies like saying the English word for an object and then letting them say it in their mother tongue. I also did a short Bible reading with them using my iPad in English with Mandarin Chinese translation. I had recorded Songs of Praise, which I played for them. My niece Julie had two Korean students, so we went on outings together.

In October 2006 I travelled to Sydney and Canberra for the tulip festival with my niece, Vicki, and her young daughter, Aimee. I seek opportunities to connect with my family and nurture relationships that need to be valued. While in Canberra I connected with my cousin Lyle Hardy and his wife, Glenys. Lyle was blessed with the musical gift passed down through our family. When he played the piano I was impressed by his musical ability.

Dave Ware of Mueller Church was putting together a team to visit Andhra Pradesh State and the hospital in Ambajipeta in November-December 2006. Some of the team members were nurses and all were eager to use their talents in ministry. Lyn Harrison and I would be flying into India before Dave's team arrived.

The Lord gave me a precious promise from Exodus chapter thirty-three. *My presence will go with you, and I will give you rest.* This assurance of God's presence in Exodus was given to God's servant Moses as he was about to enter enemy territory. It has fortified the faith of many missionaries stepping out into the unknown. In the next chapter of Exodus, the Lord God reveals Himself to Moses, *"The LORD, the LORD, the compassionate and gracious God, slow to anger, abounding in love and faithfulness, maintaining love to thousands, and forgiving wickedness, rebellion and sin. Yet he does not leave the guilty unpunished;"* Surely, we can trust such a God.

Mr Irmiah the hospital administrator, informed me that John Victor would meet Lyn and me at the Hyderabad Airport and take us to a hotel. Then he would travel by plane with us to Rajahmundry, where Mr Irmiah planned to meet us. I felt at home during the two-hour hair-raising road trip through the many villages, along the canal banks and over the dirt road to the hospital in Ambajipeta, a distance of sixty kilometres. We were greeted with garlands and smiles. Then the beautiful missionary bungalow came into view along the garden path. This had been my home for many years. I had a lot to catch up on. A new doctor to meet and opportunities to reconnect with Dr Sam, his wife Nancy and their little daughter, Ann.

One of the highlights of this visit was opening the new, well-constructed building in place of the old hospital staff quarters, which was a fire trap with only one staircase. I planned this new building to have three! From my basic sketch, the engineer had done an excellent job. It is a beautiful building. I called it 'Hebron', hoping it would be a friendly home for all staff. We had a grand opening to which many came, including the Narsapur Hospital staff. Dave Ware and his team of fifteen had arrived, settled in and enjoyed the function. The girls in the team looked beautiful in very colourful saris.

A two-storey building erected with the help of Mobile Mission Maintenance (MMM) in 1983 was used later as a post-operative ward upstairs and an infertility clinic at ground level. Now that the hospital had two skilled paediatricians, Dr Sam Ebeneezer and Dr Ramesh, a separate place was needed for sick babies and children. It was decided to set up the ground-level section as a specialised paediatric unit. A generous Hervey Bay Ladies Camp gift was used to furnish the ward. Dave Ware's team of young Australians transformed the dull white-washed walls into a vibrant display of Australian fauna and flora. They bought the paint with their own money and counted this as a service of love.

Lyn Harrison and I visited two distant tribal areas vastly different in terrain and culture. A building to house the believers from the Koya community was crowded with a smiling congregation welcoming us. Many Koya folk have become Hindus but keep many Koya tribal customs. In the simplest of Koya wedding ceremonies, the bride bends her head and the groom leans over her while friends pour water on the husband's head. Once the water has drained off the bride's head, they are said to be man and wife. They then drink milk, eat rice, and walk around a mould of earth under a pandal – a fabricated temporary structure. They then get the elders' blessings and go to their new home.

The cultural rites of other regions can be fascinating. In the past I have been invited to high-caste Hindu homes for an important ceremony when a young daughter matures. She receives a ceremonial bath, is dressed in a beautiful sari, and stands in a glass-like enclosure to be viewed by likely husbands! I was always excited when I heard a particular song that the palanquin carriers make when taking a young bride to her husband's house. I could easily see them on the open road from my side of the veranda. The young bride would be beautifully dressed and wearing garlands of flowers. Child marriages are still prevalent in India.

Lyn and I were also invited to go with Samuel Raju to the fishing village where he ministers on Sundays. Dr Sam and Mr Irmiah also came. Fisher folk are at the bottom of the caste system. How happily they received us, and our hearts were warmed to see them believing in Jesus, the one true God. Though poor, they were smiling. In all the villages we visited, opportunities abounded to speak into people's lives and pray for them. Sometimes we shared the gospel; other times we heard about their griefs and trials. Many pastors wanted me to visit their fellowships, and I saw this as an excellent opportunity to encourage and assess their needs.

You never know what's around the corner! One morning an impressive group of people, beautifully dressed and armed with cameras, came to the mission bungalow. They had travelled from Vijayawada, a distance of one hundred and forty kilometres, with the desire to interview me. They were planning a large Medical Conference and wanted to make a video to play at the Conference on the life of Dr Leeser. This interview was done with trepidation because I wanted to represent Dr Leeser correctly. They also asked me to speak at the Conference.

Mr Irmiah offered the driver to take Lyn and me to Vijayawada to the hotel arranged for us. I knew Dr Sam was involved in the Conference to speak on the doctors' panel. Dr David Prentice was one of the guest speakers. He was a renowned doctor from the USA who spoke on stem cell research.

The Conference was organised partly to honour four remarkable missionary doctors, one of whom was Dr Leeser. It was held at the River Life Worship Centre. As I stood before two hundred dedicated doctors, physiotherapists, and radiologists, the Lord filled me with a passion for the message I was to give. God was so gracious to provide me with this opportunity.

The apostle Paul wrote: *But by the grace of God, I am what I am, and his grace to me was not without effect. No, I worked harder than all of them – yet not I, but the grace of God that was with me.* (1 Cor 15:10).

The Lord by now had taught me so much during these fifty years of walking with Him. I was conscious of my need to depend on Him. How could I encourage these professionals? What did they need to hear? Some would choose to work in prestigious hospitals instead of meeting the desperate needs in thousands of villages dotted throughout this state of eighty million people. I thought of the service of Dr Leeser and Sylvia Wright and how they humbly and sacrificially served the Lord, bearing much – the attacks of the evil one and the stress of overcoming barriers to blessing. From all of these shared experiences, the guiding principles in serving the Lord could be illustrated. I learned a lot from working with Dr Leeser and Sylvia Wright.

In my message I used a very familiar event to Indians. It was something we did every harvest behind our mission bungalow. We hired two bullocks to tread out the rice crop spread on the cement mittum (a threshing space on a hard surface) to divide the grains from the stalks.

The text I chose was: *Come to Me. Take my yoke upon you and learn from me, for I am gentle and humble in heart, and you will find rest for your souls.* (Matt 11: 28-30).

Jesus has often come alongside me when I need to learn from him. Taking his yoke means that I am to be submissive to him and keep in step with him, going where he wants me to go and doing what he wants me to do. I found that when I did this I experienced the blessing of rest in my soul. The following is what the Lord laid on my heart to share.

The verses clearly show that Jesus is inviting us. It is a *Voluntary Yoke*. He wants loving hearts and willing hands to serve him, for us to serve joyfully and willingly. We are to live out the Christ-life of humility and freedom from self-effort. At the Capernwray Conferences I came to understand more about how Christ longs to live his life through us. I have experienced the yoke becoming a burden, weighing me down when one does not depend on our Lord Jesus.

It is a *Custom-made Yoke* that is *'easy'*. Jesus, as a carpenter, probably made yokes. He carefully measured the neck of the oxen. Because we are all different, Jesus has a unique purpose for each of us. He *knows* us. He fits us for service (Eph 2:10). This yoke won't chafe our neck. God wastes nothing as he transforms us and prepares us to serve others. He has given us exceptional skills that he wants to use to bless others. Even through our failures God has taught us valuable lessons. The challenge is, are we willing to give up our plans and live according to his purpose? (Ephesians 2:10). This truth still challenges me today.

It is a *Purposeful Yoke.* He works with us in our ministry to accomplish his will. He loves us and disciplines us as a Father should. We cannot go our own way or try to control every situation. Sometimes, He puts us with difficult colleagues to teach us how to love genuinely. He proposes to bring good out of everything. We are not to even try to wipe away our past. Past failures and experiencing God's amazing grace make us more compassionate toward others.

It is a *Shared Yoke.* We are yoked to him, this One who can supply all our needs. We are not alone in our struggles. Christ identifies with us in our humanity. We also have a wise counsellor in the Holy Spirit. He comes alongside us. We have a friend in Jesus who is a loving companion. We lean on him for all we lack.

It is a *Liberating Yoke. '…my yoke is easy and my burden light.'* Christ desires to free us from self-effort when we submit to being trained in his way. He wants to bless us with every spiritual blessing. He gives us rich experiences of Himself as He keeps us in his chosen place. He frees us as we release our burdens and stay in step with him. The Lord graciously enabled me to share the thoughts he had put in my heart.

At the conference, a doctor working in a small village gave a heartfelt testimony of his experiences and how the Lord had strengthened him in times of discouragement. A speech competition by a group of articulate young people was also included in the program. (I often wish that young people in our churches underwent public speaking and elocution training. This would give them confidence and the ability to express themselves well.)

Lyn and I enjoyed the warm fellowship and joyful worship service. They presented me with a figurine – a carved fish with the inscription,

> *Mrs Pauline Robins – For your dedication and tireless work in obedience to His call. From the people of India.*

This experience of being with these Christians gave me a heartening closure to my many years in India. I knew that my time in India was over.

Lyn and I planned to visit Kerala and have Christmas at the Rehoboth Orphanage with Phyllis Treasure. We caught the train from Vijayawada to Thrissur, Kerala. However, Lyn received the distressing news that her mum, Mrs Evelyn Buchanan, who was in the Residential Care Facility (RCF) at Mueller, was failing. Lyn needed to fly home. She caught a flight from the Cochin airport. On her arrival home Lyn spent precious time with her mum, who was called Home the following day. After two weeks Lyn bravely returned and we enjoyed Christmas at Rehoboth, where the children put on an entertaining concert. We also attended the wedding of Dr Lydia who had worked at Ambajipeta, to Dr Cecil. The lavish affair was beautifully arranged. Two hundred guests were fed in half an hour!

Almost ten years after this trip, I received a beautiful book produced in 2015 by the Rehoboth Girls' Orphanage Trust to celebrate one hundred and ten years of God's faithfulness to the ministry at Rehoboth. Many have written about their memories of their time there. The book is in English and Malayalam and includes grateful testimonies. Pearly, one of Mummy's girls, testified to discovering God as her Heavenly Father, the One who loves and cares for orphans.

Lyn and I were to return to Ambajipeta from Kerala State for the last two weeks as we were flying from Hyderabad. But first, we shopped in Thrissur! The theatre nurses needed more instruments to perform Caesarean Sections. These supplies are not available in any city near Ambajipeta Hospital. I also bought lots of stainless steel and rubber sheeting. Lyn wondered how we would manage the pile of equipment on the train trip back to the Godavari as the pile kept mounting. I assured her there would be porters to help, but this didn't happen. Lyn marvellously used her muscles to propel the luggage along the train corridors, for we were moved three times!

Towards the end of January 2007 I said goodbye to my friends at the Ambajipeta Hospital, and this for the last time. We received love gifts of delicacies like chutneys. In Hyderabad, Lyn and I wandered around giving away items to those on the streets to reduce the weight in our luggage. We also attended the joyous occasion of Dr T Jeeva Ratnam's marriage to Vijitha, and I could tell he was so pleased that we were with them on this special occasion. He smiled at me so often that I started to feel like his mum!

The Singapore Airlines flight home on January 28th 2007 was uneventful. I felt grateful to my friends who helped in various ways to make this time in India a worthwhile adventure and a time of proving the Lord faithful. I also experienced the closure I needed. The Lord had ordered our steps and answered our prayers.

Back in Queensland I took up where I had left off. I travelled around, giving the KYB introductions to the gospel of Matthew. This kept me in prayer and rejoicing in the Lord.

Chapter 25

Surrendering to God's Sovereignty

And we know that in all things, God works for the good of those who love him, who have been called according to his purpose.
Romans 8:28

This verse in the Epistle of Romans chapter eight gives great assurance to a child of God. It brings us to trust in Almighty God, our Heavenly Father. Truths in the Bible help us understand that God is in control. Nothing occurs in the universe without his permission. He supremely rules in history and over the circumstances of our lives. At the same time, the Bible describes God as offering humanity choices and holding them personally responsible for sinful behaviour. Not all things that occur are the direct actions of God, but he does work all things according to the counsel of his will. Sin and sinful people have left us to inherit a morally corrupt and broken world.

Many people struggle to accept that we are not in charge of our destiny and that none of us has control over our own lives (Jeremiah 10:23). At the same time we are not puppets being manipulated by an exacting God. But God does test our faith and our love for him. He wants us to grow up, to become strong believers, and to fully trust Him. I would need to hold onto these truths going into 2007 and 2008. My faith would be severely tested.

On my return from India in January 2007, I revisited the ENT specialist, and he explained how they would remove the acoustic neuroma near my brain stem. It all sounded so scary. It was going to be an expensive procedure with two specialists working together. Norm and Ruth Saunders gave me a little booklet entitled 'Fear not. Be still'. God's promises were strengthening my heart, but I had moments of anxiety when I focused on the enormity of what lay ahead.

I was looking at an alternative to surgical removal of the benign tumour. Some strongly advised Stereotactic Radiation Therapy. The more I researched, the more confused I became. I called several friends asking for specific prayers. My sister Gweneth gave me a verse in Isaiah 30:21: *Whether you turn to the right or the left, your ears will hear a voice behind you saying, 'This is the way; walk in it.'*

When I rang Dr Bevan Walker, he said he would contact an ENT specialist in Sydney. This specialist recommended Professor Paul Fagan at the St Vincent Hospital, who is well-known for his skull base surgery. Before I explored that option, I saw Dr David Schlect, a radiation oncologist at the Wesleyan Hospital in Brisbane. He walked me through the procedure. However, I decided on surgical removal. I ended up cancelling the surgery with Dr Paul Canty for March 7th with the idea of seeing Professor Fagan in Sydney. I noticed on the Web page that he operated in the public sector. This could save me thousands of dollars.

Besides these challenges weighing heavily on my mind, more opportunities arose to tell of our last mission trip in 2006. Dave Ware and I gave a presentation on our Mission Trip at the Wynnum Conference in Brisbane, which was well-received. This brings to mind one of the human tragedies we encountered while in Ambajipeta on that last mission trip. When there, I heard what had happened to a lovely Christian girl called Mary Grace. Her family worked at the hospital and I had watched Mary Grace grow up. She had become infected with HIV from her husband, who died of AIDS. I called her family to the bungalow to see if we could help and to enquire about her treatment. I wept with the family when they told me her harrowing story. Twice, mother and daughter had bought rat poison to commit suicide, but God prevented them.

When Lyn Harrison, who was with me at the Ambajipeta hospital, heard about Mary Grace, the Lord laid on Lyn's heart to help Mary Grace with the cost of medication. We informed the family that if Mary Grace attended our Bethesda Hospital in Narsapur for the proper medication, money would be sent from Australia into the hospital account. Lyn and her group of ladies in Brisbane faithfully sent money for years. Although the medication helped in the suppression of the virus, sadly, Mary Grace caught another infection and died some years later. Mary Grace is now in glory, and those ladies who gave will be rewarded.

After the Wynnum Conference I flew to Sydney to see Professor Fagan, who talked me through the surgical procedure. After seeing the last MRI films, he indicated we could wait and repeat another MRI at the beginning of 2008. I was a little surprised by this but readily accepted his decision. Before entering his rooms in Kings Cross I prayed for an hour in an Anglican Church nearby. During this time I whispered that I would accept whatever happened as if it was from the Lord. Little did I know that waiting another year was not the right medical decision. Following surgery, I would need to prove that 'in acceptance lieth peace' – the last line of a poem by Amy Carmichael. In her poem, Amy detailed the futile ways we often deal with loss. I would need God's grace to deal with the loss of normal functions due to nerve damage during the planned surgery.

Back in Brisbane I continued to seek opportunities to serve. When I visited my friend Jean Campbell in Tasmania a couple of years before this, I was impressed with the gatherings she held in her home and other friends' homes. Jean had previously served the Lord in Goa, India. On her return to Tasmania Jean worked as a teacher/principal in a Hobart school. Professional women were invited for breakfast on Saturday mornings at a Christian's home. I had the joy of speaking at one of these gatherings on the Strategies for Survival. These were strategies I put in place during difficult times in India.

The very night I thought about possibly starting something similar in Redcliffe, Jean Campbell rang me! Something she rarely did. This was truly amazing and gave me the confidence to move forward with the idea. I shared the vision with friends in the church, outlining how we could meet on one Saturday in the month for breakfast. The idea would be for Christian women to invite their non-church friends to a non-threatening place where an exciting program would centre around the truths in the Bible. I met with enough enthusiasm to approach the elders, who encouraged us to proceed with the program.

As Christian women we were to serve the Lord actively. Our purpose would be to introduce others to Christ and to grow in our Christian faith. Hebrews 10:24 says, *And let us consider how to stir up one another to love and good works.* Our first breakfast was well attended, and we planned to meet on the first Saturday of the following months. And now, in 2024 the Mueller Ladies Breakfast Club continues to meet monthly, and although the purpose has changed, inspirational speakers encourage women in their service to God. Those attending the Breakfasts support worthwhile projects and children in impoverished Asian lands needing a home and education.

Another need I became aware of was the need to have a monthly Newsletter for our Peninsula Palms Retirement Village residents. I wrote to the Residents' Committee about putting together a newsletter. When the office staff took on this responsibility, I started interviewing residents to write their stories to appear in the monthly Newsletter. I also invited friends to my unit to serve them a curry and rice meal. Eight friends from the church and village would enjoy three different kinds of curries and rice. Lyn, a friend in the Village, helped me to make it an enjoyable evening. These monthly gatherings were precious times of fellowship. I heard that I was being called 'the Curry Queen'!

Also, in 2007 I had the opportunity to speak at the CWCI gathering on the Faithfulness of God and God's vision for the future. When Ruth Graham, Billy Graham's daughter, visited Brisbane I was among those eager to hear her. Ruth emphasised the need to pray with thanksgiving. The opportunity arose for someone to lead the KYB (Know Your Bible) for women in our Peninsula Palms Retirement Village, a role I enthusiastically undertook. These activities kept me in God's Word and challenged my walk with the Lord. God has a way of running his cursor over our lives, pointing out those things that need changing.

I still kept in contact with my Indian friends and when a friend at the hospital in Ambajipeta rang me, I felt distressed at what was happening in the hospital. Staff were agitated and insecure, and patient care was such that the hospital was getting a bad name. This concerned person had no one left to appeal to, but what could I do? I was facing serious surgery. To instigate change, I would need to stay for a more extended period than was possible. What was needed was an enthusiastic Indian to give godly supervision long-term. I was pleased to hear in 2018 that a godly CEO/ Administrator was now in charge. The need was still for a Christian Medical

Superintendent. I called friends to join me in my unit on a particular day to pray. I prayed and fasted and was encouraged by those who came.

SURGERY IN SYDNEY IN 2008

Early in 2008 another MRI showed that the tumour had grown three-fold, and I needed surgery without delay. This sudden growth was out of character for this type of tumour, which usually develops slowly. Professor Fagan kept looking at the MRI films, puzzled by what he saw.

Several friends encouraged me by praying with me. My diary contains Bible verses as God strengthened me for what lay ahead. I dropped out of the Greek classes I was undertaking at Mueller College of Ministries (MCM) and went to Woodgate to meet with my Rocky family. I needed to see them as I was facing serious surgery.

In April, my sister Gweneth and her husband Russell drove me down to Sydney and supported me through the ordeal. I was admitted to St Vincent Hospital and allocated a room overlooking the harbour bridge. However, I was disappointed to discover Professor Fagan was now only operating in the private hospital system, and I would receive a hefty medical bill.

During the surgery three cranial nerves were damaged as the messy tumour had grown around them. Professor Fagan was able to save the facial nerve, although I had facial paralysis for several weeks and was left with some residual paralysis. The hearing nerve was severed, causing total deafness in my right ear. But it was damage to the vagus nerve that left me with significant loss and trauma. The vagus nerve is very long and visits all the major organs – the heart, lungs and stomach – as well as our throat, ears and vocal cords. Because of it being damaged I was left with a range of symptoms associated with the resultant gastroparesis, plus a nasty taste and an irritable cough reflex as the back of my throat had dropped down.

I had long bouts of coughing and difficulty swallowing, which led to fearful choking episodes for the first five years. The distressful condition of oesophageal spasming followed this. Because of left vocal cord paralysis I couldn't sing, and when speaking, my voice would suddenly become hoarse or strained.

When I had a follow-up consultation with Professor Fagan, he expressed his distress at the outcome of the surgery and said, "With you, I got it wrong." He had several cases in which he was monitoring the growth of the tumour with MRI scans. I quietly accepted his apology, for there was no way of knowing that the tumour would grow as it did. I had months of speech therapy, four more yearly MRIs to ensure the tumour was not growing again, and other tests to manage my distressing symptoms better. I resigned from being a speaker at the CWCI events and asked God to give me something absorbing to do to downplay my symptoms. This is how I came to write the history of my family.

I joined Ancestry.com and spent hours researching records in England, Germany and Australia to find information about my ancestors, especially my great-grandparents who immigrated to Queensland. This research became addictive, but it was what I needed. I bought birth and death certificates to ensure my facts were correct. The information I found and the results of my extensive research led me to write my first book.

After spending so much time gathering facts, I felt as if I knew my ancestors and didn't want their stories to be lost. I wrote their stories as a biography. The characters and settings may have received some embellishment. Still, the premise of their stories mirrors what they may have experienced in their home country, on their journey and settling into Rockhampton, Australia. The central characters in my book, *Life is a Journey*, were my parents Albert and Amy Hodgkinson and their five children, Margaret, Janice,

Pauline, Gweneth, and Raymond. The book was printed in Melbourne in 2014 and contained many coloured photos. All my family received a copy.

Now, with a taste for writing I joined a Creative Writing Group at the Redcliffe University of the Third Age, or U3A, which offers a learning experience for personal enjoyment for older people. The more adventurous seniors attending U3A learn languages. I was content to improve my computer skills and storytelling. My homework each week was writing a short story two A4 pages long. It was fun. Two of my stories were published in a book.

Though functioning on a surface level, behind closed doors I wrestled with my feelings of nausea, lack of appetite, and other distressing ailments. I called upon God's enabling grace. The belief that God was working in my circumstances and according to his purpose became the stabilising truth in my life.

I was brought to bow to God's voice: *Trust Me. Acknowledge Me – recognise My authority* (Proverbs 3:5-6 KJV). I needed to take hold of this verse and surrender to God's sovereign will. This was not done at one life-changing moment but in my moments of distress and weakness, month after month, year after year.

Hadn't I prayed and told the Lord I would accept whatever happened as if it were from Him? I thought of a caterpillar captured in its rigid chrysalis and hidden away as it struggles, being changed into something more beautiful than a caterpillar. Isn't this what God seeks to do with his children – to transform them into the image of his Son? Transformed to show forth the beauty of purity, humility, gentleness, compassion and a readiness to forgive others?

Dear readers, be encouraged. God is at work in your circumstances, no matter how messy or scary they may seem. He works for the good of those who love him. I continued to thank Jesus for the life He lived among us.

His incarnation brought him into our broken world. Though he walked a tear-filled path, he wasn't swallowed by grief. He endured because of the joy set before him. He often withdrew to spend time with his Father. He accepted His Father's will and went to the cross to rescue us. Such was the love of God. 'Therefore, I didn't lose heart.'

Chapter 26

Growing Older Gracefully

Therefore we do not lose heart. Though outwardly we are wasting away, yet inwardly we are being renewed day by day.
2 Corinthians 4:16

The years rolled by. Grey hairs and wrinkles warned me I was now past seventy. In the book of Isaiah, God assures us that even in our old age, he will sustain and rescue us (Isaiah 46:4). I also love God's promise in Psalm 92. We can bear fruit and stay fresh and green in our old age. These qualities spring from our living relationship with our Creator God. This relationship, like all relationships, needs to be nurtured. We need to deepen our spiritual connection through prayer, meditating on God's Word, worship, and exercising our faith. This is how we can be renewed day by day.

In 2017, I turned eighty. I had been on the Missionary Advisory Council since 1994, which kept me interested and involved in cross-cultural missions. The AMT/MAC conference held annually in different states of Australia was informative. For some time, I wrote a monthly newsletter to the Queensland missionaries on behalf of the Missionary Advisory Council (MAC). These letters contained current Queensland news and words of encouragement Though I enjoyed these activities, it was time to retire from the MAC and continue with my family responsibilities and my joy in writing of God's gracious blessings. These times of reflection proved to be therapeutic while I continued to struggle with the fallout of the 2008 surgery. I wanted to remain fresh and green.

With God's promises in mind, I continued interviewing and writing a short account of the lives of our residents in our Peninsula Palms Retirement Village. A resident's story was published in our monthly village newsletter. Not wanting these stories to be lost, I put them together in an anthology along with poems and artwork by our residents. Members of the Mueller College staff did the graphic design, and the finished book was a credit to them. I was especially indebted to Tracey Yates, a Mueller College staff member who worked with me on the project, and the Mueller Community Church who bore the cost of printing. We launched the book in 2020. Every resident receives a copy.

In 2023, I started writing my memoirs of captured memories recorded in my diaries. I hope my experiences will resonate with my readers and that God will be glorified. Words are powerful tools, and we need to use them wisely and graciously. Anna Johnson Flint was a renowned poet gifted with the ability to use words well. Anna was born in 1866 in New Jersey. During her teaching career she began experiencing excruciating pain from a severe form of arthritis. The following poem would have been written out of her personal experience. This poem is especially suited to those suffering from the afflictions of old age.

He giveth more grace when the
burdens grow greater,
He sendeth more strength when the labors increase;
To added affliction, He addeth His mercy;
To multiplied trials, His multiplied peace.

When we have exhausted our store of endurance,
When our strength has failed
ere the day is half done,
When we reach the end of our hoarded resources,
Our Father's full giving is only begun.

His love has no limit; His grace has no measure.
His power has no boundary known unto men;
For out of His infinite riches in Jesus,
He giveth, and giveth, and giveth again!

This gift of grace, God's unmerited kindness and mercy to the unworthy, can sustain us in our deepest trials. God's grace will also sustain us as we embrace the natural changes that come with ageing, whether physical changes in appearance or adjustments to our lifestyle. Acceptance can help us adapt more easily and find peace with the ageing process. This is good advice and I discovered that many living in our Peninsula Palms Retirement Village community were seeking to live this out day by day.

In May 2023 I found the Webinar on 'Bring Our Lost Boys Home' very informative. The Webinar was run by Martyn Iles and Cindy McGarvie, National Director of Youth for Christ Australia. It aimed to cover the spiritual war raging against our young men, how to win the war and bring the lost boys home, and what we can do to help reach these lost boys. 'Lost boys' refers to young men who cannot find their place in the world. Cindy, in her book, after deep research, responded to the rampage of suicide, depression and anxiety, porn addiction, fatherlessness and the feminisation of our young men.

Understanding the dangers our young people face in our rapidly changing culture is challenging for an older Christian. We become aware of these dangers when we look at the tragic numbers of young men committing suicide and those caught up in addiction, domestic violence, and pornography which has infiltrated our society. As prayer warriors, older Christians need a compassionate desire to remain connected to our young people and be aware of the dangers and deceptions they battle against every day. Young men need to know that God has a purpose for their lives according to how God created them. As intercessors we pray that young men will be restored to their true identity as sons of a loving Father. After purchasing the book '*Lost Boys—Bring Them Home*', I gave a copy to our pastoral team at Mueller Community Church.

Close to my heart was serving as an intercessor of the ministry of CWCI (Christian Women Communicating Internationally) and a study leader in our Village KYB (Know Your Bible). My visits to Rockhampton continued to spend quality time with my sister Margaret's family. Her grandchild, Zoe, was my godchild, and she was taken Home to be with Jesus in 2021. The wheelchair was left behind, and she is now surrounded by the joys of heaven until the day when she will be given a new body, perfect in every way.

Then Margaret was transported to Glory in October 2023 at ninety-one. She had often travelled a rough road but now is at peace. She said she believed when I shared the way of salvation in the Gospel of John chapter 14:1-6 not long before she left us. We miss them both, but they are in a far better place awaiting the final blessing of being in a new heaven and earth, for the old will pass away (Revelation 21). We can look forward to no more tears or death or mourning or pain. This is the final dwelling place for all those who love God our Father and the Lord Jesus, who makes all these blessings possible. I long that many more will trust in the sacrifice of the Lord Jesus on the cross to purchase our salvation. There is only one way to heaven, not by being good, for we will never be good enough. We need to trust in what the Lord Jesus has done as the bearer of our sins. We must ask for forgiveness and entrust ourselves to God.

To travel safely through this broken world, we need a personal relationship with God. We need his wise counsel, as found in His Word, his strength amid trials, and his joy to lift our spirits and give us the courage to persevere.

God has a rescue plan to meet our deepest needs. This plan was forged out of His love and grace. It includes rescue from sin's penalty, power, and presence. Sinful behaviour has wrecked the beautiful world God created. God will judge sinful behaviour if the sinner is not forgiven now.

The cross of Christ guarantees God's continuing, unfailing generosity. Out of love and as a testimony to his grace, Jesus still bears the scars of Calvary in his glorified body. In his first Epistle, Peter writes that Jesus *bore our sins in his body on the tree so that we might die to sins and live for righteousness. By his wounds, you have been healed.* Healing flows from the crucifixion of our Lord Jesus when we tap into his forgiveness and peace. Healing also comes from his resurrection, which gives hope to believers. God assures those who love him of life in the new heaven and earth where the Lord Jesus shall reign in glory.

Until that hope is realised, we live in this world that God created to be enjoyed. We can marvel at the glorious sunsets, stand in awe of towering mountains and crashing waterfalls, wonder at the intricacies of tree canopies, and enjoy their cooling effect on a sultry day. This spirit of joy can lift us out of our daily struggles and fill our hearts with thankfulness.

This is only a foretaste of the glory of God's Kingdom. I end my story with the glorious sound of Handel's Hallelujah Chorus lifting my thoughts heavenward in expectation.

Appendix

I have written this book to reflect on my life's journey. I am astonished at how God has dealt with me through his abundant grace. The following are thoughts that I would like to share with you.

LIFE-GIVING WATER

I like the verse in Jeremiah chapter seventeen. *Blessed is the one who trusts in the Lord, whose confidence is in him. They will be like a tree planted by the water that sends out its roots by the stream. It does not fear when heat comes; its leaves are always green. It has no worries in a year of drought and never fails to bear fruit.*

I love trees. I remember a song from my teenage years that I enjoyed singing. The lyrics were a poem by Joyce Kilmer, and a songwriter wrote them.

I think that I shall never see
A poem lovely as a tree.
A tree whose hungry mouth is pressed,
Against the earth's sweet flowing breast;
A tree that looks to God all day
And lifts its leafy arms to pray.

A tree is weathered by four seasons. Under the protection of the bark is its recorded history: when the tree experienced bushfires, storms, drought, and good seasons. During the good seasons, the tree comprises eighty percent water. Images of the rings inside the tree show what kind of season the tree has been through, whether drought or a good rainy season. When trees are subjected to natural forces like wind, branches are broken off, and the wound forms a hollow valuable to wildlife.

Similarly, our hearts record an inside story: all we have been through – our good years, our griefs, the times we have been hurt, our sense of loss, and our disappointments. Harmful emotions leave wounds, which become part of our story.

I like the quote by Peter Levine:

> 'When a young tree is injured, it grows around that injury. As the tree continues to develop, the wound becomes relatively small in proportion to the size of the tree. Gnarly burls and misshapen limbs speak of injuries and obstacles encountered. How a tree grows around its past contributes to its exquisite individuality, character, and beauty. I certainly don't advocate for traumatisation to build character, but since trauma is almost a given at some point in our lives, the image of the tree can be a valuable mirror.'

God grieves with us when others hurt us. At some point, He wants us to forgive, lay the burden down, and move forward in grace and freedom, to say, 'My wounds do not define me.' We need to see ourselves differently, to see ourselves through God's eyes.

We are to be like trees planted by the stream that hungrily sends out its roots to find life-giving water. Not a bonsai tree stunted in growth because its taproot and some of its feeder shoots have been severed. Such a person's soul is not nourished by the springs of living water. Roots need to go down into God's unfathomable grace, his Word, and healthy relationships. These can be life-giving.

What deprives us of experiencing God's grace in our lives? Have we sent down roots of bitterness? *See to it that no one falls short of the grace of God and that no bitter root grows up to cause trouble and defile many.* (Hebrews 12:15).

King David wrote *My soul thirsts for God, for the living God.* The quenching of thirst is powerful to the one who finds life a frustrating series of events. It satisfies the human need for meaning and purpose. We thirst for a spirit of joy to replace the weariness of the soul.

I have found that the teachings of Jesus can profoundly fulfil deep longings when acted upon. Jesus said to the Samaritan woman who came to draw water, *everyone who drinks this water will be thirsty again, but whosoever drinks the water I give them will never thirst. Indeed, the water I give them will become in them a spring of water welling up to eternal life.* (John 4:13-14)

THE SEASONS OF LIFE

Is life meant to be boring and predictable, becoming narrower and narrower and ending in a pathetic frizzle? No, a thousand times 'No.'

Life has its seasons. Each one is important and each prepares us for the next. Each beckons us to embrace it and learn from it. Each inspires hope and sharpens our expectations for the Grand Finale when faith gives way to sight.

The four traditional seasons – summer, autumn, winter, and spring – make a recognisable and beautiful statement about the seasons of life.

With the coming of summer, the Australian bushland burns with light when the earth's axial tilt points to the sun. The monsoonal rain brings relief, washing the earth and filling dry creek beds. Water rushes joyously over waterfalls or gurgles secretively in shallow creeks. Migrating birds flock to shorelines and inland lakes. Eagles soar lazily overhead. Even cows seem to chew the cud more leisurely as the sun climbs higher and the days get longer.

For humans, summer is a recreation season, a time to enjoy the leisure of these long summer days. Surf lovers are drawn to the sea by its magnetic pull. The Australian bass fish lure anglers to coastal streams. Anglers can leisurely wait under the shade of overhanging bushes for their catch. Recreational sports and leisure time foster many health benefits. The body, scantily clad, can relax in the sun's warmth on a sandy beach or cool off in a mountain stream. Summer teaches us that no matter where we are, we are to be all there – living the moment, learning patience, growing strong, and feeling free.

Yet only some Australians are capable of enjoying these long summer days. Why? Today, we have the commercial exploitation of leisure, which has led to mass leisure time occupation. Mothers become exhausted with running their children to this sport and that event. Another reason is that the productivity doctrine has stolen our freedom to do something for the sheer pleasure of doing it. We get a guilty conscience if we curl up in bed on a rainy day with a good book or spend time sipping coffee with a friend. We can so easily become prisoners of duty. However, a wise person knows that too much leisure at one time may lead to a loss of its sharp tang of pleasure.

Autumn is a season to reflect. Queensland does not have many deciduous trees, so we miss the joy of seeing the brilliant reds and gold as seen during autumn in North America. They call it the 'Fall', for the deciduous trees shed their leaves. These leaves seem to float gently to the ground like gondolas. As I reflect on this season, I realise that I am to let go of grudges that disturb my rest or bad habits that make me dull and set in my ways. It reminds me too that, as I get older, I am not to settle down to a bland, tasteless diet, for life offers so much colour and stimulation, flavours to savour and enjoy.

Winter. Even the word sounds bleak. Winter with its clear cold nights when the stars appear like platinum-headed nails in the blackened dome overhead, when night's breath freezes, becoming frost to lay crisp on stiff stalks of grass.

Yet winter is necessary, for it is a season of rest when the earth and trees gather strength for spring's burst of new life. In the long nights of winter, trees refresh their fevered life and find respite from the burning heat of the summer sun. Winter teaches us that if life is to be richer and fuller, we must take time to gather strength. A Greek motto says, 'You will break the bow if you always keep it bent.' Yet how does one relax in our stress-ridden culture with all the suffocating demands that sap our vitality?

Perhaps we need the power of a new perspective that sees life with all its seasons and is not afraid to plant roots in the Eternal – to rest in the One who gives serenity and the needed strength. Not the serenity born of indifference when one takes nothing to heart or the serenity of resignation, but the serenity of strength that is the fruit of purpose and victory over ambition and detachment. When everything seemed doomed to drabness and dryness, spring comes with its fragrance of flowers, birds busily nesting, and butterflies fluttering on painted wings. Baby kangaroos leave their mother's pouch to explore their world. Lorikeets get drunk on nectar, and Willie Wagtails don their black and white dinner suits to go courting.

Whereas autumn was a time of reflection and winter a time of rest, spring is a time of re-creation. Spring thoughts are to invade our minds so that joy takes possession of our hearts as nature sings. This joy blocks the bleakness from seeping into our souls and stops negative thinking, for spring thoughts have power. They awaken enthusiasm and inspire hope.

Thus, all the seasons of life are essential – multiple seasons, for life was never intended to be one long, monotonous marathon of pointless existence but a journey through the seasons, a journey through which one experiences various changes brought by reflection, removal, rest, and renewal.

So how can life with all its seasons and grand finale be boring or predictable? How tragic if we move through these seasons without realising their ultimate purpose – to prepare us for that grand finale when time gives way to eternity. I eagerly await that moment, which John Magee vividly described in his flying experience. His words describe that 'moment' as:

> 'I'll slip the bonds of earth and dance to skies on laughter's silver wings. High up in the sunlight silence, hovering there, I'll chase the shouting winds along and fling my eager craft through footless halls of air. Up, up into the long delirious blue, I'll top the wind-swept heights with easy grace, where never lark or even eagle flew – and while with silent wondering mind, I'll tread the high un-trespassed sanctity of space – I'll put out my hand and touch the face of God.'
>
> © Pauline Robins This is the speech I gave in the Brisbane Forum Communicators Competition.

THE MASTER WEAVER

Our awesome God is not only transcendent, dwelling in a high and holy place, but also immanent, dwelling with those who are contrite and humble in spirit to revive and comfort.

Although this great and loving God can never be wholly captured in human concepts, I know he is with me and will never forsake me. Even though life looks messy with random threads seemingly going nowhere, I have experienced God's providential care at such times.

As I meditate on these truths to make sense of events, I find food for thought in a poem by B.M. Franklin.

Life is but a weaving
Between my Lord and me;
I cannot choose the colours
He worketh steadily.

Oft times, He weaves sorrow.
And I, in foolish pride,
Forget He sees the upper,
And I the underside.

Not till the loom is silent
And the shuttles cease to fly,
Shall God unroll the canvas
And explain the reason why.

The dark threads are as needful.
In the Weaver's skilful hand,
As the threads of gold and silver
In the pattern, He has planned.

He knows He loves, He cares,
Nothing this truth can dim.
He gives His very best to those
Who chose to walk with Him.

This poem reminds me of the weavers in India who lived in a nearby village populated by weaver-caste people. I have watched these weavers work at their looms. The colourfully dyed yarn they used is stretched out on the poles to dry in the hot sun. The weaver works to a predetermined design, so he carefully chooses the yarn colours for a particular sari. He sets up his loom and begins with the warp threads. These threads stretch lengthwise on the loom and are fixed from the beginning to the end until the sari is finished. The essential purpose of any loom is to hold the warp threads under tension to facilitate the interweaving of the weft threads, which are the transverse threads. The weft threads are carefully positioned using the shuttle. The result of the weaver's artistic work is a beautiful sari.

Consider this picture as we think of God as a Master Weaver, a weaver with a Cosmic Loom stretching from eternity to eternity. Upon this loom, God is weaving His predetermined grand design. God has put a redemptive plan in place for the world He created, revealing his love and grace to straying humankind. His eternal decrees and promises in the Bible are like the warp threads stretched out and held in tension on the loom from eternity to eternity. They are anchored in God's eternal truth, which never changes. They are fixed in place and declare His unlimited power and incomprehensible holiness and splendour. He is transcendent – infinite and overall.

Some of these warp threads on the Cosmic Loom are secret things that belong to the Lord (Deut: 29:29). They have not been revealed to us. We must learn to live with the unfathomable mystery, which is too incredible to grasp. I found this one of the most challenging things until I came to know God's character better. Knowing him better, I trusted him more.

Now it is time for the weft threads to be introduced. The Master Weaver weaves the weft threads of human events and experiences across this frame. God is ever-present, active, and involved in the world He has created, and He is active in your life and mine.

Therefore, how amazing is the fact that this God stooped down, clothed himself with humanity, and revealed his heart? Jesus walked this earth, loving, healing and speaking truth into every situation. Then the unimaginable occurred. God's Son, Jesus, was crucified by people intent on silencing the message that contradicted their lives and shamed their religion. But this message of God's love can't be silenced. Every day worldwide, thousands seek him and are rescued from a life of hopelessness and shame.

MY HEART IS GLAD

One KYB study followed a selection of Psalms. I came to Psalm 16:9: *Therefore, my heart is glad, and my tongue rejoices.* God has graciously blessed us, and we are to take hold of those blessings. One of those blessings is joy. I was meditating on this psalm when making ANZAC biscuits, which I put on a plate and covered with Glad Wrap. I always find handling this polyethene wrap difficult, but it does a good job. That got me thinking about its many uses.

Glad Wrap keeps things fresh. Life can turn stale or even sour when we forget to give thanks in everything. How different life can be when our hearts are wrapped in joy. Ps 92:14: *They will still bear fruit in old age; they will stay fresh and green.* Shouldn't that be my goal as an older Christian? However, I have found this is only possible when I intentionally invite the Holy Spirit to produce his fruit in my life, as taught by the apostle Paul in the book of Galatians.

Glad Wrap holds things together. There have been times when things seemed to be falling apart in my life, where I was overwhelmed by a sense of failure. At such times, I needed to draw on strength, not from myself. I needed Jesus and his strengthening grace. I needed His joy, which remains when all else is seemingly lost. I call to mind that God is a God of joy. Heaven is a place of joy, for there is joy in Heaven when sinners repent.

Glad Wrap seals in the flavours. A grateful heart becomes a sanctuary where God is praised. I can feel my stress levels lessen when I draw upon God's peace and give thanks for even small things. I love going into a garden, carefully examining a beautiful flower, and marvelling at God's work of art.

Glad Wrap keeps out the creepy crawlies! I have found that when my heart is rejoicing in the Lord, a thief cannot creep in and steal the blessings God intends to shower upon me. Christ does not minimise the reality of all the outside forces that press in on me. My enemy, Satan, is always trying to gain a foothold through stress or even minor irritations. Christ dwells within my being and is greater than any threat from without.

Glad Wrap is transparent. I find security in the fact that God sees everything. My heart is an open book to him, and yet he continues to love me. Therefore, I don't have to pretend or even fear his rejection. He can deal with all the negative items stored in my heart, which sap my joy.

My biscuit-making effort became a blessing as I sifted through these thoughts.

THE TOUCH OF THE MASTER'S HAND

When we look around, we see people struggling; people crushed without hope; people marred by abuse; people with courage, trying to make a difference, and people some refer to as 'scum'. Yet everyone has intrinsic value because God created them in his likeness. Like God, we are endowed with language abilities, creativity, the capacity to love, and minds to plan and reason. Unlike animals, humankind possesses an eternal spirit and soul.

But humanity has been marred and battered by sin and living in a less-than-perfect world. The good news is that lives can be transformed when touched by the Master's Hand. As a teenager, I learned a monologue by Myra Brooks Welch that is worth repeating, for it tells how God's touch can transform our lives. My sister Janice was reading the book *The Finishing Touch* by Charles Swindoll when she was suffering during those last few months of her life.

Twas battered and scarred, and the auctioneer.
Thought it scarcely worth his while
To waste much time on the old violin,
But held it up with a smile.
"What am I bidden, good folks," he cried,
"Who'll start the bidding for me?"
"A dollar, a dollar. Then two! Only two?
Two dollars, and who'll make it three?"

"Three dollars, once; three dollars, twice;
Going for three...." But no,

From the room, far back, a grey-haired man.
Came forward and picked up the bow;
Then, wiping the dust from the old violin,
And tightening the loosened strings,
He played a melody pure and sweet,
As a carolling angel sings.

The music ceased, and the auctioneer,
With a voice that was quiet and low,
Said: "What am I bid for the old violin?"
And he held it up with the bow.
"A thousand dollars, and who'll make it two?
Two thousand! And who'll make it three?
Three thousand, once; three thousand, twice,
And going and gone," said he.

The people cheered, but some of them cried,
"We do not quite understand.
What changed its worth?" Swift came to the reply:
"The touch of the Master's hand."
And many a man with life out of tune,
And battered and scarred with sin,
Is auctioned cheap to the thoughtless crowd
Much like the old violin.

A "mess of pottage," a glass of wine,
A game — and he travels on.
He is "going" once and "going" twice,
He's "going" and almost "gone."

But the Master comes, and the foolish crowd.
Never can quite understand
The worth of a soul and the change that is wrought
By the touch of the Master's hand.

www.ingramcontent.com/pod-product-compliance
Lightning Source LLC
Chambersburg PA
CBHW022118080426
42734CB00006B/175

* 9 7 8 1 7 6 3 7 3 9 4 4 4 *